WHO KNEW?

Who Knew?

---

*Answers to Questions about Classical
Music You Never Thought to Ask*

ROBERT A. CUTIETTA

OXFORD
UNIVERSITY PRESS

OXFORD

UNIVERSITY PRESS

Oxford University Press is a department of the University of
Oxford. It furthers the University's objective of excellence in research,
scholarship, and education
by publishing worldwide. Oxford is a registered trade mark
of Oxford University Press in the UK and certain other countries.

Published in the United States of America by Oxford University Press
198 Madison Avenue, New York, NY 10016, United States of America.

Library of Congress Cataloging-in-Publication Data
Cutietta, Robert A.
Who knew?: Answers to Questions About Classical Music
You Never Thought to Ask/Robert A. Cutietta.
Oxford ; New York : Oxford University Press, 2016. | Includes index.
LCCN 2015045957 | ISBN 9780190462543 (pbk. : alk. paper) |
ISBN 9780190462567 (epub)
LCSH: Music—Miscellanea. | Music—Anecdotes. | Music appreciation.
LCC ML65 .C957 2016 | DDC 781.68—dc23 LC record available at
http://lccn.loc.gov/2015045957

1 3 5 7 9 8 6 4 2

Printed by R.R. Donnelley, United States of America

CONTENTS

LIST OF FIGURES

PREFACE

In 2006 I was approached by Gail Eichenthal, then program director for classical radio station KUSC, to explore the idea of starting a weekly radio segment called *Ask the Dean*. The format would be simple: listeners would email their questions about classical music, and I would answer them.

The idea appealed to me, but the thought that I, or anyone, could know about all aspects of classical music was simply unfathomable. However, the fact that I was the dean of one of the premier music schools in the country, the University of Southern California's Thornton School of Music, led us to the idea that while I might not have all of the answers, I certainly had a wealth of experts to rely on: the two-hundred-plus faculty members of the Thornton School. Thus, the segment was launched in the fall of 2006, with Gail as my cohost. The premise was that the dean may not know much, but he had "people" to whom he could turn.

The feature was an immediate success. As of this writing, it has been on weekly radio in the Los Angeles market for over ten years. This translates into hundreds of questions and answers. What is surprising is the quality and uniqueness of questions the listeners have sent in. Common responses when I approached a faculty member with a question were "Interesting, I never really thought about that" and "I never looked at it that way." Thus, what has been produced over the past 10 years is a wealth of common-sense questions and straightforward answers about music.

This book is a collection of some of the questions that have been submitted over the years that Gail and I found the most interesting. I have divided the questions into the following topics:

- The Orchestra and How It Works
- The Maestro and Music Director
- Opera and the Diva
- The Composer
- The Performers
- The Instruments of the Orchestra
- The Music
- This and That

I have not identified the listeners who sent in the questions simply because many said they did not want their name read on the air, so I doubt they would want their name in print. I suspect many were afraid they were asking a "stupid question." Nothing could be farther from the truth. Almost every question sent in, no matter how basic, led to an interesting, thought-provoking answer. In fact,

I want to thank all the listeners who submitted questions. This book would not and could not exist without their participation.

The other half of the equation is the faculty of the USC Thornton School of Music. After a few years they must have been tired of my coming to them with still *another* question. Their passion for music always won out, and their enthusiastic, thorough, and accurate answers made this a weekly joy for me. Those that contributed are listed below; I hope you take a few moments to look over this list of amazing musicians and educators. It is astonishing how much *I* learned from them in the process!

There is an important point to be made about my questioning of the faculty. This book has answers given to me by experts in the field, people who often talked with me spontaneously, without doing in-depth research. Therefore, there is a certain freshness to the answers; though accurate, they may not be as detailed as what you might find in a reference book. Nevertheless, I tried to reproduce their answers verbatim as much as possible. I think this is a strength of the answers. This is truly how musicians think and feel about these questions. It is not peer-reviewed research.

Most of the answers assume some basic knowledge of classical music and the terms used. I figure if you are interested in learning these tidbits about classical music, you probably already have some knowledge.

I also decided to use a different title for the book than I use for the radio show. The title came about just as this book was going to print. I was giving a preconcert talk before a performance of the USC Thornton Symphony followed by a question-and-answer period. Many of the questions from the audience were of the types that are addressed on the radio show. Sitting in the front row was a man and his wife. After every question he would turn to her, shake his head in astonishment, and say "Who knew?!" After the third time I heard him say this, it occurred to me that this would be the perfect title for this book.

Lastly, I want to thank the staff I work with at KUSC, the people who produce the segments and edit out all of my mistakes and tongue-tied moments before the segments air. They are Mark Hatwan, Kelsey McConnell, Katie McMurran, Brian Lauritzen, and, of course, my cohost and partner in crime when assembling this book, Gail Eichenthal. Thanks also to the President of USC Radio, Brenda Barnes.

So on behalf of the faculty and the hundreds of thousands of KUSC listeners, I hope you enjoy this book and learn about the seemingly endless aspects inherent in our great tradition of Western classical music. I certainly enjoyed writing it!

Contributing faculty from the University of Southern California's Thornton School of Music:

- Chris Bartz, saxophone
- Margaret Batjer, violin
- Bruce Brown, musicologist
- Patricia Campbell, ethnomusicologist*
- Joseph Carey, plastic surgeon*
- Ken Cazan, opera stage director
- Donald Crockett, composer
- Glenn Dicterow, violinist
- Adam Gilbert, early music
- Rodney Gilfry, vocalist

- Gary Glaze, vocalist
- Midori Goto, violin
- Henry Gronnier, violin
- Stephen Hartke, composer
- Boyde Hood, trumpet
- Elizabeth Hynes, vocalist
- Ralph Kirshbaum, cello
- Norman Krieger, piano
- Morten Lauridsen, composer
- Sharon Lavery, resident orchestra conductor
- Larry Livingston, conductor
- Brent McMunn, opera conductor
- David Allen Moore, double bass
- Kristy Morrell, French horn
- Cynthia Munzer, vocalist
- Danielle Ondarza, orchestra manager
- Giulio Ongaro, musicologist
- Josh Roach, orchestra manager
- Peter Rofé, double bass*
- Jo-Michael Scheibe, choral conductor
- Jim Self, tuba
- Bryan R. Simms, musicologist
- Carl St.Clair, orchestra conductor
- Joel Timm, oboe

*not on the USC Thornton faculty

The Orchestra and How It Works

THE SYMPHONY ORCHESTRA IS NOT just an ensemble of musicians. It is a social culture, a political system, a professional workplace, a self-contained environment, a business, and a monarchy all at the same time. It is not only the largest of classical instrumental musical ensembles; it is also one of the most structured organizations within our Western musical tradition.

Most of the customs inherent in an orchestra date back decades or even centuries. They are not easily changed, and most have a reason for still existing. Often these reasons are based on practical matters concerning the score and the ensemble, but some are based simply on a respect for musical tradition.

For the uninitiated, this tangle of traditions can be at once intriguing, illuminating, and intimidating. By providing the answers to the following listener questions, we hope to remove "intimidating" from that list and simply enhance your fascination with this most remarkable ensemble.

Why is an oboe always used to tune the orchestra?

Every symphony concert starts with the concertmaster coming on stage and indicating to the oboist to sound a pitch to which the rest of the orchestra tunes. (This nearly always happens in two parts: the oboe's first A signals the pitch for the winds and brass. Then the oboist plays a second A for the strings.) But most of us probably never give it a thought: why the oboe?

A good guess would be that the oboe's pure and piercing tone quality makes it easy to hear the pitch clearly. As logical as this sounds and as common a belief as it is, this is not the reason the oboe is given such an important role.

To understand the real reason, we need to travel back to a time when there were no specific means for communicating precise pitches. Each town would have its own approximation of A or C♯, much as every town had its own estimation of the exact occurrence of noon, which was when the sun was overhead. Since travel was not common (and was quite slow), these issues could be decided at the town level quite satisfactorily.

Often the standard for pitch was a local church organ. However, if the violinist (or any string instrument player) went to the church and tuned to the organ, the instrument would be out of tune by the time they returned to the performance venue due to the slippage of the tuning peg, changes in temperature, and simply the unavoidable jostling of the instrument. This would be true of any instrument in the orchestra except the oboe. How an oboe creates a specific pitch is different from how other instruments in the orchestra do.

The pitch of the oboe is created by the shape and texture of the reed. Most oboists spend hours constructing their own reeds to produce the exact pitch that the conductor has decided to use as the reference pitch (the idea of reference pitch is discussed later). Once the reed is finished, the pitch is stable, unaffected either by air temperature or by moving the instrument. Thus, the oboist creates the perfect A prior to the concert, transports it to stage, and shares it with the rest of the orchestra. (It should be noted that, as with other wind instruments, the oboist, even while in mid-note, can adjust the oboe's pitch by adjusting his or her embouchure; that is, the position of the lips and mouth muscles.)

The next logical question is why is this still done today when the other instruments have more stable tuning and inexpensive electronic tuners are readily available? The most common answer given to this question is that it is simply a matter of tradition. In fact, that is probably the most realistic answer, because the need for the oboist to be the "keeper of the pitch" actually disappeared around 1711, when the metal pitchfork was invented. The pitchfork is a piece of precision cut metal roughly resembling a slingshot. When struck, the pitchfork vibrates at a designated pitch, usually 440 vibrations per second, or the common A.

Since that time oboists themselves have used the pitchfork—and more recently electronic tuners—to ensure that their instrument's pitch matches the specifications of the conductor. Today this responsibility could be held by any number of instruments or by the electronic tuner itself.

At a recent concert, I heard someone ask, "At what pitch does this orchestra play?" What followed was a spirited conversation about the advantages and disadvantages of a particular pitch. What ever were they talking about?

Believe it or not, it is still a matter of opinion where the pitch A should be. While there is worldwide agreement that

A is a pitch that vibrates at approximately 440 times per second (called A 440) it is the "approximately" that is open to fairly wide interpretation.

The conductor or music director of the orchestra gets to decide where to place the pitch A that is used as a reference for tuning all the other pitches. Some orchestras prefer to put A slightly higher, at 442 or 443 vibrations per second, to give the orchestra a brighter or more energetic sound. Others place it lower, at 438, which is perceived to create a warmer sound. This is complicated by the fact that A has moved over the years. In Bach's time (the first half of the eighteenth century) A was lower, somewhere around 415. For authenticity's sake, some orchestras and ensembles use A 415 when performing music of the baroque era.

All of this is made more confusing by the fact that most electronic instruments are tuned in the factory to A 440. While many electronic instruments have a way to change this preset tuning, it is not very common. This is one of the reasons that electronic instruments have had a difficult time finding their way into symphony orchestras. One notable exception is in the movies. So many film scores use a combination of electronic and acoustic instruments that orchestras for film scores almost must use A 440.

Despite being largely an outdated holdover today, the oboist is still responsible for being the "keeper of the orchestra's A". Much as one might guard the fire for the Olympic torch, he or she must take this duty seriously and work at it diligently.

What do principals in an orchestra do that is different from what the others in the section do?

When you look at the orchestra roster in your program book, you will notice that certain members of the orchestra are designated as principals. There is *usually* one principal per instrument: a principal flute, cello, bassoon, trumpet, and so on through the orchestra. However, many modern orchestras also embrace the concept of co-principals, associate principals, or assistant principals, where two players assume the duties of leading the section at different times.

Being a principal is very prestigious. It is sort of like being class president of a section. Unlike a single class president, each principal has significant, individualized duties that contribute to the overall sound, quality, and personality of the orchestra. The duties of the principals vary according to two major divisions: winds and strings. In the winds, the principal often has his own part to play, with individualized solos. Composers for winds often write a primary line and a secondary line. The principal plays the primary line. It is also the principal who determines the intonation (or "in-tuneness") of the section. Next time you watch an orchestra perform, notice the orientation of the wind section (on some stages or from some places in the audience, it may be difficult to see this). The principals of the flute, clarinet, oboe, and bassoon are seated in such a way that they can easily hear each other.

A major duty of the principal is to listen to these other instruments and actually adjust tuning and sound quality to match the other instruments. It is up to the secondary members of each section to match the tuning and sound quality of their principal. In fact, it is the secondary member's duty to be in sync with every aspect of the principal member's playing, from breathing to intonation. In this way it is almost like the old-fashioned game called telephone, where this tuning and sound quality information is passed within and between sections. It is likewise a principal's responsibility to be in sync with the principals of the other sections and with the conductor. Both principal and secondary roles are quite challenging and, needless to say, require many years of training.

As you can clearly see from your seats in the hall, the string sections are much larger than the wind sections, so a principal string player oversees a larger ensemble. A major responsibility is marking the individual musical parts with the appropriate bowings (we cover this subject in detail in the next question). In addition, the principal strings are responsible for communicating what the conductor wants to achieve in a certain musical passage. And they have other duties.

As for the rank-and-file strings, you'll notice they tend to be seated in pairs and they share a music stand. Accordingly, each pair of string players is referred to as a stand. Conductors will often talk about having twelve stands of violins, for example. Within each stand there is an inside and outside player. The inside player turns pages and marks the conductor or principal player's requests in the score. This is to allow the outside player to continue playing, which ensures a continuous flow of music.

There is also one principal who is more influential than all the other principles in the orchestra. This person is the principal violinist, who is also designated by the name concertmaster, even principal concertmaster. The concertmaster is the second most important person in the orchestra, following the conductor / music director. The concertmaster is assumed to be the most skilled player in the violin section, and accordingly, he or she is often the most highly paid member of the orchestra other than the conductor.

Interestingly, in this day of an orchestral profession where conductors and players in orchestras come from all over the world, there is one place that this convention is not held. In the United Kingdom, the concertmaster is usually called leader, a term also used in the United States when the first violin leads the orchestra in certain baroque and classical works. If the UK was going to be the one country to have its own terminology, I would have expected its orchestras to use a more characteristic term such as "king" or "lord," but alas, they use the more pedantic term "leader" for some reason.

As you can see, there is nothing random or casual about the structure and practices of an orchestra. Every seating placement carries a unique responsibility that enables all the players to perform to the best of their abilities.

Is it true that the conductor tells the string players in which direction to move their bows for each note and that this affects the entire sound of the orchestra?

You may have noticed that within the string sections of the orchestra, the musicians generally move their bows in unison—that is, in the same direction at the same time—as prescribed by markings on their sheet music. This is not by accident. It is by design. That striking unity of motion certainly contributes to the beauty of what we see on stage, but it is also a crucial aspect of the quality of music making.

What most people find surprising is that an orchestra can play a given piece with different bowing patterns depending on the preferences of the person standing on the podium. That is because each conductor will ask for specific bowings to help achieve the sound he or she wants from the orchestra.

In its most basic form, bowing refers to the direction and speed the bow travels over the strings during a musical phrase. It can move up or down, fast or slow. (To create a different, less legato timbre, the strings can also be plucked with the fingers. This technique is known as pizzicato.)

Obviously, there is a purely practical reason that the entire string section has to decide on one, and only one, way to bow a passage. If they didn't, all the bows might bump into each other, maybe even get tangled. While that would make a great visual for a cartoon, in real life it would be a bit too distracting to the audience, not to mention dangerous to the performers and to their expensive bows. But there is a much more important reason that bowing must be unified: it defines the sound and shape of the musical phrase.

A good example of how the direction affects the sound is when a conductor decides that a specific phrase should crescendo (get louder). The best way to facilitate this would be for the strings to play that with an up-bow (the bow moving up toward the ceiling), which gives them more "oomph" at the end of the phrase. It's simply a matter of physics: the oomph is the result of the end of the bow closest to their hands being nearest the strings, allowing the player to apply more pressure. If the bows are heading downward, the tip of the bow would be on the string at the end of the phrase and it would be harder for the players to apply pressure.

The process of deciding bowings starts when the conductor decides what he or she wants from the orchestra for every phrase of a piece. When conductors are string players, they might have their own bowings for a given work. More commonly, the concertmaster works with the conductor to ascertain what is wanted, and then creates the bowings to facilitate his or her wishes. The concertmaster then notates the bowings for all of the other string play-ers, usually with the assistance of a professional orchestral librarian. Naturally these markings have to be in pencil; the next conductor will almost certainly want something completely different.

Many people are surprised that composers themselves do not specify the bowings they want when they are notat-ing the composition. It does happen sometimes, when the composer is after a specific effect. Works with great depth and scope, that is, works that allow for multiple interpreta-tions, are fulfilling and challenging for conductors, instru-mentalists, and members of the audience.

There are, and have been, some notable exceptions and experiments in regard to these conventions about bowings. Some orchestral scores of the romantic and modern era call for *divisi*, or divided strings within a section, resulting in dif-ferent bowing by subsets of the larger string section. Further, the music director of the Philadelphia Orchestra from 1912 to 1938, Leopold Stokowski, famously experimented with "free bowing"—that is, allowing the players to determine their own bow markings. He believed this free-for-all tech-nique produced a warmer, deeper sound. Not everyone agreed; when Eugene Ormandy succeeded Stokowski, the orchestra stopped the practice, and the idea never caught on.

As you can imagine, bowings are often subtle, personal, and open to debate. Ultimately the concertmaster has the final say, and you will never see a rogue string player in a professional orchestra *intentionally* bow in a different direction. A rare mistake, yes; even seasoned professional musicians are human.

Since bowings are so subjective and open to inter-pretation, not everyone in a section will agree with the concertmaster's mandate. One faculty member offered an interesting perspective on what it is like to perform with bowings with which you do not agree. In this case much of the concert is spent dreaming of deploying the bow in a somewhat untraditional manner on the concertmaster instead of on the instrument.

What is the difference between a "philharmonic" and a "symphony" orchestra? For example, what would be the difference between the Los Angeles Philharmonic and the London Symphony Orchestra? Is it the number of players in the group? Certain repertoire?

Clearly the most noticeable difference between the Los Angeles Philharmonic and the London Symphony Orchestra is the degree of suntan the musicians exhibit. Beyond that there is really no difference between ensembles that call themselves symphony orchestras, philharmonics, and simply orchestras. The different terms stem from different language and regional traditions but characterize essentially the same type of instrumental ensemble, one capable of performing large-scale works in the classical and romantic tradition, such as symphonies and concertos.

"Philharmonic" derives from French (*philharmonique*) and Italian (*filarmonico*), words designating a lover of harmony. "Orchestra" comes from Latin and Greek words meaning "to dance." In ancient Greece, the orchestra was the semicircular area at the front of the stage where the Greek chorus danced and sang. Similarly in a Roman theater, it's where senators and other important people enjoyed VIP seating. The word "symphony" derives from the Greek *syn* ("together") and *phōnē* ("sounding"), and the Latin word "*symphonia*," a term used in the Renaissance and even as far back as the Middle Ages to designate voices in concert or instrumental harmony. Today all three terms refer to a full-size orchestra (usually 70–120 players) featuring a large complement of strings, winds, brass instruments, and percussion, sometimes augmented by keyboards and electronics.

These terms are used interchangeably based on several factors. Firstly, the different names are sometimes employed to differentiate between more than one professional orchestra in a single city. London, one of the world's great musical capitals, boasts the London Symphony Orchestra, the London Philharmonic, the Philharmonia Orchestra, and many other full-size orchestras, in addition to numerous smaller ensembles. While having unique personalities determined by their respective music directors and musicians, these orchestras have basically the same instruments and play a similar repertoire. Think of it as New York boasting both the Yankees and the Mets (the baseball team, not the opera company). These teams play the same game, have the same number of players, and play by the same basic rules. New York is lucky to have two professional baseball teams, and they need to be differentiated in some manner.

The second factor in determining the name of the ensemble has to do with the sound of the name itself. While the "Philadelphia Philharmonic" (or "Philly Phil") has a certain ring to it, the combination of words probably doesn't quite offer the gravitas expected of a major city's premiere classical music ensemble.

While there is no difference between these ensembles (orchestra, symphony orchestra, and philharmonic), there are many other types of orchestras, including chamber, civic, studio, and jazz orchestras, and these name differences *do* matter.

A chamber orchestra is a considerably smaller ensemble than a symphony orchestra and will perform music that is written for the smaller complement of instruments. Music written prior to 1800 called for smaller orchestras, as does some music written after 1900. Thus, you will often hear music from these eras played by a chamber orchestra, which most commonly ranges from twenty to forty players.

A studio orchestra is one that often uses more of a jazz or popular music brass and rhythm section (and often electronic instruments) while having a full complement of strings and winds. You will find studio orchestras backing many jazz and popular singers. They also perform frequently on movie and television soundtracks. The name comes from the fact that much of the music they play originates from a studio recording.

"Jazz orchestra" is the term used for the ensemble often referred to as a jazz big band. This ensemble is completely different from the others and traditionally has seventeen members, consisting of five saxophones, four trumpets, four trombones, and a four-piece rhythm section of drums, bass, piano, and guitar.

There are also youth orchestras, school orchestras, community orchestras, flute orchestras, folk orchestras of a myriad of indigenous traditions, even kazoo orchestras.

How do orchestras determine how many musicians to employ for a piece? For example, how many of each stringed instrument perform symphonies of Mozart versus Mahler? What about a cello concerto? How many members are there in the chorus for the **Carmina Burana** *of Carl Orff or Beethoven's Ninth Symphony? What about opera and ballet orchestras? How much flexibility do orchestras have regarding head count? In tough economic times, do orchestras leave positions vacant?*

It often comes as a surprise that there is no fixed number of musicians that perform in a symphony orchestra. The size of a particular orchestra can vary from concert to concerts and even between compositions on the same program. Determining how many musicians to employ for a given concert is the result of a fairly straightforward formula. The size of the orchestra follows the basic historical line of when the piece was written. For instance, the size of the symphony orchestra increased steadily, starting with the classical period of Haydn, Mozart, and early Beethoven, through the romantic period of the nineteenth century and beyond, to Gustav Mahler's Eighth Symphony, nicknamed the "Symphony of a Thousand." While that nickname was a bit of an exaggeration—Mahler himself deplored it—the forces he specified for this sprawling work are immense: two mixed choirs, a children's chorus, eight vocal soloists, and a very large orchestra, including eight horns, an organ, a piano, a celesta, a harmonium, and at least one mandolin.

In contrast, a typical Mozart symphony uses approximately thirty strings, as well as winds in pairs—that is, two flutes, two clarinets, two oboes, and so on. Most classical era compositions have a specific number of wind and percussion parts written into the score, but there is some flexibility regarding the size of the string section. Essentially, the conductor wishes to create a good balance of sound between strings and winds.

As the orchestra grew in size and complexity during the nineteenth century, the size of the wind sections grew accordingly. In their large scores Richard Wagner, Richard Strauss, Anton Bruckner, and Mahler sometimes doubled or tripled the number of winds of the classical-era orchestra. To balance the sonic power of that many wind players, somewhere in the area of sixty-five to seventy-five string players are needed.

The same balancing strategy applies to a concerto. In a concerto there is usually at least one solo instrument (most frequently violin, piano, or cello). This means the conductor has another variable that needs attending to: the soloist must receive cues to know when and how loudly to play. Here not only does the orchestra have to be in balance with itself; it has to be balanced with the solo instrument to achieve a kind of dialogue, a musical conversation between soloist and ensemble. If the orchestra is too large or two small in relation to the sound of the solo instrument, there still might be a conversation, but one side will always appear to be shouting or whispering. A skilled composer will understand this complex relationship and write for the correct complement of winds, strings, and the rest, resulting in the appropriate overall size of the orchestra. It is not unusual, however, to take a few string players off such pieces so that the solo instrumentalist or vocalist does not have to struggle with balance issues. Again, nothing is written in stone, and the conductor makes this decision, sometimes after a trial-and-error period in rehearsal.

With regard to the size of the choir, in a work for orchestra and chorus such as Beethoven's Symphony no. 9 or Orff's *Carmina Burana*, the numbers will depend on the size and configuration of the venue. But a typical large chorus brought in for these kinds of works numbers around 120 singers, more or less equally divided between sopranos, altos, tenors, and basses. This number makes for a good balance between the orchestra and chorus.

The last factor in determining size is the occasional addition of instruments not normally found in an orchestra. For example, in his opera *Elektra*, Strauss not only called for the doubling, sometimes tripling, of the normal complement of winds and percussion; he also employed such unconventional instruments as a heckelphone (essentially a lower-pitched oboe with a wider bore and heavier tone), basset horns (members of the clarinet family. with curves), Wagner tubas (brass instruments with rotary valves that combine the tonal qualities of a French horn and a trombone), a bass trumpet, and others. If the conductor uses the full complement of strings that Strauss wanted, there are approximately 108 musicians in that pit. One can possibly cut down on the number of strings, but it takes at least forty-eight people just to cover the wind, brass, and percussion parts.

It should be clear that there is always flexibility with regard to head count, and yes, it is true that in tough economic times, especially with regional and community orchestras, there have been some improvisations in instrumentation and size of the orchestra. More common, however, is making more frugal repertoire choices to avoid those bigger, more expensive works. During lean seasons orchestras will sometimes refrain from hiring soloists altogether for some programs or at least avoid high-priced, big-name soloists.

When an orchestra adjusts its size to accommodate a certain piece of music, how is it decided which musicians

will play on which pieces? Is there a democratic rotation in place? Is it based on seniority? Or do certain players specialize in performing music from certain eras or by specific composers?

Let's get "democratic rotation" off the table. There is nothing democratic about an orchestra. Also, it really has nothing to do with an individual player's skill or affinity for a certain style of music. It has all to do with seating: if fewer instruments are needed, the back stands of the strings or the secondary winds are removed from the orchestra. If the Chicago Symphony, say, is going to perform a symphony by Mozart, the principal winds and the highest chairs in the strings are the ones who will perform. If it is followed by a late romantic symphony that demands a large orchestra, the lower chairs are brought in.

In an educational setting it will be different. At the USC Thornton School of Music, we rotate students throughout the orchestra so that more students can experience being principal, second chair, and so on. In fact, it is not uncommon for different principals to be featured in each piece on our orchestral concerts.

Whatever the size of the forces, seating in orchestras is taken very seriously and is never casually altered. For example, let's say that the inside player on the fourth violin stand resigns. The other players do not move up automatically. Instead, there are auditions for that chair (with freelance substitutes filling in for the period prior to the new hiring), and any player can apply from within or outside the orchestra. Thus, new players often enter the orchestra at a higher post than players with more seniority.

Over the past several decades, many major orchestras have instituted a policy to rotate seats in their string sections, at least after the top couple of stands, which are usually fixed. As Yvonne Caruthers, the longtime cellist of the National Symphony (of Washington, DC), explains, "With the old system new players sat at the back, supposedly to gain experience, only inching forward one seat at a time when someone died or retired from that section. That was not a healthy situation and everyone knew it. Can you imagine being stuck next to the same person for your entire career? There are many strong personalities in an orchestra, and lots of them don't blend very well. An algorithm was developed to ensure that the rotational system is as fair and random as possible. We trade seats every two weeks in the NSO. I believe rotational seating spreads out the more experienced with the less experienced players and builds more cohesive sections."

It's clear that seating in an orchestra is a very important element of the overall work environment. It determines the roles the musicians play and whether or not they play in a given piece or an entire concert. However, in regard to seating there is one very important thing to remember: do you know what they call the person who sits in the last seat of the second violin section in the Boston Symphony Orchestra? A fabulous musician.

An orchestra hires a soloist because it admires the soloist's artistry. But of course the conductor leads the soloist's performance. Whose interpretation is it? If there is an artistic disagreement, who wins?
You might think that the answer to this question would depend on whether you asked the conductor or the soloist. Therefore, I asked several of each. I was surprised how similar their answers were (with one notable difference).

Their answers were similar because it turns out that artistic disagreements between conductors and soloists happen all the time.

Both soloists and conductors bristled at the thought that anyone would regard this as "winning or losing." Great music is open to an almost endless variety of interpretations. It is exactly this fact that makes classical music so exciting to perform.

However, because of practical considerations the differences tend to be minor in most cases. A conductor (in consultation with the orchestra's artistic staff) chooses or approves a soloist to work with precisely because the conductor admires that soloist's Beethoven or Brahms interpretations or her flair for the contemporary repertoire. Therefore, in a general way a conductor knows what to expect from the soloist before the first rehearsal.

Interestingly, the more illustrious the musicians, the more likely differences will arise. That's because phenomenally skilled and experienced musicians delve into the music at deep and subjective levels, and so it's not surprising that a world-class soloist will also tend to be a highly opinionated musician. One internationally known soloist I spoke with said these differences happen all the time but the players involved rarely come to blows.

But sometimes they do. Longtime members of the LA Philharmonic well remember when the Italian maestro Carlo Maria Giulini, their normally serene, spiritually deep music director of the late 1970s and early 1980s, stomped offstage during a rehearsal of the Brahms Piano Concerto no. 2. The piano soloist, Giulini's countryman Maurizio Pollini, had presumed to tell the principal horn how to phrase his opening solo.

The Brahms piano concertos in particular seem to generate high emotions in the concert hall. A more famous controversy occurred in April 1962, when conductor Leonard Bernstein felt impelled to voice a pre-concert disclaimer prior to a Carnegie Hall performance by the New York Philharmonic of the Brahms Piano Concerto no. 1, disassociating himself from the interpretation of the soloist, Canadian virtuoso Glenn Gould, then only twenty-nine years old. Said the music director of the New York Philharmonic in part:

> You are about to hear a rather, shall we say, unorthodox performance of the Brahms D Minor Concerto, a performance distinctly different from any I've ever heard, or even dreamt of for that matter, in its remarkably broad tempi and its frequent departures from Brahms's dynamic indications. I cannot say I am in total agreement with Mr. Gould's conception and this raises the interesting question: "What am I doing conducting it?" I'm conducting it because Mr. Gould is so valid and serious an artist that I must take seriously anything he conceives in good faith and his conception is interesting enough so that I feel you should hear it, too.

Bernstein went on to address the present question: "In a concerto, who is the boss; the soloist or the conductor? The answer is, of course, sometimes one, sometimes the other, depending on the people involved. But almost always, the two manage to get together by persuasion or charm or even threats, to achieve a unified performance. I have only once before in my life had to submit to a soloist's wholly new and incompatible concept and that was the last time I accompanied Mr. Gould." The Carnegie Hall audience reportedly roared with laughter at this remark.

Gould retired from public performance at the age of thirty-one, just two years after the Brahms brouhaha.

For most concert artists, however, it is precisely these differences that make collaborations with different conductors and orchestras so rewarding. That's because it is from these divergences of opinion that a completely new and vibrant interpretation emerges. This fresh interpretation contains elements of both the conductor's and the soloist's musical proclivities. It's a type of musical marriage, exciting to share and to experience along with the audience.

You may wonder: on what issues do the soloists and conductors differ? Overall tempo, the use of *ritard* (a gradual decrease in tempo), the volume of the orchestra in relationship to the soloist, the phrasing of an orchestral solo line—almost anything. When I asked the conductors whose interpretation would be the final version if a compromise could not be reached, every conductor said the soloist's interpretation would win out. When I asked the soloists, every one said the soloist would yield to the conductor's interpretation.

Interesting paradox, don't you think?

I notice that some musicians in an orchestra play less frequently than others. The violins, for example, seem to rarely stop playing, while the brass players can sit for whole movements in silence. I've also observed some brass, wind or percussion players walk onstage just for specific pieces or movements rather than the entire concert. Is this fair?

It is true that some musicians in an orchestra seem to work harder than some of their colleagues, or at least for longer

stretches. String players hardly ever get a break from playing, and indeed some brass instruments can sit for ten to
thirty minutes during a performance and never play a note.
(These sections are referred to in the score as *tacet*, a Latin
word meaning "does not sound".) In one famous incident
in the 1970s, a member of the brass section of the world-
class Cleveland Orchestra was often seen reading a paper-
back onstage when he wasn't playing. After an article in
the newspaper taking the player to task and a minor uproar
from members of the audience (apparently unmoved by the
player's desire to expand his literary horizons), the musician was told he had to stop reading and pay attention to
the performance, whether he was playing or not.

This illuminates an important point that is true of all
aspects of music: even when a musician isn't playing, he
or she is an important part of the equation. Hardly anything about music lends itself to exact quantification. It
makes no sense to judge a symphony by how many instruments it contains or judge a solo by how many notes are
played per minute or determine the quality of a symphony
by its length. These elements simply do not matter when
it comes to the final product (except, of course, in one
of the most famous and amusing moments in the movie
Amadeus: Emperor Joseph II's haughty comment to Mozart
about his latest work, that "It's quality work. And there are
simply too many notes, that's all").

In the same way, it makes no sense to judge individual musicians by how much they "work." For example, the
brass players in a symphony may not play for the first half
of a piece of music, but when they do play, it has to be great.
Mistakes in the brass are highly detectable. Ideally, it has
to be perfect. Any mistake on the part of any musician can

ruin the entire performance. In this regard, every musician is equal regardless of the percentage of time he or she actually plays.

So how do orchestra musicians get paid? Is it proportionate to the number of notes they play? Which leads to an even bigger question: are orchestral musicians paid for rehearsals and performances or just for the performances?

Let's start with some basics. In all of the major orchestras the musicians are paid a salary plus health and retirement benefits. They are paid for a certain number of "services" per season, with every rehearsal and performance counting as a service.

The highest-paid musician in the orchestra (after the music director) is almost always the concertmaster. Next come the principal winds, brass, percussion, and keyboard players, and the principal strings (other than the concertmaster) followed by associate and assistant principals. In this regard, it is of great benefit to play an instrument that has only one of its kind in the orchestra, such as the harp, piano, contrabassoon, bass clarinet, timpani, bass trombone, or tuba. Their players are principals by default and receive higher pay.

Everyone else in the orchestra is considered to be a "section" player and basically makes "scale." Scale is generally 65 to 75 percent of what the principal player makes. Section scale is fastidiously and sometimes divisively negotiated between a committee of orchestra members and the management of the orchestra. The resulting contract that contains this and all other pertinent information (such as benefits, media agreements, vacation time, even tour accommodations) is generally renegotiated every three years.

What is ironic is that the brass and winds (the musicians who play less frequently) in general make more than the section strings. Traditionally, wind, brass, and percussion players negotiate their salaries when they win the auditions in the first place. This differential pay scale is justified because winds play their own individual part in the orchestra and frequently play heavy-pressure solos that define the very texture of a work. It seems fair that these section players make more than basic scale.

Even though there are many first violins in an orchestra, I think they play the same part most of the time. But I recently heard someone refer to different parts within the horn section. Do the wind instruments play different parts, or does each section play in unison to balance all the strings?

The wind instruments can play both in unison and as individual voices, depending on how the music is written. It is, however, actually more common for composers to divide the winds to achieve different harmonies and textures. The various wind instruments produce sounds in different ways and therefore offer different timbres (sonic textures) that enrich the sonic fabric. As noted, the winds and brass instruments readily cut through the orchestral sound, and can play with a lot of power. Therefore, a few of these players can balance the strings pretty easily, even when subdivided in such a way that single instruments play each part.

While the string sections do often play in unison (though contemporary composers frequently break up this unison sound), the wind parts have some interesting personal and musical dynamics inherent in their sections. For example, in the horn section there are four distinct roles played by the four members of the section. The fourth horn is the foundation of the section. That person anchors the team harmonically. That is, the fourth horn often plays the lowest note of any given chord. The fourth horn rarely has a solo. (Unless, of course, he or she makes a mistake counting rests.)

Third horn is really the other principal in the section but without all of the responsibilities and with slightly less frequent performance pressures. This person will often play the melodic lines with the principal (first horn) or support the principal with a secondary part in the upper register. Third horn does sometimes have solo parts or can lead the section when the composer gives the principal a rest.

Second horn is the most versatile. The job of this player is to support the principal in the section and in solo passages. This person must be proficient in all ranges of the instrument because he or she may have to play high and low. This person is really the diplomat in the section. He or she can get along with anyone and hopefully can make the principal comfortable enough to play his or her best.

The principal is the leader of the section and gets to decide the style, dynamic, color, and interpretation of the music, according to the dictates of the conductor. That person on the podium is the boss of the orchestra, and the principal horn is a liaison to the conductor on behalf of the section. In other words, if the conductor is not satisfied with the horn sound, it is the responsibility of the principal to fix the problem. The principal often plays the highest notes and most often bears the burden (and the glory) of the big solos.

THE ORCHESTRA AND HOW IT WORKS | **25**

There are similarly understood roles in the other brass and in the woodwinds. Thus, it is clear that not only does an individual player have to be an excellent performer but also must be an effective team player, understanding (and accepting) the unique role his or her part plays within the orchestra, even if it is not the most glamorous or soloistic role of that section.

In the string sections particularly but all sections in general, what is the pecking order? Who is in the top chair position? Is this done by "blind audition"?

The "top chair position" is better known as the principal position of each section. Every section in the orchestra has a principal. This means there are quite a few principals in the orchestra: in addition to the top first violin player, the concertmaster, there is principal second violin, principal viola, cello, bass, flute, clarinet, oboe, bassoon, trumpet, horn, and so on. Each principal position is both a musical and administrative leader.

The selection of a principal is taken very seriously. Principals are chosen after an exhaustive audition process by a panel of peer musicians, usually an elected committee that includes the music director. For example, if a section violist were to apply for the principal viola position, the panel of evaluators would consist of not only the principal strings but perhaps also key wind and percussion players. For a major orchestra, there are several rounds of auditions.

The first cut often takes place based on résumés—or these days, DVDs plus résumés—submitted by prospective players. Then a relatively small percentage of those applicants is invited for live auditions. These frequently take place behind a screen, making them what are called blind auditions; this is to ensure that any possible personal connection or the appearance of an issue doesn't affect the ultimate decision. Often the final round takes place directly in front of the panel, which now includes the orchestra's music director. With some orchestras, the audition committee recommends two or three final candidates. These lucky players may be invited to play a concert, sometimes a series of concerts, to determine if they are a good fit with the rest of the players. In this case, the music director often makes the final decision.

In *every* orchestra, the principal posts are leadership positions. These individuals are expected to be the most accomplished musicians of their sections.

The Maestro and Music Director

NO ONE IS AS REVERED, feared, admired, and occasionally despised as the conductor of an orchestra, the so-called maestro ("maestra" for female conductors). The maestro is the face of the orchestra to the musicians and to the public, the one person with the authority to shape the musical mission and identity of the ensemble. However, the power of this position emerges if, and only if, the individual has the leadership and musical skills to inspire the musicians to follow his or her artistic lead. Clearly it takes more than conducting technique to be a successful maestro.

In this chapter, we'll address questions from our listeners related to this larger-than-life persona, including the professional, logistical, and personal dimensions. You, too, will learn to revere, fear, admire, and occasionally despise these charismatic musicians.

What is the difference between a music director, principal conductor, principal guest conductor, resident conductor, and just plain conductor?

There are many different titles for individuals who, from the audience's perspective, do exactly the same thing: wave their arms at the musicians. But as is the case with most traditions relating to the orchestra, there is a fairly clear differentiation of roles reflected in the various titles, though each orchestra will define those roles somewhat differently.

These various conductor titles, by the way, have no impact on what happens on the podium; they pertain to the ongoing relationship between the conductor and the orchestra, as well as specific duties off the podium.

To start with the most basic term, the "conductor" is simply the person who is on the podium during an orchestral performance, taking charge of the musical interpretation. Audience members have no way of knowing if the person has a close, ongoing relationship with the institution unless they read the conductor's bio in the program book. The duties during the performance are exactly the same, whether the conductor is a music director or merely a guest.

The terms "music director" and "principal conductor" may refer to the same role. "Music director" is more common in the United States; "principal conductor" is frequently used in Europe. In both cases, the title refers to the artistic leader of the orchestra. (A high-profile exception: James Levine holds the post of music director while Fabio Luisi is principal conductor of the same great ensemble, the orchestra of the Metropolitan Opera.)

Whatever they're called, these chief conductors enjoy great latitude in programming, that is, choosing the music for the coming seasons, often with input from the orchestra's artistic administrator, as well as the hiring and firing of musicians. The music director is also expected to help cultivate major donors and generally serves as the public face of an orchestra.

It stands to reason that the personality and public image of an orchestra is a direct reflection of the music director's artistic vision and musical priorities. For example, it is the music director who would decide during the course of a given season to highlight contemporary music, collaborate with a particular soloist for special projects, deepen the orchestra's commitment to local schools, or champion neglected or underrepresented composers. It is this vision, realized in conjunction with top administrative leaders of the orchestra, that defines how the programming for a season is shaped, as well as what will drive the orchestra's long-term goals.

The music director / principal conductor is also the person who usually conducts more concerts during the season than any of the guest or assistant conductors. He or she therefore influences the orchestra's personality in other ways.

Each conductor has strengths and weaknesses. If a conductor is renowned for his or her interpretations of Mahler, for example, this will become, by default, a characteristic of the orchestra. If the conductor is uncomfortable with the baroque repertoire, the orchestra is unlikely to earn renown for its performances of Bach and Handel, though a visiting or guest conductor can help fill in the gaps.

If a conductor possesses a strikingly clear beat, fosters crisp and accurate rhythms and transparent textures, the orchestra becomes known for its technical mastery. George Szell's reign with the Cleveland Orchestra is a case in point, as is Fritz Reiner's with the Chicago Symphony and previously with the Pittsburgh Symphony.

However high-spirited the temperament of some music directors, past and present, their stature in the musical world is equally lofty. As such, it is not uncommon for such an individual to serve as music director of more than one orchestra. These well-compensated maestri are also in great demand as guest conductors with major orchestras around the world, at least those ensembles that can afford their fees. For this reason, it is likely the music director / principal conductor will be absent quite frequently during a given season. Since musicians flourish in a stable atmosphere and require continuity of vision to move steadily toward their loftier artistic goals, some orchestras and opera companies also hire what is called a resident conductor.

The resident conductor functions exactly as the name implies: this is the person who is "in residence" with an orchestra or opera company much of the time. The resident conductor provides the artistic continuity for the ensemble, especially in the absence of the music director.

The duties of the resident conductor are many. First, this person has to be in close communication with the principal conductor or music director to ensure that the orchestra is constantly moving toward the overall musical goals that have been identified. The first rehearsals are often prepared and conducted by the resident conductor before turning the baton over to the person who will eventually conduct the concert. At least several times a season the resident conductor will also prepare the orchestra from start to finish and conduct the public performance.

Though the audience will not see most of the work of the resident conductor, he or she is the most important person, after the principal conductor and top administrator, in determining the success of an orchestra.

A guest conductor, who is exactly what the name implies, is approved for work with the orchestra by the principal conductor. A guest conductor is on the podium for a specific concert or series of concerts and may or may not have an ongoing relationship with the orchestra. A principal guest conductor does enjoy an ongoing relationship with the orchestra and functions more or less as the guest conductor of first choice.

Orchestras frequently hire assistant conductors as crucial backups. Very often at short notice, an assistant conductor fills in for an ailing or geographically stranded resident conductor or music director or even for a guest conductor who, for whatever reason, can't fulfill his or her duties. In this capacity, assistant conductors, most often young musicians on the rise, are said to "cover" rehearsals and performances, much as opera singers and musical theater performers lean on understudies. Assistant conductors are expected to know the score well enough to conduct it at a moment's notice; while attending rehearsals, they may also serve as a consultant to the conductor on orchestra balances in the hall.

Two other titles are sometimes used: conductor laureate and conductor emeritus. Both are usually reserved for a conductor who has enjoyed a long and fruitful relationship as a former music director with the orchestra and has either moved on or retired. For example, if an extremely popular or influential principal conductor were to retire from an orchestra, he or she could be given the title conductor emeritus or conductor laureate. The implication is that such conductors are welcome to return (if still active) and upon returning will be treated with the respect and dignity their years with the orchestra have earned them.

How many of these positions to use is the decision of the orchestra management. Not every orchestra employs a principal guest conductor, resident conductor, or conductor emeritus. Some ensembles, following a model used more frequently in the United Kingdom, have multiple music directors: the Saint Paul Chamber Orchestra, for example, is run by the orchestral musicians themselves, in collaboration with a diverse group of what they call artistic partners, including pianist Jeremy Denk and violinist Joshua Bell.

Confusing? You betcha.

Finally, a word of caution: if you are ever invited to go backstage after a concert or interact with a conductor, there is a very important protocol that you need to know. The orchestra players, staff members, and even the audience refer to a prominent conductor as Maestro. Thus if someone named, say, Roberto Cutietta is the seasoned conductor engaged for a concert, he would be addressed as "Maestro" or "Maestro Cutietta." To call him "Mr. Cutietta", "Conductor Cutietta," "Roberto," or, heaven forbid, "Rob" would be viewed as a sign of disrespect. Break this protocol at your own risk. Do so and you can expect to glimpse that fire-and-brimstone glare musicians have come to know in rehearsal.

Lately, I have noticed that a music director is absent for much of an orchestra's season. Guest or resident conductors lead the rest of the programs. This can be disappointing or at least disconcerting to the audience and, I assume, to the orchestra. Is this something relatively new?

The life of a conductor of a major symphony orchestra has certainly changed over time. Today's conductors are jet-setters. As noted, they sometimes juggle posts with multiple orchestras, often in different countries. Rare is the prominent maestro who conducts one and only one orchestra in a season.

There are three basic reasons for this phenomenon. First of all, conductors *can* work with multiple orchestras because of the ease of worldwide travel. The schedules that some of today's preeminent conductors maintain would have been physically impossible a few decades ago. Los Angeles Opera General Director Placido Domingo has been known to hop an overnight flight following an opera performance in Los Angeles (either as the lead singer or conductor) to rehearse the next day at New York's Metropolitan Opera or in Madrid. And there's no rest in flight for the weary singer/ conductor; Domingo says airplanes are his favorite environment for learning new roles and studying scores.

Secondly, everything is quicker than it used to be behind the scenes. Today members of a topnotch orchestra are expected to show up to the first rehearsal with their individual parts learned to concert perfection. As a result, the entire program can be polished in just three or four rehearsals. In the past, sometimes dozens of rehearsals were required (and were more financially feasible) to explore, practice, and polish the music. Today's orchestras are lean and efficient organizations that can effectively prepare a concert in a very short time. This allows the principal conductor, for example, to take a week off, conduct another orchestra, and return home. It also allows a guest conductor to be in residence with the orchestra for only one week, making scheduling easier.

Lastly, this game of "musical chairs" is tolerated because the conductor's home orchestra, to a degree, actually wants its music director to travel the world. A conductor who works with multiple world-class orchestras brings prestige and attention to his or her home orchestra. The more famous the conductor, the more renowned the orchestra with which he or she is most closely associated.

The players, too, have adapted to the current pattern of showcasing a variety of conductors during a season. Many even prefer this arrangement. There is a certain freshness that comes with working with different conductors. Naturally, each player has his or her preferences, but over the course of a season or two, presumably everyone has had a chance to work with his or her favorite.

A side benefit for the musicians is that the days of the tyrant conductor are largely behind us. In no way do conductors "own" the musicians, as they tended to do in the past: union regulations protect the players in major orchestras from unpaid overtime, verbal abuse, unfair suspensions, and, as noted, impulsive firings. Nor do music directors necessarily crave total devotion: after all, they can't claim fidelity to one "band" (as orchestra members themselves often refer to an orchestra); the conductor is frequently off gallivanting with other orchestras!

Clearly an argument can be made that for all these reasons, today's music directors tend to place less of a personal stamp on their orchestras. Yet on the plus side, this state of affairs provides both audiences and musicians with variety, freshness, and new energy, hopefully sacrificing neither performance quality nor cohesiveness. It is the poor maestros who must be pitied: spending so much of their precious time trying to calculate what time zone they are in.

Every orchestra conductor seems to have a different baton technique. Is there any consistency of gestures

and cues? If not, how can orchestra musicians figure out how to play with so many different conductors?

It is true: there are as many conducting styles as there are conductors. Some styles are so personal to the individual that you would swear no player could possibly follow them. Carlo Maria Giulini's beat was sometimes indecipherably wobbly, yet the purity of his musical vision and his fiery intensity often resulted in performances of epic grandeur. He is still spoken of in reverent tones by veteran audience members and orchestra players at the Chicago Symphony, where he was principal guest conductor from 1969 to 1972, and in Los Angeles, where he was music director in the late 1970s and early 1980s.

Some conductors are reserved and restrained; others are flamboyant, extroverted, and even larger than life—think of Leonard Bernstein, especially early in his career. "Often, in moments of excitement, he would leave the podium entirely," wrote Donal Henahan in his *New York Times* obituary for Bernstein in October 1990, "rising like a rocket, arms flung aloft in indication of triumphal climax. So animated, in fact, was Mr. Bernstein's conducting style at this point in his career that it could cause problems. At his first rehearsal for a guest appearance with the St. Louis Symphony, his initial downbeat so startled the musicians that they simply looked in amazement and made no sound."

Bernstein, of course, was a peerless, highly engaging orator on music, lecturing at Harvard and becoming a beloved television commentator on the prestigious series *Omnibus* and with his New York Philharmonic Young People's Concerts. Composer and conductor André Previn scored in a slightly more modest vein with his witty PBS series *Previn and the Pittsburgh* and on numerous radio broadcasts. More recently, San Francisco Symphony Music Director Michael Tilson Thomas earned accolades for both the television and radio series *Keeping Score*.

Other conductors let their baton do all the talking. Some, such as Pierre Boulez, Georges Prêtre, Leopold Stokowski, and Dimitri Mitropoulos, often didn't use a baton at all.

However, there are basic techniques to which most conductors adhere. Otherwise, they would be unable to communicate their musical intentions. Let's start with the hands. If you notice, the right hand is where the conductor nearly always holds the baton. The baton helps the conductor communicate the tempo and flow of the music. In this regard, the right hand is the timekeeper. The time is communicated by very specific conducting patterns that all conductors use. These patterns change based on how many beats there are in any given measure, but some things stay constant. For example, the first beat of every measure is always expressed by a downward stroke. This is why the first beat of a measure is called the downbeat; the conductor's hand, with or without a baton, lays down the foundation to designate this all-important starting beat.

The last beat of the measure is always communicated with the hand heading upward. The logical reason for this: what goes up must come down—for the next downbeat. In between these two beats there are various specific patterns that can be executed, depending on how many beats per measure.

So the right hand demonstrates when the piece starts and ends and how fast the music should be played. But there is more. The right hand also shows how the music flows. If the conductor wants a heavy beat, like in a march, the pattern will be angular and very specific. If the beat is to be flowing, like in a waltz, the pattern will be smooth and connected. Naturally, there is every possibility in between. But even if you were hearing-impaired, by watching the conductor's right-hand movements you could sense both the tempo and the overall feel of the music.

Sometimes the left hand mirrors the right hand, simply executing the beat pattern in reverse. This technique is used when the conductor wants to communicate that everyone is playing and "we are all in this together." But this mirroring is used only for certain passages. More frequently the left hand functions independently as a kind of pointer, cueing certain players to begin or finish a particular solo or passage. Sure, these entrances are notated in the music. But a precise cue from the conductor results in a more accurate and confident entrance. It assures the player that he or she did not miscount; this is the moment to shine.

It goes further, however. The conductor's left-hand cue tells the player not only *when* to begin a passage, but *how* to begin. The player has to enter seamlessly into the overall sound of the orchestra in a way that matches how everyone else is playing. It is much like a relay racer starting to run prior to grasping the racing baton so that he or she is moving at the same speed as the first runner. Soloists and, for that matter, an entire section about to entire the fray must match their colleagues already playing in sound and style. The gesture of the conductor communicates how the entrance should proceed: forcefully, almost imperceptibly, bombastically, softly . . . the possibilities are almost endless.

These hand functions compose the main tenets of conventional conducting technique, but experienced conductors boast two additional tools to communicate their intentions to the orchestra: the face and the rest of the body.

The emotion in a conductor's face helps the players feel the music. A conductor whose eyes are closed as in ecstasy is trying to portray a very different tone from the conductor whose eyes are full of fire and brimstone. Inevitably, the conductor's face may sometimes also register either high approval or barely masked chagrin with a solo passage just performed.

Though in most concert halls, the audience can't see the conductor's facial expressions during the music, quite a lot of private nonverbal communication occurs between conductor and players. One of the treats of sitting in the less expensive seats behind the orchestra in certain venues, such as the Berlin Philharmonie and LA's Walt Disney Concert Hall, is observing this unique dynamic in action. Like the orchestra members, the audience members seated in these sections face the conductor. It's Conducting 101, without the quizzes.

Lastly, the conductor uses his or her entire body to help convey emotion. Like the trajectory of the baton, sharp, percussive body movements and gentle swaying express very different things.

These are the basic methods that a conductor uses to try to get the orchestra to play in a manner that matches the sound the conductor is hearing in his or her head. But there is great variation and even some outright ignoring of all of this. When an orchestra and a conductor have worked together cohesively and productively for years, there is a deep, often wordless, understanding, much as in a long marriage. In these cases the conductor can drop many of these conventions and still the orchestra will know what is expected. I recently went to a concert where the orchestra was playing so magnificently that the conductor literally stopped conducting and just stood on the podium for a while, seemingly taking in and enjoying the orchestra's performance. The orchestra played on, and this might have been the highest compliment the players could have been paid. I just hope the conductor's pay was not reduced for the time he "wasn't working."

Some orchestras work regularly with no conductor, and they seem to do it well. I thought that the position of conductor was fundamental for any serious musical ensemble. Was I wrong? Do you think this tendency of conductorless orchestras will spread in these difficult economic times?

There are indeed some smaller orchestras, or chamber orchestras, that do not employ a designated conductor, but there is always a leader. You may not immediately recognize the leader because he or she is also playing an instrument in the orchestra. The sole determinant of whether there is an actual conductor has nothing to do with economics but instead the size of the orchestra, the music being performed, and the preference of the musicians.

Think of it as a continuum. String quartets, jazz combos, rock bands, piano trios, wind quintets all play quite well without a conductor. Ensembles can get larger, even the size of a small orchestra, and still function quite well without a conductor. For example, the Orpheus Chamber Orchestra was founded in New York in 1972 without a designated music director or conductor. According to its website, Orpheus "rotates musical leadership roles for each work, and strives to perform diverse repertoire through collaboration and open dialogue." The experiment is working: to date, the Grammy-winning group has made over seventy recordings and enjoys an annual concert series at Carnegie Hall as well as tours throughout the world.

Typically, the repertoire of this and other chamber orchestras consists primarily of music from the baroque and classical eras, plus modern works, traditionally performed by a group numbering forty players or fewer. There is a historical precedent: through the eighteenth century, the concertmaster often served as leader, directing the orchestra from the first violin chair or, as is sometimes seen today in a nod to authentic performance practices, standing up with the ensemble. Composer–keyboard players such as Bach, Haydn, and Mozart led the orchestra from the cembalo (or harpsichord) as they played.

But beginning in the early nineteenth century, as both the orchestra and the musical works expanded in size and complexity, it became necessary to have one person (who was not also performing) lead the orchestra. Violinist, composer, and conductor Louis Spohr, a sometime chamber music partner of Beethoven's, claimed to be the first person to use a baton. He did so to keep the players together— as an extension of his arm, so that everyone could see him. (Some also credit Spohr with the invention of rehearsal letters, placed strategically throughout a player's part; that is, his or her sheet music. To save time in rehearsal, conductors refer to these letter markers, as often numeric nowadays, when requesting the orchestra to repeat a given passage, such as "Let's start at four bars after D" or "Take it from three bars before 33.")

At the borderline of the classical and romantic eras in music, large-scale orchestral works, such as Beethoven's

Eroica Symphony, premiered in 1805, required a conductor to take on the role of musical traffic cop for both practical and musical reasons.

On the practical side, many of the players in a large orchestra sit a good distance from their colleagues and from the conductor. For example, the distance between any given bassist and second violinist can be equal to the entire proscenium of the stage. Likewise, the entire depth of the orchestra often separates the percussionist and the concertmaster.

This distance creates several problems. Firstly, it's impossible for all of the players to see each other. Secondly, as the sound travels, there is a time lag between sections. If you have ever seen a marching band on a football field you have probably noticed that the music can seem to be falling apart when the band is widely spread out. The ensemble is in fact not falling apart; it simply takes more time for the sound to travel from the far end of the field to your ears. Consequently, those band members on the field have to learn to trust the conductor instead of what they are hearing; not an easy task.

The same phenomenon happens, to a lesser extent, on the orchestra stage. Without an agreed-upon standard, the sound lag from one end of an orchestra to the other could throw the musicians off their timing. To prevent a musical catastrophe and preserve the sense of ensemble, early conductors literally hit a stick on the floor to maintain the beat. But this quickly gave way to today's more sophisticated hand movements after one famous musician, the French court composer, dancer, and conductor Jean-Baptiste Lully, accidentally hit his foot with the stick while leading a performance of his Te Deum in a Parisian church on January 8, 1687. The infection spread to his leg, and he died of gangrene a few months later. While I believe every orchestral player at some point or another has wished this exact fate on his or her conductor, Lully's death pointed out that there had to be a better way to conduct.

As I indicated, the conductor's role grew in importance in direct proportion to the music's increasing complexity, not only rhythmically but also in terms of its dimensions and its expressive potential. Conductor's beats became more fluid to better communicate the wider range of expressivity. Also, dynamics (changes in volume) grew more subtle and changeable. Someone needed to be the arbiter of all these musical variables. Thus, the post of conductor was born, a position vital for any serious large musical group, choral or instrumental. Again, smaller ensembles constitute the exception. But even there, while it may not be obvious to the audience, there is almost always one musician empowered to lead the group in performance.

It should be clear that we will not be seeing a trend of conductorless orchestras due to financial constraints or for any other reason. Large orchestras need conductors. To cut costs, it's not unusual for orchestras to program some pieces—or even entire concerts—requiring fewer musicians. But a conductor is too critical to the success of an orchestra to be eliminated.

In many chamber orchestras one of the musicians is actually the conductor as well. How can one play the piano, violin, flute, or other instrument and effectively conduct the orchestra at the same time?
Being a musician who is playing and also conducting the orchestra is not for the faint of heart. It might be the ultimate example of multitasking in a musical setting.

Only small orchestras can perform without a stand-alone conductor. The reasons for this are explained in the answer to the previous question. However, even without a person standing on the podium, musical groups need a designated leader, someone they can see and follow. This individual is responsible for all of the normal tasks of a more conventional conductor. He or she must lead the ensemble through tempo and dynamic changes while also cueing other instruments to enter and cut off. He or she is the player everyone should turn to (figuratively) if something goes wrong: one of the sections or musicians getting lost, missing an entrance, forgetting to repeat a passage, or somehow getting out of sequence with the rest of the ensemble.

There are certain instruments that lend themselves to this role better than others. The most common are the concertmaster (lead violinist) or a solo keyboard instrument, such as piano or harpsichord.

Location is a great advantage for the concertmaster. The concertmaster sits closest to where a traditional conductor stands on the podium. Therefore, musicians are used to looking for leadership in that general direction. Nearly all the musicians can see the lead violinist, and the lead violinist can watch nearly all of the players.

Secondly, without much difficulty, a violinist can simultaneously play the instrument and move to the beat of the music. The violin can be lifted or "pointed" without interfering with the sound or intonation of the instrument. For example, when a trumpeter or oboist moves the instrument, the movement immediately alters the relationship between the mouth of the performer and the instrument, thus affecting the sound. This does not happen with the violin. Therefore you will most often see the first violinist as the leader. The only other instrument that really has as much flexibility of movement is the flute. It, too, can be moved to indicate entrances or tempos and is less influenced by the performer's head movements than most other wind instruments. Unfortunately, the traditional seating location of the flutes within the orchestra is not as advantageous as the first violin.

The violin also has the extra musical advantage of often playing the most prominent melodic part in the music. Thus from a musical standpoint, the first violin is at the center of things; even without adding extra hand or facial gestures, the first violinist tends to embody the musical content.

The piano has certain advantages over the violin but also limitations. Obviously, in order for the keyboardist to conduct, there must be a piano or harpsichord part written into the music. This is not a problem with much of the music written prior to 1750; a harpsichord was viewed as a regular part of the orchestra, acting, often in concert with a lower stringed instrument, as part of the continuo, establishing the harmonic anchor of a work. When that tradition began to fade, orchestral composers used the keyboard only sporadically.

However, if a keyboard instrument is available to lead, the advantages are several. First, as the instrument is often placed smack in the center of the ensemble, it affords clear visual cues. Secondly, the keyboardist can often continue playing with only one hand and use the other hand more in the manner of a traditional conductor. Hand gestures can be used for cueing entrances, tempo changes, and even expressivity. Even if the musician cannot always free up one hand to make a gesture, his or her head is free to make eye contact, nod, or effect any number of gyrations that can communicate to the other musicians without interfering with the performance.

All of this being said, there are probably examples of just about any instrument in a chamber orchestra being used to lead the ensemble. This would almost certainly be the result of the individual behind the instrument having exceptional leadership skills, being the administrative leader of the ensemble, or having earned the respect of the other players. Still, violinists and pianists dominate the landscape of what are sometimes referred to today as player-conductors.

All of this leads to another, slightly touchy question: what are the advantages or disadvantages of having an orchestra play without a conductor? Indeed, there are both. Rehearsals can be less efficient without a conductor; the leader must explain and verbalize all aspects of the music, from phrasing to dynamics, to be sure everyone in the orchestra understands the musical goals and can deliver a cohesive, sensitive performance in response to only a nod, glance, or tip of an instrument. However, musicians find it very exciting and rewarding to play in such a tight-knit ensemble, in which each performer has a heightened level of responsibility to listen intently and to pull together as a powerful team. Plus, every now and again, most orchestral musicians just want to remind the maestros of the world who in an orchestra is *truly* indispensable.

Sometimes there are other, more ceremonial, reasons for an orchestra to perform without a conductor. For example, the New York Philharmonic often performs the overture to *Candide* without a conductor as a tribute to Leonard

Bernstein, its composer, who was also the New York Philharmonic's music director for many years.

Another example results in a situation that sometimes arises that is often fun to watch. Recently, it has become somewhat common for a donor to an orchestra to "buy", usually at a gala auction, the opportunity to conduct the orchestra in a concert. Usually the donor will conduct the national anthem or some short overture after a private conducting lesson with the maestro. If you are lucky enough to attend a concert such as this, watch the orchestra members while they are performing. Almost no one will be watching the conductor. Instead they will be watching the concertmaster, whom they know they can trust for their tempos, cues, and phrasing. This might be evidence that even the largest of orchestras sometimes perform without a conductor even though there is someone standing on the podium seemingly conducting.

Why does the conductor leave the stage between pieces? Is it to generate more applause?

While the reputation of some conductors might lead you to believe they will do anything for more applause, the reason the conductor leaves the stage between pieces is more complicated. However, *controlling* audience applause does indeed factor into the stage-leaving convention.

When a piece in a concert is finished, the conductor will take a bow, accept the applause, and then leave the stage. If the audience continues to show its approval by continuing to applaud, the conductor returns to the stage and uses the accolades as a platform for sharing the applause with the orchestra. If there was a soloist, the conductor will be sure to allow the soloist to receive the additional praise.

If there was not a soloist (or even if there is) the conductor will sometimes use this extra bow as an opportunity to acknowledge individuals or sections of the orchestra that played a significant role in the performance.

If there were principals who had a key solo or an important part to play, the conductor might gesture for them to stand in turn and be acknowledged by the audience. (This is known as a solo bow.) If the applause continues, the conductor's gestures will sometimes continue to additional players or sections that might have had a slightly smaller but still important role. Each section duly stands until the entire orchestra is upright. In this way, the conductor shares the audience's enthusiasm with the entire orchestra, indicating the performance was truly a team effort.

But it is not all about the applause. Conductors exit the stage between pieces to provide themselves with a little breather between performances, perhaps grab a sip of water backstage, or wipe their sweaty brow. The concentration required to conduct an extended work such as a symphony—or even a brief, complex contemporary score—is enormous. Leaving the stage affords the conductor an opportunity to gather his or her thoughts before proceeding to the next piece, which is often in a completely different musical style.

Lastly, there are logistical reasons why the conductor leaves the stage. Different pieces of music require different numbers and combinations of instruments and musicians. Thus, it is not unusual to see personnel changes or even changes in the physical setup of the orchestra between pieces. If the next piece on the program is a concerto, for example, not only will the makeup of the orchestra change, but perhaps a piano might have to be rolled onto the stage by backstage crew members. Or an entire string section might have to be reconfigured to make room for a solo cellist. Even if the stage or orchestra is not reconfigured, the conductor leaving the stage allows the performers to check tuning, adjust their seats, or even talk to their stand partner.

These are the three basic reasons the conductor leaves the stage between pieces. Usually at least one of the three is in play. Therefore, unless for musical reasons the conductor prefers to segue from an overture directly into a symphony, for example, the conductor always exits the stage between compositions.

While this might seem to break the overall mood and continuity of the concert, it actually provides two very important cues for you, the concertgoer. First, it makes it very clear when to clap. Second, it signals "at ease" for the audience: an acceptable time to cough, clear your throat, unwrap that hard candy, uncross your legs, or whisper those all-important disparaging remarks about the maestro's interpretation of the music.

Why are there no female conductors, even now?

It is not true to say there are no female conductors. High-profile examples include Marin Alsop (Baltimore Symphony), JoAnn Falletta (Buffalo Philharmonic and Virginia Symphony), Joana Carneiro (Berkeley Symphony), Jeannette Sorrell (Apollo's Fire), and Gisèle Ben-Dor (former longtime music director of the Santa Barbara Symphony). Emmanuelle Haïm, Jane Glover, Xian Zhang, and Simone Young have conducted major ensembles throughout the world. Rachel Worby, Lucinda Carver, and Sonia Marie De León de Vega are familiar presences on Southern California podiums. As I write this, three female conductors have earned rave reviews within a matter of weeks from the *Los Angeles Times* music critic Mark Swed: Karina Canellakis, an American; Lithuania native Mirga Gražinytė-Tyla, and Susanna Mälkki, a Finn. However, it is true that the list of women in the driver's seat of major orchestras remains relatively short.

Almost everyone would agree that it is not because there are no competent women to take these roles. Instead, the situation probably exists because of long-held traditions and, perhaps prejudices.

It was not long ago that male players dominated the orchestras themselves. For example, incredibly, it has been less than two decades since the Vienna Philharmonic even allowed women into the orchestra. It wasn't until recent history that the musicians' union started requiring blind auditions for orchestra members. Today the player mostly auditions from behind a screen precisely so the listening committee cannot determine gender, race, or age. This simple change has transformed the makeup of orchestras in a just a few decades. Female orchestral players now constitute a healthy proportion of most orchestras (unfortunately the same can't be said for certain minorities, which is a different topic).

The major conductors tend to be advanced in age; thus, their careers began during the male-dominated times. There is some indication that this situation is changing. Many smaller orchestras, where conductors get their start, today have female conductors. Further, there are now far more females in graduate conducting programs than in generations past.

There is probably more going on than just a generational change, however.

Audiences play a part in this movement. Conductors have historically held a certain mystique, a charisma, that captivates audiences (and sells tickets). Audiences have been slow to embrace female conductors in the same way. But I believe it is coming.

For example, the Los Angeles Philharmonic broke the traditional mold in appointing Gustavo Dudamel as music director and conductor when he was just twenty-six years old. His youth was surprising, even shocking to some, but I believe no one would have been any more surprised had an established female been appointed to this major American post.

In other words, it seems that audiences and orchestras are becoming much more willing to break the mold of times past. It will take a few more bold and forward-looking presidents of orchestras to simply appoint some women to major posts and show how successful they can be: fully the equal of their male counterparts.

Why do orchestra conductors use a baton, while choral conductors do not? Also, I have noticed that some opera conductors switch back and forth, using a baton during part of the production, no baton in other sections of the same opera. Why is this?

To baton or not to baton, that is the question! There is so much variation in performance practices that it can indeed be confusing for concertgoers.

First of all, there are a number of choral conductors who do use batons, particularly with large choruses, and almost always when there are orchestral musicians accompanying the chorus. Still, it is true that in general, choral directors do not tend to use a baton and orchestral conductors do.

A baton is used because it helps communicate the beat and tempo to the ensemble. In a symphony orchestra the physical distance between the conductor and the back rows of the orchestra can be a sizable gap. The baton helps the players see the precise beat, without ambiguity.

Choirs, even if they have the same number of performers as an orchestra, tend to be physically closer to the conductor. Choirs don't need to leave room for instruments and music stands, so even the farthest members in the back row are considerably closer to the conductor than their counterparts in an orchestra. A tuba player, for example, has to peer at the conductor through rows of other instruments, players, and stands. A singer in the bass section of a choir has a much more direct view. Thus direct communication between the choral conductor and his or her singers does not require a baton.

There is another, less practical, reason as well. In the choral ensemble there are no mechanical instruments. All sound is produced by the singer's voices. Therefore, there is something very personal about a conductor using hand movements to actually mold the sound. The hands can shape clarity of expression but also affect the choral sound. As one conductor said to me, "There is a difference between a fixed piece of metal or wood in an instrument and the flexibility of human tissue in the voice." Introducing a baton between the conductor and the singer removes some of this intimacy. Also, choral conductors are dealing with words and the shaping of syllabic information. These considerations may lend themselves better to the nuances of hand motions.

Very generally speaking, early choral music tends to be more about sound and beauty of line than rhythmic intricacy. Orchestral music traditionally has a much wider range of rhythmic complexity, for which a conductor with a baton may be a better navigator.

Still, some orchestral conductors, the exacting (and recently deceased) Frenchman Pierre Boulez being a particularly memorable one, do not use a baton, further complicating the landscape. It may be that the music itself is the ultimate determinant. When conducting slow, lyrical, and deeply expressive music, whether choral or orchestral, the hand might be better suited to expression than the rigid baton.

This answer satisfies the issue of choral and orchestra directors, but what about that question of opera directors who sometimes switch back and forth? Again, it is totally the preference of the conductor. In an opera the distances involved can be even greater, with the orchestra in the pit and the singers onstage, at a much higher level than the conductor. In most cases these distances necessitate the baton. (More recently, video cameras are sometimes employed as well.) Still, some conductors seem to feel that in slower, more expressive passages, it's nice to put down this inanimate object (the baton) and shape the music with their hands—which, again, are capable of far more subtle movements.

The bottom line in all of this is that there is no hard and fast rule regarding when and with what type of music a baton should be used. The decision is based on the conductor's preference, the physical arrangement of the ensemble, and the nature of the music being conducted. After taking these three aspects into consideration, the conductor decides what method of conducting will best communicate his or her intentions to the ensemble, then goes for it.

It seems as if classical music audiences stand ready to embarrass newcomers if they don't follow the rules and protocols of concert etiquette. This, in turn, discourages the newcomers from coming back. I believe the conductor can ease this potential embarrassment by simply turning around and explaining expectations. "In this piece, the three movements are closely linked—so closely that applause might interrupt the mood, so please hold applause until the end. I will signal the end of the piece by laying down my baton."

Or for another piece, the conductor might say, "Music history tells us that when this piece was written and for many years afterward, audiences applauded after each movement. Please feel free to continue that tradition if you are so moved."

Why don't all conductors do this? I, for one, thoroughly enjoy the few words some conductors offer before a piece. Is the conductor's usual aloofness considered more sophisticated and appropriate?

This is perhaps one of the most-talked-about topics in concert music today: should conductors speak to the audience from the podium, or not? If conductors choose to speak, what should they say? And how long should they keep talking?

In the past, this was simply not done. It's almost comical to imagine such venerable maestros as Bruno Walter, Carlos Kleiber, Carlo Maria Giulini, or George Szell amiably chatting with the audience before plunging into Beethoven's Seventh Symphony. Today, while still not the norm, it is not unusual for a conductor to address the audience prior to the start of a piece. Some conductors frequently speak, some make occasional comments, and some use only the baton to communicate. There is no set standard.

There are many factors involved in the decision to speak or not to speak. The conductor is the primary person responsible for the overall mood and content of a concert. Conductors and music directors put much thought into the pairing of musical pieces at any given concert. Decisions about what pieces should be performed, in what order, for what precise flow and effect, dominate the discussion when a concert is being planned. There is always concern for the overall impact on the audience. For this reason, even conductors who like to speak from the podium might decide for a specific concert that speaking could break the mood or detract from the planned juxtaposition of pieces.

Another determinant is the comfort level of the conductor as a public speaker. While some are supremely confident picking up the baton and conducting the orchestra, they are very uncomfortable, sometimes petrified, of speaking to an audience. I have known many musicians who are comfortable performing solos in front of thousands of people but shudder at the prospect of speaking to a small group of individuals, even elementary students. Performing music, either as instrumentalist, singer, or conductor, is not always paired with the gift of gab.

Often there is also a language issue. In today's closely knit global network of orchestras, conductors often find themselves in front of audiences who do not speak the language they themselves do (except the musical language). In this case, speaking is out of the question. Of course, there are also situations in which a conductor is just not very interesting or articulate, let alone concise. I have been to concerts where I have had the uncharitable thought: "Just stop talking and conduct!"

To be fair, shifting gears from verbal communication to music making can be a very difficult adjustment. It is not every conductor who can effortlessly flow from intense musical concentration to effective and informative speaking.

Lastly, there is tradition. Not all audience members like hearing the conductor speak. They feel there are program notes, preconcert lectures, and website content enabling interested audience members to learn more about the music if they desire. These individuals may feel they came to the concert to hear the music, not hear *about* the music.

Still, habits are clearly changing. Talk seems to be proliferating, especially with chamber groups and orchestras, even at choral concerts. The economics of running a symphony orchestra or choir—really any musical organization—are daunting, and classical audiences are aging. With fewer options for studying music appreciation in school settings, classical music groups are seeking other means to build and diversify their audiences. So just as you've suggested, they are aiming to demystify the art form just a little.

Many major conductors of the twentieth century had the reputation of being autocratic, even dictatorial in manner and fiercely impatient with those who did not comply with their orders. But more recent conductors do not seem to have this reputation. Does this represent real change in directorial style and personality?
Talk to any seasoned orchestral musician, and you will be told that times have changed. Because of rules put in place by the musicians' union and, perhaps more importantly, changing expectations in society of what is acceptable behavior, music directors can't get away with some of the legendary tantrums of yore. Sixty years ago, a music

director could fire a musician on a moment's notice to pun-
ish the player for a wrong note in rehearsal, for trivial non-
musical reasons, or for no reason at all.

Fritz Reiner had a hair-trigger temper and demanded
perfection from his players. His small, vest-pocket-sized
beat required the musicians to remain on high alert.
According to Pittsburgh Symphony lore, an exasper-
ated double bass player once hoisted a telescope during
rehearsal. When he explained to Reiner that he was "trying to find the beat," the conductor fired him on the spot.

George Szell was another perfectionist autocrat. As
recounted by music writer Tim Page, a professor at both
USC's Thornton School of Music and the Annenberg School
for Communication and Journalism, "in 1946, Szell's first
year as music director of the Cleveland Orchestra, he fired
22 of the 94 musicians in the group. He later dismissed the
orchestra's brilliant principal oboist of almost two decades
for a single insubordinate comment at a rehearsal. Most of
his players were terrified of Szell; some frankly despised
him. After Szell's death, one Cleveland violinist refused to
cut his hair, letting it grow down to his waist in posthu-
mous rebuke to the martinet who could no longer object.

"And yet Szell's accomplishments in Cleveland cannot
be overstated."

Likewise, Arturo Toscanini was one of the most
renowned conductors of the first half of the twentieth century, praised for his perfectionism, his uncannily accurate
ear for orchestral sonorities, balances, and phrasing, and
his intensely dramatic performances. But there was ample
drama behind the scenes, as well. The great Danish-born
tenor Lauritz Melchior was present for many of Toscanini's
"explosions," as the singer called them, including one that

occurred at Bayreuth during a production of *Tannhäuser* in the early 1930s. The title role that season was being sung by a tenor Toscanini didn't like, wrote novelist and filmmaker Ib Melchior in his biography of his father. "The singer's endeavors at this particular performance, in the opinion of Toscanini, left so much to be desired that the angry conductor exploded in a torrent of Italian and repeatedly shouted "Cane" ("Dog!") at the startled singer, almost drowning out the poor man by bellowing along in his own rather awful voice. Composer Paul Creston, whose works were championed by Toscanini, well remembered the conductor shouting the ultimate insult to a player who displeased him during a New York Philharmonic rehearsal of Creston's music: "*Porco del vostro dio*" ("pig of your God!")

Thanks to the increasing clout of musicians' unions, there are protections in place today for the players of major orchestras, reducing the ability of the conductor to ruin lives at a whim. Still, the conductor has lots of power over an orchestra and needs to exert it. Conducting is not a democracy. It is a form of artistic dictatorship. The conductor has the final say on the musical interpretation and is ultimately the person responsible for the both the artistic concept and its execution. It is he or she who will get the credit or blame for the way the orchestra performs in a given concert. Conductors will do what they need to do, within limits, to get the job done. This attitude is necessitated by the limited rehearsal time available to conductors and can still lead to some fairly gruff or cranky behavior. By and large this is both expected and accepted by the musicians. But if it goes over the line, rules are now in place to defend them from an unjust maestro's acting out.

As long as we have orchestras and conductors, increasingly difficult music, limited rehearsal time, elevated performance expectations, and the pressures of public performance, there will be some degree of forceful, sometime abrasive, leadership by conductors. However, by and large, the tyrants of the past (and the pleasure they received from having that reputation) are gone.

3

Opera and the Diva

THERE WAS AN OLD BUGS Bunny cartoon in which Elmer Fudd said about opera, "*Everyone* either loves opera or hates opera. Me? I could take it or leave it." Things have not changed much since Elmer said those words decades ago. Those who love opera *love* opera. Those who don't seem to spend an inordinate amount of time ridiculing it.

The opera lovers can't seem to get enough of it, even after a six-hour production of Wagner's *Die Meistersinger*. It only makes sense that an entire culture has grown up around opera, much like the culture of the symphony orchestra. One important difference between opera and symphonic music is that in opera the center of attention is not the conductor, not the composer, not even the story. It is most frequently the female lead, known as the diva. The word "diva" is derived from an Italian noun for a female deity—or in other words, a goddess. What more does one need to know?

As it turns out, this is only the tip of the iceberg when it comes to opera. In this section we provide answers to questions about opera you didn't even know you had.

After a recent opera production, I was talking with some of my friends and the question of vibrato came up. I've heard some people, often sopranos, whose vibrato is so extreme that I'm not sure what note they're on; I'm not convinced they know either. So my question is, why do opera singers use so much vibrato? And why do some singers use little or no vibrato?

To many people, the vision of a hefty soprano or tenor singing with a wobbly vibrato is their very definition of opera. And while a singer can certainly use too much vibrato, there are good reasons that almost all opera singers use some.

First of all, let's loosely define the term. When applied to the voice, the Italian term "vibrato," from the Latin verb *vibrare*, "to shake," is a rapid fluctuation of pitch, intensity, or both, imparting an extra measure of warmth, expressiveness, or power. The key is how much vibrato is enough to add warmth and when does it just evolve into a annoying wobble. As the *New Grove Dictionary* icily opines, an "exaggerated, slow, or irregular vibrato ... is a technical fault," not to be regarded as a genuine vibrato.

Why is this vocal effect so pervasive? First of all, opera singers are rarely amplified. They have to produce enough volume to be heard in every corner of the performance hall, usually over the sound of an orchestra. Vibrato helps the voice carry. Some people describe this as adding "size" to the pitch. As noted, it also tends to make the sound warmer and easier on the ear. A soprano singing full throttle can be quite loud. If the sound were too pure or shrill, it could be uncomfortable for the audience. Vibrato can "even out" the sound. Vibrato is never intentionally used to allow the singer to be less accurate in hitting the pitches—at least we *hope* it is never intentional. We can only hope that three-time Olivier Award–winning actor Philip Quast was joking when he told interviewer Tim O'Connor that when he can't quite hear the pitch he's supposed to be singing, "I just increase my vibrato so I cover all the bases."

It is important to note that singers today are more selective about when to use "so much vibrato." For most of the twentieth century, vibrato was liberally applied not just for opera performances but for most vocal music. However, since the 1970s, when greater emphasis began to be placed on historically accurate musical performance, this has changed. Today, for example, vocal music from the baroque period is often performed with minimal vibrato. When vibrato is used, it is for emphasis or to underline a character's high emotion. Likewise, some contemporary art music is meant to be performed with little or no vibrato, and the composer will sometimes state that clearly in the score. An example: John Cage's 1979 choral work entitled *Hymn and Variations* is inspired by hymn tunes of the eighteenth-century American William Billings, tunes traditionally belted loudly, with straight, forceful sound. Cage gives his performers explicit instructions here to produce a "non-vibrato" tonal quality.

Similarly, in performing David Lang's spooky 2002 chamber opera *The Difficulty in Crossing a Field*, the vocalists are asked to avoid an obviously "operatic" style. "We sing with more of a pure sound and not a lot of vibrato," says mezzo-soprano Jennifer Rivera, who took the lead role of Mrs. Williamson in a production by Nashville Opera.

But even music of the classical and romantic eras is generally handled more delicately on today's major operas stages. The stereotype of a large singer (with or without horns and breastplates) perpetrating a huge, pitch-indeterminate vibrato is much less accurate today than it was even a decade ago.

I gather that opera was invented somewhere around 1600, when it was discovered or discerned that Greek tragedy was sung. How was it discovered or discerned? No one has ever been able to answer this for me, in America or in Italy!

Probably the reason no one has been able to answer this question is that the answer is actually quite complicated. To truly understand the roots of modern opera, one has to understand some of the artistic tensions afoot in the late 1500s.

The standard and accepted style of music used in the Catholic Church was polyphony, which signifies the weaving together of multiple differentiated voices. In polyphony, the harmony is created when multiple voices or melodies intertwine. The easiest way to understand the concept is to imagine in your mind's ear an old-fashioned round, such as "Row, Row, Row Your Boat." Each person starts the melody at a different time. The weaving together of multiple strands, known as counterpoint, creates both the harmonies and the multifaceted texture. Some people are singing "Row, row, row, your boat" at the same time others are singing "Merrily, merrily, merrily, merrily." While this sounds musically interesting, it is sometimes hard to understand the words. Yet a sophisticated version of this style was considered the highest form of music in the late sixteenth century and was *the* approved style for the Catholic Church.

A contrasting style to polyphony is monody, which refers to a single vocal line. It was a style of song for one voice and "continuo," which is a chordal accompaniment typically played on a lute, harpsichord, theorbo, or guitar. These were generally secular Italian songs, but the style was also incorporated into such religious works as oratorios. With monody, the harmonies supported the melody. The words were clear as a bell. This innovation, introduced by Giulio Caccini, Emilio de' Cavalieri, Jacopo Peri, and other composers and enhanced by the printed publication of their works and the patronage of music-loving aristocrats, formed the basis of early opera.

But back in Italy at the end of the sixteenth century, this became a big musical controversy: which was better, the "old-fashioned" style of polyphony or the newer style of monody? This is the backdrop upon which the old Greek documents about music were "discovered" and interpreted. Hold that thought for a moment.

The next piece of the puzzle indeed stretches back to ancient Greece. The Greeks were quite philosophical about their music and the importance of music to society, as well as to an individual's intellect and overall well-being. We have extensive writings *about* music from the Greeks but know very little actual Greek music. Only a few small fragments have come down to us, including two Delphic hymns praising the god Apollo. Imagine having a few measures of music to try to figure out what music has been like in Western culture from 1700 to the present, without even knowing if these musical scraps were typical, of high quality, or perhaps an anomaly.

So we knew how the Greeks described their music and how they philosophically felt about it but not what it sounded like. Beginning in the 1570s in Florence, a group of scholars known as the Florentine Camerata met on a regular basis at the home of Count Giovanni de' Bardi to discuss trends in the arts, especially music and theater, and to debate the future direction of these art forms. They pored over Greek descriptions of theater and music and learned that Greek tragedies involved both singing and dance. In fact, one ancient text claimed the best way to move an audience's emotions was through solo singing.

Of course there is really no way to know precisely what was meant by that. For example, when the writings said the tragedies were sung, did that mean literally sung, or did it perhaps mean chanted? But the Florentine elders seized on these writings to support their contention that monody (solo singing) was superior to polyphony. Who is going to argue with the ancient Greeks when it comes to art?

It would be imprecise, however, to imply that opera was suddenly invented during this period. Opera evolved from the medieval shows and pageants, which often dealt with mythological ideas and featured solo singing balanced with chorus and sometimes included special effects. The first full-fledged opera is generally regarded to be *Dafne*, by Jacopo Peri and Jacopo Corsi, produced in 1598. Alas, most of that music is lost, though the libretto by Ottavio Rinuccini survives. The earliest opera in the active repertory today is Claudio Monteverdi's *Orfeo*, on the Greek myth of Orpheus, first presented as part of the 1607 carnival season at the court of Mantua.

Whew. This history is not exactly enticing cocktail conversation! It is no wonder no one was willing to try to explain it.

I recently attended a production of the **Merry Widow** *and was surprised to hear so much spoken dialogue from the stage. I also remember being sharply corrected by an opera buff for calling* **Les Mis** *an opera even though it is completely sung. So what am I missing here? Is this just some sort of elitism going on, or is*

there actually a well-accepted definition of what constitutes an opera?

This is one of our most frequently asked questions over the years. Nothing separates the opera purists from the more casual operagoers than the question of what constitutes a "real opera."

One of the misperceptions is that an opera is always completely sung and anything that has dialogue cannot be a true opera. In fact, opera has a long tradition of dialogue interspersed throughout. It might be sung as recitative, a style first described by Jacopo Peri, who referred to its presence in his opera *Euridice* (1600) as a middle ground between speech and song. Or it might actually be spoken, such as the German dialogue in Mozart's *The Magic Flute*, a work the composer himself characterized as a "singspiel," a song-play. However, operas with dialogue tended to be lighter fare, as opposed to the more dramatic "grand opera." *The Magic Flute* was based on fantastical Masonic themes and, as I mentioned, was written in the layman's language of German. Bizet's *Carmen* was written as an opéra comique, a form close to musical theater. It, too, had spoken dialogue and even opportunities for comic relief, exotic gypsy dances, and other elements of local Spanish color (though, amazingly, the Frenchman Bizet never stepped foot in Spain).

The Merry Widow is actually an operetta, a term that implies a work lighter in both thematic content and musical weight. You could argue that operetta was German musical theater.

None of this was really an issue until the twentieth century, when opera started to be differentiated from "musical theater," a style shunned by true artists. (Thankfully, the genres are moving closer together today. Many major opera companies, including Chicago Lyric, Houston Grand Opera, and New York's Glimmerglass regularly mount beloved musicals by the likes of Rodgers and Hammerstein and Stephen Sondheim as part of their regular seasons. The English National Opera has staged such musicals as *Pacific Overtures*, *On the Town*, and *Kismet*. In September 2015, the Royal Opera invited the audience to sing along with professional vocalists at a screening of the Oscar-winning film version of the Lionel Bart musical *Oliver!*

It is true that classic American musicals are very different from opera. *Oklahoma!* and *The Sound of Music*, for example, are largely plays in which the actors occasionally break into song and dance. In more recent works, such as *Les Misérables* (*Les Mis* for short), *Sweeney Todd*, and *Next to Normal*, the texts are nearly always sung.

So, what *is* the difference between an opera and a musical? While there are many subtle differences, there are a few general rules: First, the style of the composition is often very different. In opera, the text is king and dictates the rhythms and melodic phrasing. As a general rule, the theme is often tragic, or at least more serious than is usual in traditional musical theater. Opera plots tend to be more convoluted. Likewise, the music is often more complex and varied.

The style of singing is different, too. An opera singer is rarely amplified. But today even topnotch Broadway stars use microphones, and if a high school can scrape together the resources, their musical theater stars are amplified, too. Renowned American baritone and USC Thornton faculty member Rodney Gilfrey, both an acclaimed *Don Giovanni* and Émile de Becque in *South Pacific*, says the very vowel sounds in the two art forms are different, and accordingly he uses different vocal techniques and a different physicality for each. Finally, opera singers, as noted,

usually employ a sizable amount of vibrato; musical theater singers tend to use vibrato less frequently, though it
often provides dramatic emphasis or poignancy at the end
of a song, such as the so-called eleven o'clock number—the
big showstopper that occurs late in the second act of a two-
act musical, which in the old days of Broadway fell around
11 p.m., since the curtain rose at 8:30 p.m.

Female musical theater performers also typically make
liberal use of their "chest" voice, or lower range, to achieve
what is affectionately known as belting (the ultimate
example might be Ethel Merman singing the title song in
Hello, Dolly!).

But again, the genres are blurring. Stephen Sondheim's
gripping musical thriller *Sweeney Todd* began life on
Broadway in 1979 and was introduced in London's West
End the following year. But it has also been staged with
great success by the Finnish National Opera, the English
National Opera, the Royal Opera, the Israel National Opera,
the Chicago Lyric Opera, the San Francisco Opera, and
even the Icelandic Opera, among others. Acknowledging
that only about 20 percent of *Sweeney* is spoken dialogue,
theater critic Martin Gottfried asks, "Does so much singing make it an opera?" He answers his own question with
a resounding no: "Opera is not just a matter of everything
being sung. There is an operatic kind of music, of singing,
of staging. There are opera audiences, and there is an opera
sensibility. There are opera *houses*. *Sweeney Todd* has its
occasional operatic moments, but its music overall has the
chest notes, the harmonic language, the muscularity, and
the edge of Broadway theater."

Operas usually have more elaborate instrumental support than musicals; except for chamber operas and some
contemporary works, operas are usually accompanied by a

full symphonic orchestra. Partly because of economic considerations, musicals tend to use smaller ensembles, called pit orchestras, often augmented by synthesizers or other electronic instruments.

These are some means of differentiation, but I could also point out valid exceptions to each. For example, in the spring of 2014, I saw a production of Puccini's *Madama Butterfly* at Sydney Harbor with the audience situated along the shore. Naturally this mandated that the orchestra and all the singers be amplified.

This gets us back to the original point. Sometimes the difference between these two art forms is clear, but increasingly, the lines are blurred. The important point that every opera performer I spoke with emphasized is this: it is OK, even understandable, to be confused. You should have the confidence to tell elitist opera buffs to "get off their high horse and settle down" (using more colorful language if you prefer; this *is* about opera). It is just not that clear cut.

What is the major difference between opera, oratorio, and choral music? Also, George Frederic Handel turned from opera to choral music and ended up writing the most famous oratorios of all time. Was this purely an artistic transformation or were there other reasons, such as availability of singers, scenery, or even religious factors?
The major differences between opera and choral music are that opera tells a story, relies heavily on solo voices (in addition to choral passages, duets, small vocal ensembles), and features costumes, sets, and staging. Choral music is not usually narrative, relies primarily on choral textures (though vocal soloists are sometimes employed), and rarely involves staging or costumes beyond basic choir robes and

risers. Oratorio, often written within a religious context, is a kind of hybrid that intersperses solo and choral sections, tells a story, but rarely uses costumes, sets, or staging.

Choral music goes back to medieval times and was a major musical form during the Renaissance. As we've seen, opera developed in Italy at the turn of the seventeenth century and quickly spread to other European music centers. For all its popularity, there was a problem: the church prohibited "entertainments" during Lent, which meant there were forty days when opera could not be performed. Composers are a creative lot, and a loophole was found. Works with religious texts, without staging, could be mounted as devotional or didactic presentations rather than entertainment. Thus the oratorio was born. Such pieces were regularly performed in the Oratory of the Church of St. Philip Neri in Rome, known in Italian as the Congregazione dell'Oratorio, hence the name.

Recent research has pointed to contemporaneous origins in Florence in the late sixteenth century and the early seventeenth, when greater dramatic content began to creep into sacred musical works. The first known oratorio was Emilio de' Cavalieri's *The Representation of Soul and Body*, a morality play set to music and performed in costume in 1600, right around the time of the first opera.

The progression that Handel went through that is described in the question is often cited but not quite accurate. Handel had always been involved in writing various kinds of choral works for the church. He had also delved into the oratorio genre while a student in Italy during the first decade of the eighteenth century. He also composed a few oratorios during his first two decades in London while becoming enormously famous as a composer of

Italian operas. Handel began focusing on oratorio in the late 1730s and early 1740s. The triumphant success of several of his new oratorios in Dublin in 1741 and 1742 (including *Messiah* and *Saul*) apparently bolstered Handel's confidence; he now felt his stature as England's leading composer would be secure even if he walked away from Italian opera to embrace English oratorio. There were also the practical advantages that oratorios were cheaper to produce than opera and Handel would have complete artistic and production control over the performances, something he could never have with opera.

While he wrote in all three styles in the early part of his life, it is true that from about 1739 on, the oratorio was Handel's primary form of compositional outlet. It is clear that this shift was caused by financial considerations. For example, the immense success of John Gay's English-language *Beggar's Opera* in 1728, performed sixty-two times during its first season, did not go unnoticed by Handel. Gay was a pal of Handel's and even wrote the libretto for Handel's oratorio–pastoral opera *Acis and Galatea* back in 1718. In any case, there is no evidence that religion played a part in Handel's decision. His oratorios were originally designed for performance in theaters, not churches, and they were not intended to fulfill any liturgical function.

The bottom line: Handel was an entrepreneur who produced his own works by mounting concerts funded by subscriptions. Since oratorios generally did not require costumes, staging, sets, scenery, or the like, the production costs were much lower than for opera. This naturally appealed to Handel the businessman.

One hears about the superstitions and rituals that rock musicians indulge in before going on stage. Some will

eat only red M&Ms, some light a candle, some insist on
a certain amount of time alone. Accommodating these
rituals is often written into their contracts. Do clas-
sical performers have rituals they enact before every
performance besides musically warming up?

All classical music performances require an intensive
amount of focus and concentration. To help with this concentration and allow the mind and body to focus, soloists
have a dressing room or "green room" backstage, where
they and only others whom they personally approve can
enter. This allows them to get in the zone. Even orchestral
musicians generally have a lounge or backstage area where
audience members are forbidden to enter without a special
dispensation.

Opera singers, especially, need this time. If they are
playing a lead or principal role, they have to get into character and then spend several hours singing, acting, perhaps
dancing, at the top of their game. This is no small task.

I am sure that some performers have specific rituals
and contracts that accommodate them, but the opera singers I spoke with didn't know of anyone with those types of
specified demands. On the other hand, it seems that every
opera performer has some preperformance ritual.

One established singer always follows a strict preconcert ritual that begins twenty-four hours in advance. In her
many years as a major performer she has never varied from
this schedule:

> Have a steak dinner the evening before the performance to
> provide protein.
> The morning of the performance, sleep in.
> The time from 3:00 to 7:00 p.m. is spent alone while
> strictly doing the following:
> 3:00: review music in her head while resting

4:00: exercise
4:30: shower
5:00: warm up voice
5:30: eat lots of pasta for energy and quick digestion
6:00: go to theater
6:30: hair and makeup, eat a banana
7:00: costume on
7:30: last warm-up of voice
7:59: send up a prayer!
8:00: show time

This singer feels that it is the exact repetition of these rituals that make them effective. She also stressed that the protein (as well as the potassium and vitamin B_6) in the banana was very important. In fact, she used to label the difficulty of a show as a one-banana, a two-banana, or for something like *Aïda*, a three-banana show.

A second opera singer had a totally different routine. He was concerned that if he had a specific demand like green M&Ms or a certain bottled water, the first time it was not delivered correctly, it would destroy his concentration and perhaps the performance. He prefers a routine that he can completely control.

He warms up his voice starting a few hours before the performance, then completes the following routine before getting into costume. He repeats it once he is in costume. Here's how he describes it:

I stand, feet apart, arms at my side. I inhale through my nose and blow it out very slowly. I do this until I'm internally calm. Then I find an object about 8 feet away that's below my line of sight: maybe an electrical outlet or a spot in a wall. I stare at it intensely, as if I'm trying to make it burst into flames with my

super-power gaze. I stop JUST before it ignites, because a fire
would stop the performance. Through this exercise, I feel power-
ful, focused and calm. I feel like a superhero. Then I walk onstage
with so much confidence that nothing can stop me.

You can see that these performers approach the task
of getting ready quite differently. However, they both do
what they need to do to have their voices warmed up and,
importantly, their confidence and concentration at the
highest possible level.

I spoke to about six professional performers to answer
this question and literally every one had a ritual of some
kind, starting hours before the scheduled concert or opera
production. Surprisingly, almost all of them, instrumentalists as well as singers, included the eating of a banana.

From an audience member perspective I think it is
important to realize that the performance starts well
before the curtain goes up. While you are stuck in traffic
or having a relaxing dinner before the show, the artists are
already in intense performance mode so they will be ready
when you take your seat.

Why are there never altos in operas or mezzo-sopranos in choirs? Do these terms refer to the same voice part? Are the terms simply different for choral and operatic singing?

It is interesting and quite true that women with lower
voices are generally referred to as altos in choirs and mezzo-
sopranos in opera. Your confusion is understandable.

To make some sense of this, let's look at the Italian
(or Latin) roots of some of the words we use to designate
voices and voice parts. "Soprano" derives from the word for

"highest" and is reserved for the top line in vocal music. A boy soprano is also known as a treble, and in the seventeenth and eighteenth centuries the term "soprano" was also used for adult male castrati—a painfully self-explanatory term—with a high range. "Alto" is the Italian word for "high" and in choirs designates the voice part that is *second* highest. Thus in choral music it has been the common practice for several centuries to have the two top parts called soprano and alto, or highest and high. Importantly, these words are meant to designate the musical part, not a voice type. So to be accurate, in a choir you have a person who is *singing* alto, not an alto (though the latter is now common parlance). Some practical examples of this difference: in early music it was not unusual to exchange a recorder or violin for the voice when playing the soprano or alto parts. Further, through much of the Renaissance and baroque periods, following Saint Paul's dictum that "women should be silent in churches," boys sang these parts. Clearly these terms were not intended to define a type or texture of voice, just the range.

However, over the years, even though common usage does refer to females with higher voices as sopranos and lower voices as altos, it still describes a voice range rather than a voice type.

Now, to switch to mezzo-soprano, we indeed move to the realm of opera. Since solo singing is (for the most part) the name of the game, it would make no sense to name the vocal roles in reference to another voice part, such as highest (soprano) or second highest (alto).

In early opera, all women's characters were referred to as soprano, regardless of the precise written range. An example would be the Three Ladies in *The Magic Flute*. The score calls for three sopranos, though today several of the parts are just as likely to be sung by mezzos.

At the dawn of the era of bel canto (literally, "beautiful singing"), in the early nineteenth century, composers such as Rossini, Bellini, and Donizetti began to extend the upper range of their soprano roles, and the term "mezzo-soprano," or "medium soprano," simply designated a slightly lower voice part that didn't necessarily ascend to those new heights. The disappearance of the castrato contributed to the establishment of the mezzo-soprano's important place in opera. Indeed, many of the early mezzo-soprano roles, such as Mozart's charmingly confused Cherubino in *The Marriage of Figaro*, are so-called pants or travesty roles— that is, male roles played by women.

Importantly, mezzo-soprano is a wide-ranging voice type, ideally with a rich, lustrous texture. Generally speaking, operatic mezzo-sopranos sing a wider range and with a darker tone than their alto sisters who sing choral music. When a chorus is combined with soloists, such as in Verdi's Requiem, the second highest female choral parts are listed as altos (contraltos actually), and the lower female soloist is indicated to be a mezzo-soprano, though the parts are in essentially in the same range. The two designations are to differentiate the vocal sound that Verdi desired.

There are other, more current examples of this designation. In the twentieth century, Benjamin Britten upheld the English tradition in his opera *Peter Grimes* by indicating alto for the female chorus parts that lie below the soprano line, while the soloists are specifically labeled soprano and mezzo-soprano.

There is also a still lower female part below mezzo-soprano in the opera world. This voice range is called contralto; while less common than mezzo-sopranos, there are still significant numbers of female singers who identify themselves as contraltos.

So the bottom line is that "alto" refers to a specific line in the music, while "mezzo-soprano" refers to a voice type. To be totally correct, there is no such thing as an alto, but in common usage one can find them all the time.

By the way, it is not uncommon for singers to switch voice parts as their voices and their careers develop and grow. Marilyn Horne, widely regarded as the greatest living mezzo-soprano, sang soprano roles early in her career at the municipal opera house in Gelsenkirchen, Germany. Horne went on to conquer the Metropolitan Opera stage as a mezzo, helping to revive long-neglected works of such composers as Rossini and Handel and mustering star power equivalent to the true divas, her soprano colleagues. Interestingly, she has, nonetheless, remained humble. Maybe it's a mezzo thing, but this USC Thornton School of Music alumna has none of the trappings that many divas do. "Whenever you think that you are getting too big for the people around you," she wrote in the prologue to her memoirs, "remember all that separates you from the guy sitting next to you is a little piece of gristle in your throat."

Why does Italy seem to overflow with operatic tenors and Russia boast so many operatic bassos? Do voices get deeper as you head north in Europe? Are there really ethnic differences?

From the circumstantial evidence it would seem pretty clear that ethnicity plays a role in producing certain types of singers. However, there is probably a better explanation for this phenomenon.

Singing must reflect the qualities of the spoken language being sung. For example, you will often hear vocal coaches tell their students: "This is Rachmaninoff. Sing it with an open-throated sound." Or "This is a Neapolitan song. Please sing it with portamento" (connecting two notes by gliding audibly through the intervening pitches— derogatorily referred to as "scooping" or "swooping" in the mid-twentieth century).

When they say these things, they are referring to the natural inflections or sound of the language that is being sung. For instance, the Russian language has an open-throated *L*, articulated in the back of the throat, which opens up the preceding vowels in a very distinctive manner. The Italian language requires pure, forward vowels in the spoken language, which contributes to a wonderful legato sound in singing—moving smoothly from vowel to vowel, enunciating the consonants, creating a flowing sound from note to note and word to word.

It is clear that the language of each country has its own particular vowels and consonants, which change the acoustical quality of the sound. In Russia, men's choruses are popular and have helped promote that country's reputation for basses. However, if you listen carefully, you will see that the sound emanating from all Russian voices— not just basses—is full and open, much like the Russian language. Sweden has a reputation for resonant sopranos and tenors because of that language's extremely forwardly placed vowels and consonants.

You may be wondering why the native language makes any difference, since the singers perform in the language in which the opera is written. For example, it is true that almost all European singers have been influenced by Italian language instruction, since Italian operas are the heart of the repertoire. Even in earlier centuries, Italian singers and teachers were present at the royal courts of Germany, Austria, and Russia. Today, European and American voice teachers have carried the traditions of Italian singing to South Korea, Japan, and China, where both Western and indigenous opera flourish.

But even after years of language training, a singer's diction is inevitably influenced by his or her native language. While on the surface it may seem that the ethnicity of the singers makes a difference, it is the singer's native language—and the relative rigorousness of their language and diction training—that determine how convincingly they sing in a certain language.

I am often amazed at the mastery of opera singers in singing different languages. When they are interviewed, from the way they pronounce different languages it is clear they pronounce like native people (the same is true for some radio announcers), and my question is whether the singers are required to learn languages when they are in school?

Learning to be an opera performer is one of the most daunting tasks in music. Almost every successful performer has advanced degrees from either a music conservatory or music school. There is simply so much to learn and develop.

Like any musician, an opera singer has to learn all the basics about music: theory, ear training, history, analysis, plus private lessons and ensemble singing, and they're usually required to have proficiency at the piano. However, for the opera performer it does not stop there.

The opera performer also must be trained as an actor, trained in stage movement or dance, and must be able to sing convincingly in at least three or four languages. All singers must develop the proper diction and pronunciation of French, German, Italian, and English. Some go on to learn even more, perhaps Russian, Czech, Spanish.

However, there are only so many hours in the day to do all this, so a great deal of work is required outside the conservatory or music school. Many aspiring opera singers feel they must study abroad to immerse themselves in a language. This cannot be done during the regular school year, as it would take them away from their private teachers and also exclude them from holding parts in the school's opera productions. Thus, summer study abroad is advised for young opera singers. There are many excellent summer programs across Europe; they provide intensive vocal and language coaching while also immersing the student in the European language and culture.

But this is still not enough. In addition to the regular classes offered, schools hire both acting and diction coaches to work with students in their productions. This instruction is on top of everything else they are doing. Majoring in opera singing at the collegiate level means no spring-break vacations to Hawaii for these young students.

Still, it seems that no amount of study is ever enough. Almost all professional vocalists have done extensive study beyond the undergraduate college years. Vocalists are constantly seeking out opportunities for further study as musicians, as actors, and in languages they haven't yet mastered—not to mention, as new roles require, in vocal and interpretive techniques. It is common today for even the most prominent opera stars to continue studies with a voice teacher or vocal coach in whom they trust.

I recently heard the fine San Francisco-based group Chanticleer and have a question about male voices. In times past, the voices of talented young male singers were prevented from changing through grueling surgeries. Hopefully we don't encourage that today. So why is it that some of the men in Chanticleer have voices that sound like sopranos?

You are absolutely correct that in the distant past, high male voices that persisted after puberty were made possible by castration. In the Renaissance period, sacred choral works were largely intended for performance by male choirs, including men and boys with unchanged voices. This was not for artistic reasons but rather because women were not welcome in the choirs of the early Catholic Church. From the sixteenth until well into the eighteenth century (particularly in Italy), the practice of castrating young boys before their voices changed was widespread. What this practice produced were male soprano and alto singers who retained the larynx of a boy coupled with the physical strength and maturity of a man's body. The resultant voices had a unique timbre, great volume, and a wide range that could brilliantly execute sustained as well as highly florid music. Composers wrote for this particular combination of sounds, and to be historically accurate, it often needs to be performed by men and boys or by men with voices that can capture these vocal ranges. It is this sound that is an important element in giving so-called early music its distinctive character.

Some of the men in the Chanticleer ensemble have cultivated the art of singing in the female or boy soprano vocal range because of their interest in authentic performance practices for medieval, Renaissance, and baroque era music. How do they do it? Some men have naturally high voices because of their physiology and a natural inclination to sing in the higher range. Many men sang as boys and retain a pleasant memory of how it felt to sing in the soprano range. Cultural influences, such as the gospel choir tradition, can play a role as well. Some feel more comfortable singing in a kind of falsetto voice, which is the "light" mechanism of the male voice. Many baritones who have a particularly beautiful falsetto voice often train to a high level of ability. Those who can integrate the purity of the falsetto with the richness of the middle voice are the most successful. The training involves learning to coordinate the musculature of the high falsetto voice with the fullness of the normal chest register. No doubt, some of the singers in Chanticleer are true falsettists, or male sopranos, and others have integrated registers. Such countertenors, as they are called, embody the range of a female contralto or mezzo-soprano.

Interestingly, high-pitched singing is still very popular today even outside the realm of opera. In the pop field, the baritone "crooners" of the late 1930s, 1940s, 1950s and early 1960s (Bing Crosby, for example) gave way to a new wave of high-voiced male pop singers, including the Bee Gees, Paul McCartney, the Four Seasons, Johnny Ray, Michael Jackson, Little Richard, Hanson, and many more.

There are men performers who sing very high, even in the soprano range, yet I have never heard of a female bass. Why is this?
It's a physical thing. Generally women have a smaller larynx (voice box) than men, and their vocal cords (folds) are

shorter than those of men. That's why there are no true female basses. Some women who by inclination or nature sing almost exclusively in the low, or chest, register do sing in choirs as female tenors but rarely, if ever, as basses. However, in the colorful universe of barbershop quartet harmony, the more than twelve hundred registered quartets and six hundred choruses that belong to the collective group Sweet Adelines International divide their female voice parts into tenor, lead, baritone, and bass. The bass, similar in range to a second alto in conventional SATB (i.e., soprano, alto, tenor, bass) choral music, provides the foundation of each chord and generally sings with greater volume than the higher parts.

As a pulmonologist, I've wondered if opera singers have supernormal lung capacities. Since lung capacity is generally proportional to height, are most opera singers tall?

Actually, it does seem that most opera singers are tall but probably not because of lung capacity.

While lung capacity may relate to height, there are so many other factors that go into producing a successful singer that lung capacity is just one ingredient. Other factors include innate musicality and the abilities to sing on pitch, to project one's voice to the back of the opera house, and to act convincingly. In fact, these qualities can overshadow the natural advantage of lung capacity. It is less lung capacity than a combination of breath control and physical coordination that produces marvelous singers. In fact, there have been many wonderful singers who were not tall—legendary Swedish soprano Birgit Nilsson (described as "small, though sturdy in stature"), early twentieth-century tenor Joseph Schmidt (just under five feet) and, more recently, the powerful German bass-baritone Thomas Quasthoff (just under four feet five—as a result of a birth defect; his mother was given the drug thalidomide during pregnancy to offset morning sickness).

Still, legendary Russian bass Fyodor Chaliapin, known as a riveting stage presence, checked in at over six feet tall. Pavarotti topped out just under six feet. Maria Callas stood five feet eight. Dame Joan Sutherland towered above many a tenor costar; she was six feet two, the same height as Placido Domingo. And if Domingo's colleagues at recent Los Angeles Opera productions are any indication, many great voices do come wrapped in bodies blessed with impressive height. I am not convinced their height gives them more of an ability to sing long lines of music; rather, they are wonderful singers who happen to be tall. That height can afford them terrific stage presence.

A postscript about the towering impact of the diminutive Swedish soprano Birgit Nilsson, who died at eighty-seven in 2006: Regarded as the greatest Wagnerian soprano of her day, Nilsson's very vocal power sometimes got her into skirmishes with those she shared the stage with. Her extraordinary breath control enabled her to hold flawless high notes for what seemed like forever. A frequent combatant in the battles of the high Cs was the powerhouse Italian tenor, Franco Corelli, who was six feet one.

In Nilsson's obituary in London's *Telegraph*, the story was told of how on one occasion during the second act of Puccini's *Turandot*, Corelli was so enraged at being unable to sustain his top note for as long as Nilsson's that, in the third act, he took his revenge by biting her on the neck during their love scene. Birgit Nilsson is said to have pulled out of the next performance, explaining, "I have rabies."

*I recently saw a performance of Gustav Mahler's **Resurrection Symphony, his Symphony no. 2. The conductor asked the members of the chorus to remain seated during their first musical entrance, which was very quiet and a cappella (unaccompanied by instruments). Then he had them stand when they sang a much louder passage with orchestral accompaniment. Is it not true that vocalists can perform better standing than sitting? Doesn't standing up afford the singer better abdominal support for the voice and better overall control of the vocal apparatus? And is it not also true that just as much if not more freedom and control are needed to sing softly as when singing full-throated passages? Do you know why the conductor had them sit, then stand?***

It is a common misconception that a choir has to stand to have the proper posture for breath support. It is true that standing enforces good singing posture, but the same appropriate posture can be achieved with training from a sitting position.

Test this out by standing, then sitting with your upper torso in a "standing position." There is actually not much difference. However, how to keep the standing position while seated needs to be learned, practiced, and maintained. This is usually reserved for professional or trained choirs.

In Mahler's Second Symphony the choir is almost always sitting for the first four movements, collectively about an hour in length. And you're quite right; it is common practice for them to remain seated for the hushed, otherworldly entrance with the words *"Aufersteh'n, ja auferstehn' wirst du"* (rise again, yes, you will rise again from the dead). This powerful moment in the symphony is marked extremely soft (*ppppp*) and requires great breath support. I believe the character and nature of the sound required for this entrance is actually enhanced by being seated.

Lastly, standing has its own issues, such as lightheadedness. I can't tell you the number of times I have seen choral members pass out onstage during very long concerts or works (especially during Southern California summers in venues with no air conditioning). Another problem with standing is that in a soft section like this, it could be more likely for someone to sway and cause the floor or risers to squeak. Lastly, the sound of them eventually sitting down (if they were standing) would be a distraction.

So all of these factors are considered when the conductor decides if the choir is to stand or sit, and in this case keeping them seated for that famously quiet, serenely beautiful entrance was probably the right decision.

By the way, if you're not yet a fan of this piece, it's a fantastically exciting symphony, as that almost inaudible choral passage leads the way to a shattering climax. Here's how Mahler described the music that follows: "Then God in all His glory comes into sight. . . . A feeling of overwhelming love fills us with blissful knowledge and illuminates our very existence." Mahler later told a friend, Natalie Bauer-Lechner, about the uncanny experience of conducting this immensely dramatic piece in the concert hall: "The increasing tension working up to the final climax is so tremendous that I don't know myself, now that it is over, how I ever came to write it."

I enjoy attending the Metropolitan Opera Western Region Auditions each year, and I like to keep track of my favorites to see if I agree with the judges. But

I really don't know anything about the voice business nor do I have the vocabulary to express my impressions. Can you help? What are the top five vocal qualities professionals listen for?

First of all, don't feel bad if you do not always agree with the judges. The judging of vocal performance can be quite subjective; believe me, the judges themselves don't always agree. This is why there is often such a long wait while the judges are conferring. In fact, they may be in heated or at least pointed debate about the pros and cons of certain performances.

That being said, there are basic qualities that professionals listen for when judging classical voices.

THE IMMEDIACY OF THE VOICE

Since classical singing is almost always unamplified, it is crucial that a voice project an individual character yet still possess the carrying power to be heard in every corner of the hall. It also must have resiliency and, melded with the singer's personality, the ability to reach or touch a listener. Usually the best singing comes across as free and effortless, full of emotion and feeling. Tension in singing is a huge no-no and is generally audible as a harsh, unpleasant, or pinched vocal quality or off-pitch singing. Physical tension manifests in stiffness or "holding" the body: raised shoulders, stiff arms, clenched jaw. Imagine how hard it is to sound free and effortless at the biggest audition of your life. As one young musician put it, "You have two minutes to show what you've accomplished in all your years of training."

THE SHEER BEAUTY OF THE VOICE

Judges are listening for a certain resonance, overtones, a "ringing" quality, burnished with mellowness, warmth, and roundness. (Singers in earlier times sometimes called such balanced tones pear-shaped.) Too much of a bright or "forward" quality tends to create a harsh, edgy, strident, or shallow sound. Yet an overabundance of mellow or dark tones could make the voice sound muffled or dull.

Judges listen for an acoustical balance of these two qualities. A wide vibrato or wobble—or the other extreme, a fast tremolo, or tremor in the voice—is considered undesirable in classical singing today. It is true that some famous singers had hints of these qualities, but other aspects of their artistry (such as great acting ability) overcame this deficit. A wobble, or unusually rapid tremolo, suggests technical flaws, fatigue, or physical limitations. Highly nasal singing is also frowned upon, except when used to comic effect.

VOCAL COLOR

The two primary vocal colors are usually referred to as the head register and the chest register. The head register is so named because singers feel or sense the vibrations of high tones in the head. Similarly, the chest register's lower tones (for a female voice) or higher notes (for a tenor) reverberate in the chest. The area in the middle of the singing range, which is often a blending of head and chest registers, is referred to by singers and teachers as middle voice or mid-range. However, there are places in the musical scale where an actual shift of registers occurs going down to low tones or heading up to high ones. The areas of three or four semitones in a musical scale where these register changes occur are referred to by the Italian word for a passageway: *passaggio*. Skillful classical singers endeavor to make register shifts (or breaks, as some inappropriately call them) appear seamless by slightly altering vowel shapes.

In most singers one can hear a slight shift in the registers, an acoustical change in a voice's color; it is a pleasurable experience, as when a tenor or baritone lifts into head voice, or the "loft register," or a soprano or mezzo-soprano descends into the lower chest register (sometimes described as sexy). It's a trick the shameless Ms. Carmen employs to stunning effect in Bizet's opera.

TEXT EXPRESSION

What is the meaning of the words you are singing? How does a character feel about her plight? This all-important quality of expression is evidenced through musical phrasing and meaningful delivery. Articulation, enunciation, and idiomatic diction (in English or another language) must come together to heighten expression and underline the meaning of the libretto. In a great performance, diction and musical phrasing meld into a whole to convey the musical and emotional content of a poem, aria, or dramatic monologue.

THE PACKAGE

The "package," admittedly a vague term, is nonetheless used quite frequently by judges, teachers, casting directors, and singers themselves. It is basically the coming together of all the above elements, combined with palpably dramatic presentation, poised physical appearance, a natural feeling for the stage, and a strong sense of self. It is called a package not only because it combines all these qualities and more; it is also an artistic product that is highly marketable.

4

The Composer

ULTIMATELY THE MUSIC WORLD STARTS and ends with the music itself. Without music there would be no need for maestros, divas, principals, concertmasters, instruments, audiences, or anything else we are discussing in this book. Therefore, almost everyone (divas being the possible exception) agree that the composer is the most important person in the musical equation. While great instrumentalists or conductors can take an average piece of music and make it sound better than it is, they cannot take a mediocre piece and make it sound like a great one. In the world of pop music, it is often said that the secret to having a hit record is to start with a hit song and not mess it up. Likewise in classical music, a great performance ideally starts with a great piece.

In this chapter we will address questions that help us understand how composers work, and how they think about their creations.

Why do composers write in different keys? Wouldn't it be easier to write everything in C major?
This is a very, very good question. If everything was written in the key of C major (the white notes on the piano), we could do away with sharps, flats, and naturals, eliminating those pesky symbols on the printed score. We could build

pianos consisting of white keys only, which would be so much easier and inexpensive. Life would be a breeze for both composers and performers. The loser would be the listener, as all classical music would become bland, simplistic, "plain vanilla." Let's hope this never happens. Or as one composer asked rhetorically, "Why don't we all wear beige every day?" Perhaps the most thought-provoking answer comes from Morten Lauridsen, a composer and longtime professor of the USC Thornton School of Music, who replied, "I don't choose the key. I let the composition pick the key."

There are two basic reasons that composers don't dwell exclusively in C major. The first reason is the perceived emotional impact of each particular key. This belief goes back at least as far as the ancient Greeks, who felt that each tonal center (mode or key) embodied a distinct emotional character. One key radiated joy. Another key was pensive in quality. This belief far outlived the ancient Greeks. Beethoven felt A major (the key of the Seventh Symphony and the serenely beautiful Piano Sonata op. 101) was joyous. For Beethoven, D minor, the key of his Ninth Symphony and "Tempest" Piano Sonata, was serious. Chopin gravitated toward A♭ major more than any other key for his grand solo piano works; he associated it with a fiery quality and a wide emotional range. Mozart felt G minor was dark but not frightening. It's the key of his somber Viola Quintet K. 516; one of his first undisputed masterworks, the Symphony no. 25 (it reverberates throughout the film *Amadeus*), and the towering Symphony no. 40. Mozart reserved D minor for some of his most shattering music: the Piano Concerto no. 20, K. 466; climactic moments in the opera *Don Giovanni*, and the Requiem left unfinished at the time of his death.

Though Morten Lauridsen insists the keys choose him, the "warm" key of D♭ frequently comes calling in his most radiant choral works, such as "Sure on This Shining Night" from the *Nocturnes*, and "Dirait-on" from *Les chansons des roses*. It's a key, Lauridsen says, which seems to resonate with the human voice.

If this idea is taken to its extreme, we find ourselves in the fascinating world of chromesthesia, also known as sound-to-color synesthesia, a rare phenomenon affecting a tiny percentage of the population, wherein a heard musical pitch evokes the experience of a particular color. These cross-sensory color associations differ from person to person but seem to be consistent over time. Play a C♯ and the person sees orange. A♭ yields bright blue. The innovative early twentieth-century Russian composer Alexander Scriabin is probably the classical world's most celebrated "chromesthete." He went as far as building a color wheel to correspond with music theory's circle of fifths as a reference tool for his own composing. Anticipating the light shows of the 1970s and today's increasingly common multimedia extravaganzas, Scriabin even invented a "clavier à lumière" ("piano of lights"), a color-coded keyboard that projects different hued lights as the keys are depressed.

Even for composers who don't involuntarily see colors with each heard tone, most seem to associate certain keys with a particular musical character or emotion. But it goes further. Even if every composer *did* begin every composition in the key of C, the piece probably would not stay there for long. For example, Mozart's Jupiter Symphony starts in C major but does not stay there; modulating to a different key is one of the principles of sonata form, on which the classical symphony and concerto is based. In fact,

modulation is one of the most powerful tools at a composer's disposal and is used in just about every style of music.
An example of this is the abrupt change from one key to
another, a device employed in much contemporary church
music, not to mention the pop tunes of Barry Manilow
("Mandy"), Beyoncé ("Love on Top"), and that perennial
American baseball stadium sing-along, "Take Me Out to
the Ballgame." A gradual modulation through different
keys is a much more subtle way of achieving a similarly
dramatic effect.

The second reason a composer chooses a key is a purely
practical one: to comfortably fit the instruments that
will be performing the piece. For example, if the key signature has multiple sharps, a wind player may be forced
to play with awkward fingerings or to transpose the key,
simply because of the way the instrument is constructed
(Chapter 9 has more on this). Even among stringed instruments, certain keys lay on the fingerboard better than
others. Each key change subtly shifts the timbre, the very
texture of the sound. A clarinet sounds different in its different registers, as does every other instrument, including the human voice. In all registers, eighteenth-century
French composer André Grétry always associated the
instrument with a quality of melancholy: "The clarinet is
suited to the expression of sorrow, and even when it plays a
merry air there is a suggestion of sadness about it. If I were
to dance in prison, I should wish to do so to the accompaniment of a clarinet."

Another practical consideration: the level of performer. If the piece is being written for beginning band,
for example, it is wise to favor the keys of B♭ and E♭, as it is
easier for band instruments to play in these keys without

having to resort to unconventional fingerings. The importance of this fact can be readily seen when a composition that was written for one set of instruments or for voice is transcribed for a different set of instruments. For example, a choral piece that is rewritten for band will almost certainly be cast in a different key from the original to accommodate those instruments. If the piece is transcribed again for strings, it will almost certainly be transposed to yet another key. Even if the piece was originally written for a mixed choir and then transcribed for a men's choir, the key will likely be changed to fit the vocal ranges of the male singers.

Lastly, composers seem to have favorite keys, keys that "speak" to them. At least they tend to start in that key. Where they end up is where the composition takes them as it emerges from the imagination.

Why were so many composers throughout history prominent pianists? Is there something inherent to the piano that makes a person a better composer? Which is the chicken and which is the egg?

While it is true that many great composers, including Bach, Mozart, Beethoven, Chopin, Liszt, Brahms, Prokofiev, Rachmaninoff, and Debussy, were all splendid keyboard players, there are some significant exceptions, such as Berlioz, Sibelius, and Hindemith. Still, it is probably true that the number of pianist-composers is disproportionately high.

There is a considerable difference of opinion about why this phenomenon exists. On the one hand there are people who feel that piano study is the "egg" that leads to a person being a composer (the "chicken"). A young person who studies piano grows up thinking in a holistic way about music. The pianist thinks in multiple voice parts, understands the difference between melody and harmony, and is exposed at an early stage in his or her musical training to counterpoint, the interweaving of melodic lines. Given this background, it makes sense that being a pianist could lead eventually to composing. The person who has facility playing the piano has a definite advantage as a composer because of all of these factors.

Other composers I spoke with feel differently. For them there is no inherent advantage to playing the piano. Some feel that playing the piano might actually be a disadvantage; it might inhibit a composer from hearing the notes as pure orchestral colors and thereby limit his or her tonal palette. The composer may also be hampered by the limits of his or her own keyboard technique in striving to create new sounds. They're also somewhat anchored to the piano, unable to scribble melodies on a napkin in a café, as both Mozart and Schubert were said to do on occasion. Further, since the piano is often a solo instrument, the typical piano student may lack a sense of ensemble or the ability to follow a conductor, a consequence of missing out on potentially formative group music-making experiences.

These experts believe the reason there were so many pianist-composers is simply a function of their training: Almost all classical composers were (and still are) trained in the European model, the basis of which is keyboard harmony and theory.

This group also points to the fact that outside of Western classical music, the dominance of pianist-composers is much less prevalent (in traditional Chinese music or American pop, for example). Which leads us to another interesting, related question:

In pop music it seems that you can often tell whether a song was written on the piano or the guitar just by listening. For example, The Beatles' "Blackbird" was clearly written on guitar, while "Let It Be" was written on piano. Is the same true of classical music?

On this point every classical composer I spoke to said that in classical music one cannot identify a composer's primary instrument from hearing a particular composition. For example, listening to Esa-Pekka Salonen's award-winning Violin Concerto from 2009, one would never suspect that Salonen's principal instrument of study was the horn (in addition to the baton).

Of course, since most composers even today have keyboard training, isn't it a safe bet that the piano is their main instrument? What was that question about the chicken or the egg?

In crafting a piece for orchestra, does the composer write all the music for every instrument? Or does he or she write only the melodies and then turn them over to an orchestrator?

Many aspects of how a composer works are a mystery, but the answer to this particular question is clear. Perhaps the best way to explain it would be with a visual arts analogy. Does a painter simply sketch the main subject in pencil and let a colorist do the rest? Of course not. The entire color palette is what an oil painter uses on the canvas, foreground and background, to focus attention, create a feeling, and capture our attention.

So too with the composer. The reason composers love writing for an entire orchestra is that it provides them with an almost limitless palette of colors from which to choose. Write a melody for flute and a violin and you get one "color"; bring together a trumpet and cello and get another, in an almost unending number of possible combinations. Two orchestral works of the twentieth century in which the composers offer practically a sampler of the vast panoply of orchestral textures are Ravel's *Boléro* and the Concerto for Orchestra by Béla Bartók.

The way the composer uses the available instruments is perhaps as important as the notes themselves. In fact, the overall message the composer is trying to project might actually dictate the instruments for which the piece is written. If the composer is wishing to portray a certain mood, then hushed strings might be chosen over heavy brass. For a different occasion or mood, the same composer might choose brass over strings.

If the composer is commissioned to write for a specific ensemble, the instruments at his or her disposal can help formulate the composition. So while the composer might write while sitting at the piano, we can assume the composer's mind is hearing the piece as if the intended instruments were actually playing.

Besides using the sounds of the instruments as part of the composition process, there are practical reasons a composer writes the notes for specific instruments. Each instrument produces a set range of notes, from highest to lowest. If a composer writes a melody without regard for where it sits on the instrument's particular fingerboard, it might not even be playable. The trained composer knows the range and sonic textures of every instrument throughout its register. That knowledge becomes one more tool in the composer's toolbox.

Beethoven is a great example of how this all works. His music is conceived differently depending on the instruments or ensemble for which he was writing. So the overall sound of one of his symphonies is quite different from one of his string quartets, and the piano sonatas introduce a sound world of their own.

Being the perceptive reader that you are, you are probably saying to yourself, "If this is all so important, why are there orchestrators?" Good question!

An orchestrator is a person who takes a piece a composer has written and then assigns those notes to different instruments in the orchestra. While this would rarely happen during the composition of a concert work for orchestra (for the reasons explained above), there are times when it makes good sense.

The need for orchestrators started in the mid-1800s in the opera house. The solo singers needed more time to study and memorize their scores than did the members of the orchestra, who would be using music at the performances. Therefore, long before the first orchestral rehearsal, the composer would give a complete score with all the voice parts plus a piano accompaniment to the singers so they could start learning their parts, mastering the staging, and memorizing. While the singers were working on all of that, the composer would then take the piano accompaniment and write out the orchestra parts in time for the dress rehearsal many weeks later. It was just a matter of time until enterprising composers realized that if they turned the orchestration over to someone else (perhaps a music student or assistant), they could embark on their next opera, a more lucrative career strategy. Thus the orchestrator came into being: a musician who excels in writing idiomatically for the instruments of the orchestra, forming a sonorous orchestral blend and balance. Though Arnold Schoenberg would later turn the classical music world on its ear by dissolving the notion of conventional tonality as an organizing principle in his compositions, he earned extra income early in his career orchestrating operettas, cabaret tunes, and waltzes. By the 1920s orchestrators were commonplace on the rosters of theaters and opera houses in Europe and America. As a case in point, Missouri-born composer, arranger, and conductor Robert Russell Bennett began orchestrating for the theater when he was in his midteens, about 1920. He went on to orchestrate more than three hundred scores, including such classic stage works as *Porgy and Bess, Show Boat, Kiss Me, Kate, Annie Get Your Gun, Oklahoma!, Finian's Rainbow, My Fair Lady*, and *The Sound of Music*.

There is another area where orchestrators are necessary: film music. It's all about time and money. The score is often one of the final steps in the completion of a movie, as the music cues are specifically timed to the completed visuals. Therefore, a composer faces incredibly tight deadlines: perhaps just a few weeks to write all of the music for a full-length feature. In this situation, the composer requires the assistance of an orchestrator—or multiple orchestrators—to get the parts to the orchestra in time to record the score and make the film's release date. There are exceptions here as well. Bernard Herrmann, Ennio Morricone, Rachel Portman, and John Williams are prominent examples of film composers who have chosen to go the extra mile and complete their own orchestrations whenever possible.

In summary, for pure concert music, orchestration—the choosing of the instruments—is integral to the composition process. In fact, the instruments chosen dictate the shape of the composition as it develops, and a composer would never willingly rely on someone else as orchestrator.

In theater and film music, where the melody or text is king, an orchestrator is often used.

Why would any composer write for an annoying instrument like the piccolo?

Many people have probably wondered about this, but few would have the courage to ask the question openly. Bravo to you for your bravery. Yes, the piccolo can be piercing and annoying to many listeners, especially older listeners who might have a bit of hearing loss, but the instrument plays an important role in the whole scheme of things.

The basic answer is that composers are always looking for as wide a tonal palette as possible with which to express their musical ideas. Like a painter who is always mixing colors to achieve the perfect blend, the composer seeks just the right tonal colors to enhance his or her melodies and harmonies. The piccolo expands the range of an ensemble by playing an octave higher than a traditional flute, affording the composer a unique, brilliantly high profile voice with which to work. Such composers as Vincent Persichetti, Karlheinz Stockhausen, Judith Weir, Meyer Kupferman, Franco Donatoni, and even Vivaldi (writing for a sopranino, or very high, recorder) showcased the piccolo in solo works, as have many others (likely commissioned by the piccolo players themselves).

That being said, it is true that the piccolo is not often heard as a solo instrument. However it is very common in orchestral works as an added tonal color, often doubling the violins or flutes. Composers describe the resulting effect as adding sparkle or brilliance to the sound. Of course, one notable exception is John Phillip Sousa's *Stars and Stripes Forever*; this infectious "official American march" has a spectacular piccolo solo near the end. Who doesn't love that?

But for most composers, the piccolo is simply one very special instrumental texture they employ, usually in combination with other instruments, to enhance the overall effect of their composition. It's not normally featured as a solo instrument because by itself it is . . . well . . . kind of annoying.

In tonal languages like Chinese, Thai, Vietnamese, and others, how is the lyricist able to compose lyrics that match the tune but require the actual tone of the word it is presenting? When a tone is changed in these languages, the meaning of the word also changes. So if a lyric is required to meet the tone, I can't figure out how the meaning is not altered.

The idea of tonal inflections in music is important to all music, but you are right: it is most pronounced in the tonal languages. Indeed, it is true that in Chinese classical vocal music the shapes of melodic lines are determined to a large extent by the tones of the language. The composer must write the melody in a way that is cognizant of the original pitch and inflection of each word. This is so important and pervasive in these languages, that if you were to hear a classical vocal work set in Mandarin Chinese (which has four tones and one neutral tone) followed by one in Hong Kong Cantonese (which has six) you would hear that the results are strikingly different, even if you do not understand the language.

What is truly surprising, however, is that while classical vocal composers' melodies are inspired by the natural tones, the same is not true in the melodies of popular music. In the bulk of current Chinese pop music, little attention is paid to the inherent melodic tendencies suggested by these tones. How this practice does not affect the meaning, or comprehensibility, of the words is something I do not understand.

However, while not as pronounced, the practice of constructing melodies in classical music based on natural inflection is not all that different from what composers do in Western languages—languages that are much less tonal. Even here, the natural inflection of language powerfully influences melodic shapes in opera and song. Leoš Janáček is a great example of a composer who took a 'nonstandard' operatic language (his native Czech) and beautifully adapted his musical settings to the language's vernacular speech patterns in such powerful works as *The Cunning Little Vixen* and *Jenůfa*. Similarly, Bartók's rhythms and melodies reflect the patterns of Hungarian speech in *Bluebeard's Castle*. In the operas of Henry Purcell and Benjamin Britten, English texts and haunting music come together to brilliant and memorable effect. For a more idiosyncratic setting of English texts (by a composer far more comfortable in Russian and French), there is Igor Stravinsky's *The Rake's Progress*.

Stravinsky's librettists on this work were eminent poets, W. H. Auden and Chester Kallman. Conductor Robert Craft, one of Stravinsky's closest musical associates, met with the composer on the very day Auden delivered the completed libretto for *The Rake's Progress* in 1948. Here's how Craft described Stravinsky's scrupulous efforts to idiomatically set the English words, few of which were familiar to him:

> He would ask me to read aloud, over and over and at varying speeds, the lines of whichever aria, recitative, or ensemble he was about to set to music. He would then memorize them, a line or

a couplet at a time, and walk about the house repeating them, or [do so] when seated in his wife's car (a second-hand, ancient and dilapidated Dodge) en route to a restaurant, movie, or doctor's appointment. Much of the vocabulary was unfamiliar to him but he soon learned it and began to use it in his own conversation, charging someone with "dilatoriness," or excusing himself for having to "impose" upon us, which sounded very odd from him.

It's safe to say all composers, regardless of what part of the world they come from or the language they're working in, likewise look for the "music" in a libretto or song lyrics by repeating the text aloud to hear its innate rhythms, pitch patterns, and inflections. From there a melody is created that best captures and expands upon the natural tendencies of the language.

Spurred on by a casual comment on KUSC, I recently estimated that the snare drummer in Ravel's Boléro plays on the order of 8,100 notes in the course of an approximately fifteen-minute piece. This caused me to wonder in awe at the capabilities of our great composers; not only their musical genius but their physical skills in being able to put that much ink on paper. I recently heard John Williams say he still composes at a piano with pen, ink, and staff paper. Considering the size of an orchestral score, the very task of putting it on paper seems Herculean.

Which leads to my questions:

- *How many notes are there in a typical symphonic score?*
- *In Mozart's day, how did the scores he composed get typeset and printed?*

- *Do any Thornton composition students still use pen and ink?*
- *Do film composers have staffs of orchestrators to help with this task? Did Mozart?*

Composers do much more than compose the actual melodies and harmonies of their pieces. They also have to assign each pitch to a specific instrument to perform. The result is indeed often a finished score that looks like a huge book.

It is hard to determine how many notes there are in a typical symphonic score without actually counting them (and I don't plan to do that any time soon). But it is safe to assume it is in the tens of thousands. Over the course of a composer's lifetime it could go well into the millions.

Most composers feel it is this process of working with all these notes that helps them to develop what is called a personal "voice," or style. Young composers who have only manipulated tens of thousands of notes are already beginning to develop certain tendencies. But when a composer get into the millions of little black dots, he or she is bound to develop certain habits, certain musical proclivities, which crystallize into what is call a voice.

Until as recently as the 1980s and 1990s, all of this composing was done by hand: sketching, orchestration, even professional engraving. Composers tediously notated their works in ink on vellum (a transparent onion-skin paper), using rulers and other gadgets to enhance a professional look. A ruler was used for every stem, every beam, and every hairpin dynamic. If a mistake was made, the composer either scratched it off with a razor blade or used an electric eraser designed to remove ink from vellum. The whole process required an unimaginable amount of physical labor that young composers of today cannot even fathom, nor do they need to fathom it.

It would take several hours to complete a single orchestral page and perhaps weeks or months to orchestrate an entire piece. It was tedious work, but it fostered skills, nurtured an attention to detail, and taught the importance of advance planning to get the project done in a timely manner.

Today, most Thornton student (and faculty) composers still sketch in pencil but at some point in the compositional process move to the computer. For some it's a back-and-forth sort of process. For others, the move to the computer occurs only after a penciled sketch is complete. One way or another, for just about all composers today, the computer has become an essential tool and a great time-saver.

The process for a film composer is quite different from that of a concert composer. As I mentioned earlier, a film composer nearly always has to work in a tight time frame. I have talked with many composers who lament the fact that films frequently fall behind schedule, but the release date rarely changes, leaving them even less time than they originally thought they'd have to write the music.

If the film composer has achieved a certain level of success and is in hot demand, he or she will most likely rely on a staff of orchestrators to help complete the score. The time crunch simply demands it. But with concert composers the time demands are less stringent, and as I mentioned, orchestration is a key part of the creative process. It must be said, however, that there are notorious procrastinators in this world: According to an oft-repeated story, Rossini always put off the overtures to his operas until the last minute, and in the case of *The Thieving Magpie* he worked right down to the wire. The theater manager at La Scala accordingly was said to have locked up the composer in a room; Rossini was instructed to drop each completed page of the overture out the window for copyists to pick up and complete. The manager threatened that if there were no pages forthcoming, Rossini himself would be dropped out the window instead. The threat worked, resulting in one of Rossini's most beloved overtures.

Until the relatively recent addition of computers to this process, copying was not that much different for Mozart or Rossini (or any other composer, for that matter, through the 1970s). In Mozart's time, if a work was to be performed in a specific city, it would be copied out entirely by hand, with Mozart showing up to conduct if he wanted to be paid. There were lots of copyists who worked very hard for very little money. But they performed a necessary task and, in a way, helped to contribute to some of the greatest works of all time. That is because if it weren't for copyists, the composers would have had to do all of this themselves, taking precious time away from their next project. Mozart would surely have left us fewer symphonies and operas as a result.

Composers relied on engravers to help with the publishing of the individual parts, but that's just a copy job involving no creative work whatsoever. In Mozart's day, copyists were hired for the same purpose. However, the down side of this practice is that we have conflicting versions of many famous works. The question is often asked, "Did Mozart mean to have an F♮ in that measure or an F♯?" because whoever wrote out the part was sloppy. Beethoven often admonished his hired copyists for illegibility or errors.

Here is an except from a letter written by Mozart's father that gives some insight into how last-minute some of the processes were:

> *The Piano Concerto no. 20 in D minor, K. 466, was written by Wolfgang Amadeus Mozart in 1785. The first performance was at the Mehlgrube Casino in Vienna on February 11, 1785, with the composer as the soloist.*
>
> *A few days after the first performance, the composer's father, Leopold, visiting in Vienna, wrote to his daughter Nannerl about her brother's recent success: [I heard] an excellent new piano concerto by Wolfgang, on which the copyist was still at work when we got there, and your brother didn't even have time to play through the rondo because he had to oversee the copying operation.*

With all of this handwritten work being done under strict time constraints and by multiple copyists, it is no wonder that today questions remain about certain pitches or other markings in classical music scores. This is one of the reasons there are often multiple editions of a certain work.

The 36th and the 38th symphonies by Mozart are well known as the Linz and the Prague, but I never hear about a 37th symphony by that composer. Was it lost?
The reason you never hear Mozart's Symphony no. 37 is that Mozart didn't write it. Michael Haydn wrote Mozart's 37th as his 25th.

Huh?

To clarify, Mozart himself did not number his symphonies. After his death, scholars studied his output and numbered his symphonies chronologically according to when they believed they were written. Later scholars determined that what was originally labeled Mozart's 37th symphony was actually the work of Austrian composer Michael Haydn, the younger brother of Joseph Haydn. However, this fact was not confirmed until 1907, and by then all of the Mozart symphonies were well known in their original numbering. It would have been very confusing to renumber them at that point, so the numbering stayed, and the 37th was eliminated or carries an asterisk.

How could this situation happen? Actually, Mozart himself added to the confusion. Composers of Mozart's time (and earlier) learned their technique by copying the works of their predecessors and contemporaries. No YouTube back then. No iTunes. Not even classical music radio. There were no recordings and few live public performances to hear because most classical concerts were given for the nobility and other dignitaries. Therefore, the way composers learned from others was to literally copy compositions by hand. In this way, a composer could better understand how an earlier (or contemporary) composer crafted his work. Further, it was a compliment or a tribute to actually take something from an earlier composer and use it in your own work. This practice was common through Beethoven's time, so much so that Beethoven once wrote in a sketch for a piano sonata "Dies habe ich von Haydn gestohlen!" ("This bit I have stolen from Haydn!"). Taking melodies, themes, and almost anything else became thought of as plagiarism (stealing) only much later. Mozart was known to have copied out and transcribed excerpts from Bach's *Well-Tempered Clavier*, which he encountered at the home of Baron van Swieten in Vienna in the early 1780s.

Mozart also likely copied out the score of Michael Haydn's Symphony no. 25 in order to learn from it; this is the manuscript that was found in Mozart's hand and assumed to be his creation. But there are two other factors that added to the confusion. First, this symphony was performed in the same concert in 1783 where Mozart's Symphony no. 36 received its premiere. It would not have been unusual for two symphonies by the same composer to be presented; as composers were constantly under pressure to provide new music for the hungry Austrian concertgoers. Secondly, Mozart did not simply copy the Haydn work but felt he had to improve upon it. First, he wrote a new Adagio maestoso introduction for the symphony. Then he went through and made other small changes, like removing a bassoon solo from the middle of the Andante movement.

This situation isn't the only instance of eighteenth-century-composer confusion. The so-called Mozart Second Symphony is now known to be the work of Wolfgang's father, Leopold Mozart; and scholars now attribute what was originally dubbed Mozart's Third Symphony to the elder German composer Carl Friedrich Abel. In that case, the eight year-old Wolfgang Amadeus Mozart had copied Abel's work while visiting London. Again, since it was in his hand, it was believed to be composed by him.

It should be pointed out that Mozart never claimed these pieces as his own. Instead, scholars compiling his output incorrectly attributed the compositions to him. One also can forgive the scholars their mistake. Several early symphonies that were once attributed to Wolfgang survive in manuscripts that simply say "Mozart" on them. Since Symphony no. 2 is now thought to be by Leopold Mozart, the experts really only got the first name wrong. Plus, in the nineteenth century, when these works were being catalogued, we didn't have many of the tools we have today, such as analysis of handwriting, inks, and papers. But occasionally the owner of the manuscript looked to profit by putting the name of a more famous composer on a piece. In the case of the 37th Symphony, it just took a long time to actually sort out the conflicting information and determine that it was not actually written by a young Mozart.

Here is one fun fact concerning this topic that is a wonderful intermission conversation starter if you are so inclined. You have just read that Mozart learned from copying the symphonies of Michael Haydn. Mozart was also mentored by the more famous composer named Haydn, Michael's older brother, Joseph. This leads to a very natural question. Ask someone why it took so long for anyone to find Mozart's composition teacher. When he can't answer, simply tell him, "Because he was Haydn."

How does a composer decide whether to write a concerto, a symphony, a choral piece, or a chamber work?

A composer has almost unlimited possibilities when sitting down to write a piece of music. A piece for full orchestra and chorus would be wildly different from a piece for two bassoons. Yet the composer has these possibilities plus literally thousands of other potential combinations.

The first determiner for the composer is whether the piece is a commission or not. Usually if an institution commissions (i.e., orders and pays for) the writing of a piece, it will indicate what is expected or choose the composer based on his or her expertise or style. If the Mormon Tabernacle Choir commissioned a piece and it came back for orchestra alone, no one would be very happy. The institution will usually ask for a concerto or symphony or fanfare based on its programming needs, the purpose of the commission, and the budget. The institution will also indicate the length in minutes of the desired piece. So the musical format for a large number of compositions, especially by established composers who are awarded commissions, is dictated by the ensemble that is requesting the commission.

If the composer does not have a commission, then a prime consideration is how to get the work premiered. There are many established ensembles, including string quartets, piano trios, and chamber orchestras. Composing for a conventional ensemble will increase the likelihood of a performance compared with, say, writing for such an unusual duet combination as timpani and flute.

Beyond these two key considerations, there is no one answer to the question. The composer may decide to write a piece for a pianist or violinist friend or for another musician whose playing moves him or her. Or the composer may indeed be inspired by the possibilities of unique pairings or an unusual space for performance. Further, the composer may be inspired to write a piece that communicates something specific, feeling that a particular combination of instruments, a text, or a distinct musical form presents itself as the best vehicle for expressing what the composer is trying to say.

Composers are problem solvers and like to challenge themselves in new ways. Each musical form and each combination of instruments presents its own unique sets of limitations and possibilities. These are the challenges for which composers live. For this reason, composers will often try a new musical form or instrumental grouping simply as an artistic challenge.

In an ideal world the musical form would come from the composers' artistic inspiration. In the real world, the form is more often dictated by the nature of the commission or the makeup of the ensemble. The great composers are able to compose based on the second factor and make it sound like the first.

To what extent do contemporary composers write what they think audiences will like? When a piece is commissioned, is the composer given specifics for the piece?
Ask any serious composers whether they are concerned about the audience's reaction to their piece, and they will say that the public's response doesn't matter. They lie.

If we go back in time, composers such as Mozart, Berlioz, and Mahler all craved popular success and wrote what they thought people would like. In their time public opinion mattered to them because their livelihoods depended upon their popularity. Interestingly, for the three famous composers mentioned above, success in their lifetime of the magnitude for which they aimed largely eluded them.

Because Mozart and other composers were not widely popular in their own lifetime, it became common during the twentieth century for composers to take this concept to an extreme and think that if the public *did* like their music, they were a failure. At least that is what they said. Still, many waited anxiously for the applause and critical acclaim when the piece ended.

In fairness, during the twentieth century a huge industry based on popular music arose, especially in the United States, which tends to judge music solely on popularity. The actual value of the music is often not what is considered or discussed. Instead the worth of a piece of music is determined by record sales. Perhaps the "art" composers' striving for *un*popularity in the 1950s through the 1970s—a period in which much austere music that avoided conventional harmonies and tonality was written—was partially a response to this trend. Great music, especially contemporary classical music, often doesn't have the "first hearing" appeal of some popular music. By definition this music is more complex and will often require multiple listening sessions in order for the listener to begin to grasp the composer's intent. It's hard enough to get a first hearing; a second performance is even rarer.

Even here, it's safe to say the composer is interested in the audience's response. But the composer and the rest of us may define "audience" differently. A composer tends to work within a certain tradition, a tradition understood by the composer's peers. So it is not that the composer is ignoring the audience but instead may be more focused on his or her peer group of composers, musicians, and conductors than on the general public.

In the nineteenth and early twentieth centuries there endured the romantic ideal of the solitary genius composer locked away in his garret, feverishly writing in isolation with no thought to public taste. It is a romantic fantasy, but it is not entirely dead. There are still composers who essentially feel the same way, especially in academia. But even these composers are probably more concerned about audience reaction than they might readily admit.

Why don't today's serious classical composers write recognizable melodies or "tunes" anymore?

This is an excellent and oft-asked question, and it cuts to the heart of issues of musical style and the relationship of folk music, commercial music and older music to the compositions of today. Tunes are alive and well across genres and mediums, including those used by so-called serious classical composers—modern opera and musical theatre, modern jazz, new art song, chamber music, choral music, orchestral works, and so on.

A "good tune" is generally shorthand for emotionally accessible, harmonically conservative, relatively simple music ... and there is no doubt that this type of tune, or very accessible melody, is today primarily to be found in popular music and musical theater. Truly great and accessible melodies are alive and well.

But in classical concert music, melodies have certainly changed. They are still there, but in a much more complex form; they have evolved to the point that they do not immediately jump out at you or get stuck in your head.

We can go back to Béla Bartók as a good example of this change in the first part of the twentieth century. Bartók devoted his early musical life to collecting his native Hungarian and also Romanian folk tunes, painstakingly visiting village after village, and preserving the tunes on very primitive recording equipment that utilized wax cylinders for storage. He used this music as the basis of his considerable output of compositions. However, most people who are yearning for tunes in modern music probably would not rank Bartók as one of their favorite composers. He could have written melodies that would be accessible to the general public, but instead he used the common folk melodies as the basis for expanding the entire idea of melody with dissonance.

Why would anyone in his or her right mind do this? Bartók took something that everyone loved (the traditional melodies) and deliberately altered them to be more complex and inaccessible. One of the most basic reasons he did this is that he was an artist of his time. Throughout history great pieces of music have reflected and been influenced by the times in which they were created. For example, there was an inescapable complexity and heaviness of style that pervaded a great deal of European music during and after the First World War. You can see this same trait in the visual arts of the period, especially emanating from central Europe. This often thorny, angry, alienating music reflected the horrific, devastating, and alienating experiences resulting from a progression of wars and oppression that saturated civilization during those years. Composers' music was the cultural expression of their era.

Because Europe had been the cradle of serious art music for centuries, this direction in music spread throughout the world. The movement created some of the greatest musical works in history. Benjamin Britten's *War Requiem*, Dmitri Shostakovich's Seventh Symphony, Olivier Messiaen's *Quartet for the End of Time*, Igor Stravinsky's *Symphony of Psalms*. These are perhaps not easy pieces to perform or even listen to, but they are life changing, profound, necessary works of art.

The great American composer Charles Ives wrote a wonderful and imaginative piece just over a century ago called *The Unanswered Question*. The question is a five-note "melody" played by the trumpet and repeated at intervals throughout the quiet, roughly ten-minute work. It is memorable but not easy. The piece itself is haunting and transcendent but also irrational and at times chaotic. For Ives, the short melody represents the perennial question of existence. And in his way, Ives makes a bold and true claim that music cannot and should not be captive to narrow tradition but must be free to express anything and everything.

Even complex melodies can become accessible, but it takes effort on the part of the listener. An interesting example of this happened to my son, Nathan. He works as an editor for television and educational videos. A few years ago he was working on an hour-long show about Hindemith's Symphony in B♭. If you have ever heard any music by Hindemith, you probably did not leave singing his melodies, and the Symphony in B♭ is no exception. There are melodies but they are complex, inaccessible, and hidden in the texture of the music. Nathan is a casual musician and played drums in a variety of rock bands as he was growing up, but he is not formally trained. As an editor he had to listen to this piece repeatedly while he made the visual edit to the performance. One day he and I were driving together, and he started humming one of the melodies from the symphony. Clearly it took repeated active listening sessions, but even these complex melodies got stuck in the head of an untrained listener. If he could learn to like them, you can, too.

I do think things are changing as we move through the twenty-first century, however. In the past several decades many composers in the United States (in particular) have loudly challenged the dark complexity of their forebears. In my city, the Los Angeles Philharmonic regularly performs new music that is powerful in its emotional and melodic directness. For example, it recently performed John Adams's nativity oratorio, *El Niño*, a work of extraordinary melodic joy, featuring a children's choir, chorus, orchestra, and vocal soloists. Contemporary composers Morten Lauridsen and Eric Whitacre write ravishingly beautiful choral music that is nothing if not filled with melodic invention, much of it hummable. Stephen Hartke's Third Symphony, commissioned to commemorate the tragedy of 9/11 and premiered by the New York Philharmonic and the extraordinary four-voice Hilliard Ensemble, is an ode to expressive melody that binds us to ancient sounds and times.

So the bottom line is that melody is alive and well but has transformed and matured into something that is not as immediately accessible as it once was. But that is what art does; it grows, matures, and transforms itself. A listener might have to work a bit more to find the melody in a modern piece than in the *Nutcracker*, but in the end the effort will be worth it. If you don't agree, you might just wait a while. Music is always evolving, and who knows, we might see a revival of the notion of music based on lyric melodies.

5

The Performers

WHEN WE THINK ABOUT ATTENDING a concert, probably the first thing that pops into our heads is, who will perform? In the popular music world, we say, "We saw Josh Groban" or "We went to a Lady Gaga concert." We don't say "We went to a 'Poker Face' concert" or "We went to hear 'I Left My Heart in San Francisco.'" When it comes to concerts we usually go to hear the performers first; what they choose to perform is usually a secondary consideration.

This is not too different in classical music. We might choose which Philharmonia Orchestra concert to attend based on what is being performed on a specific night, but we usually have already decided we want to see the Philharmonia and perhaps its conductor.

So it makes sense that there is much fascination with these instrumental virtuosos and what their lives are like when they are not on the stage. Our listeners have also wondered how they work together as a team and what protocols, politics, and even superstitions drive what they do.

This chapter is about classical musicians: the people who make it happen.

I am wondering how musicians memorize a score? I am especially referring to those who play the solo parts in lengthy, virtuosic piano concertos, like those of

Rachmaninoff, Liszt, and Beethoven, works that contain thousands of notes, yet artists play them from memory.

The idea of performing classical music from memory (outside opera, where it is necessary) was almost unheard of until the middle of the nineteenth century. Prior to the 1850s, music was most commonly performed from the printed page. Part of the reason for this is that musicians seldom had the luxury of having adequate time to prepare music to the level of memorization. The few "professional" musicians that were around had to perform music for a great number of occasions and events; thus they had to learn an immense quantity of music.

During the so-called romantic era of the 1800s, things would start to change. Pianists such as Clara Schumann and Franz Liszt began to perform their music from memory. There were several reasons for this change.

The first reason was the democratization of classical concert music. Increasingly, musicians performed at public concerts given for a rising middle class rather than, say, for ceremonial banquets honoring royalty or the name day of a benefactor or for church services, as had been the common practice in earlier times. This change actually prompted a change in both the quantity and characteristics of the music being composed.

The example of a composer who wrote for a benefactor was Haydn. At the age of twenty-eight, Haydn landed a plum job: he signed a contract as "Vice-Kapellmeister in the service of his Serene Highness Paul Anton, Prince of the Holy Roman Empire, of Esterházy and Galantha, etc. etc." What all that fancy verbiage meant was that for nearly the next five decades, until shortly before his death, Haydn would be a salaried employee of the Esterházys, under the benevolent patronage of the finest princely house of what was then part of Hungary. This entitled the composer to a high standard of living and a superb house orchestra but also required him to produce, rehearse, and perform a large quantity of music. In addition to this, he also wrote many symphonies and other works commissioned by others. In all, he composed 109 symphonies plus many other works. This kind of performance schedule did not lend itself to memorizing music.

In part because of this, Beethoven, who came after Haydn and did not have a single employer, left only nine symphonies. Most of those Beethoven symphonies are more complex and longer than those of Haydn. Beethoven wrote them, for the most part, on commission to be performed at public concerts, but also to satisfy his own creative spirit. An example of how this played out is that for the princely theaters, Haydn composed some twenty Italian operas and five singspiels, now mostly forgotten. Beethoven left us a single opera.

The increasing dependence on public ticket sales resulted in musicians needing to develop something of a wow factor. By performing technically challenging music from memory, the artist was able to display his or her devotion to the music (a romantic-period ideal for an artist) and also create excitement for the audience in the same way a trapeze artist creates a buzz by performing without a net.

Since the musicians had a bit less music to contend with, they could more thoroughly prepare for each performance. Therefore, the printed score was less of a necessity at the performance because of the great preparation involved in learning the music: by the time of the performance, the music was often memorized. Many composers (Mozart, Beethoven, Chopin, Liszt, Rachmaninoff) also performed their own concertos, so much of it was already in their head. But even for pianists who were not composers, the more complicated and virtuosic music of this time demanded much more practice. On stage, having the music present actually might be a hindrance due to the need to turn pages and the danger of possibly losing one's place in a poorly lit hall.

Music has become ever more complex since the nineteenth century. Therefore the preparation needed to perform music has only increased. The accepted norm for pianists today is that standard repertoire presented at recitals and in concerts with orchestra is played from memory. However, for complex modern scores, it is very common for the featured soloist or recitalist to follow a score on stage.

I understand that pianists often memorize large works like concertos; it's part of the act in playing with an orchestra. But what puzzles me is that the same artists, such as Emanuel Ax or Yefim Bronfman, need someone to turn pages for them when they play chamber music, such as a piano trio or piano quartet. Isn't this a contradiction?

Yes, this does sound like a contradiction. There is no rule about whether to use music in chamber music, but it is certainly the convention to do so. There are several reasons for this. In playing solo repertoire, if pianists make a mistake or have a slip of memory, an accomplished artist can do a "work-around" to get back on track or to cover a mistake. After all, they are playing alone; no one (except musically knowledgeable audience members and possibly their spouse) will be the wiser if they veer from what is actually printed until they find their proper place. Skilled pianists are actually quite good at this.

While it wouldn't seem likely, the same thing is true in performing a piano concerto from memory; even if the pianist somehow gets lost or has a memory slip, the conductor (who has a score) can keep everyone on track while the soloist recovers.

In chamber music, all the performers are considered equals, rather like individual soloists who are playing as one. Each person has an equally important musical part that is carefully integrated with the others. If the pianist (or any member of the ensemble) tried to play chamber music from memory and became lost, the results would be devastating to the ensemble as a whole. (The term "train wreck" comes to mind). Therefore, most pianists (and other performers) play chamber music, including art song recitals, with the score in front of them, out of respect for the others in the group and for what might transpire if there is a problem. Even when a singer or a violinist performs from memory at a recital, accompanists have the music in front of them as a safety net.

As logical as this sounds, the classical world is not quite as clear cut as that. Some pianists perform even solo recitals with music, at least some of the time, especially for a new and complex piece or simply because the pianist's touring schedule is so hair-raisingly busy that he or she lacks sufficient time to memorize or rememorize the program. Then, too, there are a few pianists who memorize chamber music repertoire. Two notable examples are the Canadian pianist Glenn Gould, who was said to be able to practically memorize any piece at sight, and the American pianist Warren Jones, *Musical America*'s Collaborative Pianist of the Year in 2010 and a member of the Camerata Pacifica, based in Santa Barbara, California.

So the bottom line is that there are no hard and fast rules. There are general conventions and logical reasons behind those conventions, but exceptions to the rule are not hard to find.

Is there such a thing as a left-handed violinist?

Let's clarify what is implied in the question. First of all, there are many left-handed violinists, pianists, guitarists, clarinetists, and the like. My guess is that the percentage of left-handed musicians more or less mirrors the percentage of lefties in the population at large. There are debates as to whether this is an advantage or a liability. Left-handed people generally learn to live in a right-handed world. Instrumentalists are no different. Most lefties simply learn to play in the traditional right-handed manner. In fact, one of the most acclaimed violinists of all time, Jascha Heifetz, was left-handed but was trained at a very early age to play the violin in the right-handed manner.

However, the person who asked the question was probably wondering whether anyone has ever played the violin "against the tide"—that is, with the bow in the left hand instead of the right. The answer to this question is also yes.

Comedian Charlie Chaplin was a proficient amateur violinist who also composed many of the scores to his own films. By his midteens, he was a recognized artist in the English music halls, and according to his 1964 autobiography, at this time he was also practicing violin several hours a day: "Each week I took lessons from the theatre conductor or from someone he recommended. As I played left-handed, my violin was strung left-handed, with the bass-bar and sounding post reversed. I had great ambitions to be a concert artist, or failing that, to use it in a vaudeville act." Chaplin went on to play the violin in two of his movies, *The Vagabond* (1916), in which he seduces a young gypsy woman with the sound of his playing (though one of the sight gags shows his fourth finger trilling uncontrollably), and *Limelight* (1952), in which he plays a faded music-hall star who plays the violin with Buster Keaton at the piano. The violin doesn't fare too well here: Keaton is shown walking around the stage with the smashed violin under his foot.

The late Finnish conductor Paavo Berglund started his musical life as a violinist who played left-handed—and joined the ranks of the Finnish Radio Symphony Orchestra in 1949 at the age of twenty. The orchestra accommodated his need for extra space around his left bowing arm until 1958, when he began to focus on his rising career as a conductor. At one point the concertmaster of the Buffalo Philharmonic played a violin specially configured for a left-handed fiddler.

The prominent Austrian-born violinist Rudolf Kolisch performed with the bow in his left hand as a result of a serious injury to the middle finger of his left hand suffered in a childhood accident, after he had begun violin lessons. He made the adjustment without missing a beat. He went on to become a founding member of one of the leading string quartets in the world from the late 1920s to the early 1940s, the Kolisch Quartet, which premiered major works by such composers as Arnold Schoenberg (who became Kolisch's brother-in-law), Alban Berg, Anton Webern, and Béla Bartók.

Similarly the contemporary violinist Philip Bride lost
the use of some fingers of his right hand in an accident. He
had to relearn how to play the instrument, bowing left and
holding the violin with his right arm. This must have been
awfully difficult. But he was able to master the specially
configured instrument and impress audiences, even recording such virtuosic works as Mendelssohn's Violin Concerto
in D minor and the same composer's Octet for Strings with
the chamber group he leads, Ensemble Instrumental de
France.

There are examples of left-handed orchestral cellists
as well. Obviously they really need to keep their distance
from their colleagues in the cello section.

Despite these examples, playing left-handed is definitely the exception. First of all, there are very few violins
made to accommodate the reversed playing technique, and
none of the great traditional instruments were set up that
way. Plus, most left-handed violinists do not feel disadvan-
taged bowing right-handed since both hands are so intri-
cately involved with playing.

An interesting sidebar: in all of these cases the left-
handed violinist who wanted to play in a left-handed manner used a left-handed violin. In the guitar world, there are
guitarists who simply take a right-handed guitar and turn
it around. Thus, all the strings are "backwards." I have seen
this several times, and it actually changes the entire sound
of strumming and how they play.

Jimi Hendrix was left-handed and, as a young man in
Seattle, learned to play the guitar upside down. (He also
was reportedly encouraged by his father to learn to play the
instrument right-handed and could do that quite well, too.)
But Hendrix's favored left-handed technique included the

use of the right thumb to form unusual chord fingerings. Hendrix's signature guitar was the Fender Stratocaster, which he played upside down and restrung backwards.

So, yes, left-handed musicians can make just as indelible an impact as their right-handed brethren.

I once heard the late composer-conductor Johnny Green say that an orchestra will test guest conductors during rehearsal to see if they really know what they are doing. Is this true? Does this happen?

I had always heard this also and I was pretty sure it was common practice. However, when I asked musicians who perform in major orchestras, I was surprised to find that the practice was neither as overt nor as openly hostile as I had suspected.

Classical musicians are professionals; as such, they want every concert to be something they can be proud to be a part of. That being said, as professionals, they want to see a conductor come to rehearsals well prepared, with a deep knowledge of and familiarity with the music, and the confidence and ability to impart this vision to the orchestra. They also want to see the allotted rehearsal time used as efficiently and effectively as possible. This is where the rubber meets the road, so to speak.

Musicians can tell almost immediately if the conductor is prepared. They can also sense if they and the conductor are on a similar musical level. If they intuit that the conductor is not prepared, the musicians will have very little patience. They will let it be known subtly through attitude, questions, or their manner of playing. As one prominent orchestral musician told me, "In this situation a rehearsal can go south pretty quickly." Sometimes a musician might ask an obvious question about interpretation meant to expose the conductor's lack of preparation. Other times musicians might play an entrance or passage exactly the way it is being conducted even though they know that is not the way the conductor really wants it; in such a case the conductor simply didn't know how to accurately convey his or her own interpretation. One prominent musician recalled in detail an actual scenario where "enthusiastic brass players" wanted to demonstrate to a conductor that his baton technique was inaccurate. They played their entrances exactly as conducted (instead of as notated in the score) in a way, shape, and form that was out of sync with the rest of the orchestra. Everyone (except the conductor) knew what they were doing and what they were trying to communicate to the conductor, and "it became a very uncomfortable situation for all." In this case what the conductor was subjected to could almost be considered cruel and unusual punishment.

Interestingly, all the musicians I spoke with said that they never engaged in these sorts of shenanigans as a game, nor was it the way they ever approached a first rehearsal. Instead, they felt it was their way of sending a strong message that it was not appreciated that the musicians came prepared; the conductor did not.

Frankly, it's not often as dire as that statement by the belligerent brass. A conductor's personality, reputation, age, and other extenuating circumstances can all play into how the orchestra responds. For example, even if a conductor is not prepared or in some other way not quite up to the task, how that conductor responds to the orchestra can make a difference. If the conductor feels threatened and becomes defensive or dictatorial—say, carping about small intonation issues or demanding many repeats of a particular passage just to throw his weight around—the orchestra players will dig in their heels and put up resistance. On the other hand, a conductor who responds with respect or admits that something needs to be given more thought is likely to be granted a bit more leeway.

Likewise, elderly conductors of great esteem or highly respected younger conductors who are known to be experiencing personal or professional challenges will be given some slack.

The one scenario that is different and where the orchestra does test the person on the podium is when the conductor is auditioning to be the ensemble's music director. In that scenario, orchestra musicians do feel it is their responsibility to "test" the conductor and then communicate to the orchestra's management how they feel about the person, either in a written survey or possibly as a member of the music director search committee.

It is clear from all of this that orchestras do test (or at least judge) a conductor almost from the moment he or she steps on the podium. This is not to say it's the "open hunting season" mentality often depicted. Still, conducting is clearly not for the faint of heart (nor the faint of baton technique). One orchestral musician summed it up as follows: "It's not so much that we enter the rehearsal prepared to judge. But if a conductor does not respect the orchestra or the conductor is not prepared, it ain't gonna be pretty."

Bassists seem to be the unsung heroes of orchestral music. They never get a solo, they stand in the back row, and they have to lug around the biggest instrument. How has the role of the bass player changed in music over the last sixty years? Also, upright vs. electric—who wins?

Let's start with the fact that most music needs a bottom line to sound complete. In a string quartet that role is provided by the cello, which has the lowest range in the group (which also consists of first violin, second violin, and viola). In wind music the bass notes are provided by the tuba. From the time of Johann Sebastian Bach (1685–1750) until the start of the twenty-first century, just about every other ensemble, from an orchestra to a rock band, has had the lowest part—the very foundation of the music—played by some form of string bass. This makes the bass one of the most important instruments in the ensemble[1]. So any answer regarding the bass will depend on which genre of music we are discussing.

In symphonic music the double bass provides the lowest part. But a common problem is that many composers write notes for the bass that can't be played; they are lower

---

1. Yes, my primary instrument is the bass, but that is not why I gave the instrument such an important role in the music of the last 250 years. There are many exceptions to the generalization that the bass is responsible for the "bass part" in most music. In a piano trio, for example, the piano will often play the bass part, leaving the cello to interact melodically with the violin. In many non-Western cultures, the bass part is played by some sort of percussive instrument, and in recent pop music the bass part is often created digitally by computer or synthesizer. Still, for the vast bulk of classical ensemble music of the last 250 years, the string bass has been primarily responsible for the lowest part. Even with the many exceptions, what is not disputable is that bassists are always the best-looking, coolest, and smartest members of any ensemble regardless of genre.

in register than the lowest string can go. Talk about composers not respecting an instrument! I would like to see them try doing that to the violins!

Let's leave that discussion for another day and explore the two common ways to deal with this awkward situation. In Europe it is common to add a fifth string to the bass that goes a fourth lower than the conventional lowest string. In the United States it is more common to add an extension to the instrument that allows the player to descend to the lower notes as needed. For example, a C extension extends the register to a low C. The extension itself frequently costs over a thousand dollars. Look for these extensions the next time you attend an orchestra concert; you will see what looks like an extra narrow board or stick rising up above the tuning pegs and scroll.

In orchestral music, the bass is frequently bowed, which brings out the instrument's lyrical quality and also projects a more intense sound. Orchestras always have a group of bassists playing the same part; in such a low register it takes several instruments playing together to be heard among all the other instruments on stage.

With the advent of jazz, things started changing. The double bass still provided the bottom line, but it was rarely bowed. Instead it was plucked, or played pizzicato. This plucking makes the bass much more of a rhythm instrument. In fact, with the drums, piano, and guitar, the bass makes up what is called the rhythm section of a jazz orchestra. I have never seen a C extension in jazz.

In jazz, the bass is an improvisatory instrument, just like every other instrument in the ensemble. For that reason, it would be very difficult to have multiple basses; they would have to play the same thing, which is contrary to the independent spirit of jazz. (It would also force the audience to pretend to politely listen to multiple bass solos instead of just one). However, the sound of the bass would often be drowned out by the brass and drum instruments. This is why the bass was the first instrument to frequently be amplified for jazz (usually by placing a microphone in front of the bass).

Early rock and roll groups featured a double bass played in the jazz pizzicato style and often in a moving or running line that interacted with the beat. Unfortunately, as guitars started to be amplified, the bass was often very hard to hear.

Then came 1951, when Leo Fender introduced the Fender Precision Electric Bass. The electric bass quickly replaced the stand-up bass in most pop music because it could be amplified and blend with the electric guitars. (It was also easier to carry to a gig, until you added the weight of the bass amplifier).

The electric bass and a jazz string bass are played differently. The electric bass provides the foundation of the harmony; thus the pitches move less than in jazz. In fact, it could be argued that the electric bass functions musically more like the symphonic bass than like the jazz bass.

In the 1990s the electric bass started having the same pitch limitations as the symphonic bass: it couldn't go as low as the songwriters wished. Especially in country music, many songs mandated notes that were lower than the lowest note on the traditional four-string bass. Thus, five-string electric basses started becoming very popular. Today, the four- and five-string electric basses are at least equally popular, and there are six-, seven-, and more string basses.

The electric bass colors all types of music, including some contemporary art (or "classical") music, but it is mainly confined to pop styles. You also do see electric basses in jazz from time to time.

You can see that the questioner was quite perceptive in asking how the bass has changed over the years. Its role and function have probably shifted more than any other string instrument in the orchestra.

Now for the final question: who wins ... electric or acoustic? As with most decisions requiring artistic judgment, we can't really answer that. For each genre, each composition, what instrument most aptly fits the musical style?

Unless, of course, you are talking volume ... then the electric bass wins hands down!

I worry about the musicians of the orchestra; isn't their hearing likely to become impaired since they sit so close to each other? And many of them sit right in front of the heavy brass, the horns, trombones, and tuba. I realize rock musicians (and their listeners) may suffer from hearing loss. But a far greater loss would seem to be with classical musicians.

We live in a very noisy world, and hearing loss should be of concern to everyone. However, musicians are especially concerned because having good hearing is critical to their livelihood.

There are basically two broad types of hearing loss; age-related (called presbycusia) and noise-induced. Age-related loss will affect everyone, although not equally. But as of now there is not much that we can do about it. There are some really exciting prospects on the medical front; they may be able to slow or even reverse age-related hearing loss. But as of this writing, these developments are still on the far horizon.

Therefore, what most musicians must concern them-selves with is noise-induced hearing loss. First of all, this condition is misnamed. Noise-induced hearing loss can be caused by any loud sound, even the beautiful sounds of Beethoven; it does not have to be "noise." The ear is pretty indiscriminate when it comes to loudness.

There are three factors that interact to cause hearing loss: loudness of sound, length of exposure, and heredity. For example, a short but very loud sound can cause instant and irreversible hearing loss. A nearby explosion or gun blast will often cause hearing loss.

This type of experience is often unavoidable (rarely do we hear: *"Johnny, stop playing with that grenade!"*). All too frequently, the listener simply happens to be at the wrong place at the wrong time. The frustrating part is that two people experiencing the same phenomenon may be affected differently. This is where heredity sets in.

Perhaps surprisingly, less loud sounds over a longer length of exposure are just as damaging as the short burst of explosive noise. The government sets guidelines on safe exposure to sound levels. For example, a loud sound might be considered safe for fifteen minutes a day but deemed unsafe if the exposure is increased to an hour. This is the type of exposure that is of most concern for musicians.

The loud sections of a symphonic work can certainly reach "dangerous" levels, but these sections tend to be short lived, often measured in seconds or a couple of min-utes. This is in contrast with many popular styles, where the music is loud and does not have the dynamic range of classical music (unless you consider starting loud and get-ting louder a dynamic range).

In general, we might assume classical musicians tend to practice for longer hours in a given day than pop musicians. And while a clarinet might not be as loud as an amplified electric guitar, remember that it is that formula of volume plus length of exposure that creates the problem. Eight hours of violin practice per day could be of very much concern.

Many people ask why musicians don't wear earplugs (ear protection). Some do, even some members of the Los Angeles Philharmonic and other major orchestras, during subscription concerts. (You can sometimes spot them removing their earplugs if you look closely as softer passages approach.) However, most musicians I know (myself included) find it very distracting to perform with earplugs. Most earplugs make it very difficult to judge (or at least be confident) that you are blending and balancing your sound with the musicians around you. Just as with hearing loss, the medical field has here made some promising advances, and we may be close to truly useful musicians' earplugs.

In the meantime, knowledge and good acoustics are the best ways to combat this problem. Today we know so much about good acoustics that rehearsal rooms, concert halls, and practice rooms can be designed to at least partially offset the negative effects of exposure to loud music. Even within an orchestra it is totally accepted to place sound baffles between certain musicians. This would have been unheard of a few decades ago, but knowledge of the effects of long exposure to loud sounds has changed policies. (More powerful and protective musician unions help, too.)

My biggest concern in this general area of inquiry is for younger musicians who play in school bands and orchestras that rehearse in rooms not designed for that kind of performance or were designed so long ago that the acoustical miseries therein are simply no longer acceptable. I have seen marching bands forced to rehearse in a school cafeteria or a gymnasium because the school did not have a dedicated music room. This is of great concern not only for the young musicians but also for the music teachers, who often spend the entire day, every day, rehearsing ensembles in these rooms.

I have noticed that percussionists don't play as much as other instrumentalists in an orchestra. Yet it seems there is more percussion in twentieth-century music than any earlier music. Is that true or just a coincidence of the pieces I have seen performed?

The first thing to realize is that the percussion section is probably the most visually striking (and varied) within the orchestra, and people often listen with their eyes. When a percussionist gets up to play a glorious cymbal crash in the climax of a Bruckner symphony, everyone notices (and perhaps also notices that the percussionist then sits down for another hour). However, when the alto, tenor, and bass trombones fail to play until the fourth and final movement of Beethoven's Fifth Symphony, hardly anyone one notices they were sitting idle for the first three movements.

Still, it is true that the strings and woodwinds play the most notes in an orchestra. These sections produce the basic sound palette that we associate with an orchestra, so composers tend to give them a lot of notes to play.

In regard to the percussion, there is a historical reason for this section playing less continuously. While the timpani were an important voice in the orchestra as far back as the baroque period, other percussion instruments were developed only more recently.

In the classical period, percussion instruments, introduced from other earlier cultures, were often used for novelty effect or to add color to the overall sound. Percussion was not considered at the core of the orchestral sound. It wasn't until the nineteenth century that percussion became an integral part of the orchestra, with composers beginning to explore a wider range of textures, instruments, and effects.

In the twentieth century percussion blossomed. This might have something to do with the popular music of the twentieth century, which was very rhythmically based. But composers certainly explored this phenomenon in art music, as well. Some examples: the great hammer blows in Gustav Mahler's Sixth Symphony. To achieve the proper effect, the percussionist strikes a huge mallet against a wooden block. Mahler called for an effect "like the stroke of an axe." Then there's the vast percussion battery called for by Igor Stravinsky in the ballet *The Rite of Spring*, including a wildly insistent bass drum, antique cymbals, and the guiro, commonly used in Latin American music. The guiro is a hollow gourd with notches on one side. It is played by rubbing a stick or sticks along the notches to produce a scratchy sound. George Antheil's *Ballet mécanique* (1923) is an early example of a composition written exclusively for percussion. Béla Bartók made a big splash with his *Music for Strings, Percussion, and Celesta*, written in 1936, and his Sonata for Two Pianos and Percussion, a pioneering chamber work from the following year.

Twenty-first-century composers have followed their examples. Percussion ensembles are proliferating, including Nexus, So Percussion, Third Coast Percussion, and in a somewhat more popular vein, Blue Man Group and Stomp. Today we have concertos, chamber music, and solos written for a wide variety of percussion instruments. At the

2015 Ojai Festival, Stephen Schick gave the first solo percussion recital in the festival's nearly seventy-year history.

It is not your imagination. Percussion arrived ready for
its close-up just after the turn of the twentieth century,
and it carries an ever more reverberant voice in the world
of music.

**_Percussionists in orchestras seem to spend a lot of time
sitting around waiting to play. Is there a certain personality type that is attracted to an instrument that
plays only part of the time?_**
Research has shown that different personality types are
attracted to playing different instruments. So the stereo-
types you find attached to different sections of the orchestra have probably just a bit of grounding in reality.

It makes sense that a certain personality type would
be attracted to percussion. You probably remember these
folks from school when you were growing up. In the music
world, they are a bunch of guys (and gals) who get away
with sitting in the back of the class and contributing less
but getting the same pay as everyone else. As if that isn't
enough, they always have the coolest toys in the room.

At least that is how _they_ see themselves.

Seriously, there are some personality traits that are
probably found in many percussionists. First of all, there
is a lot of testing of ways to play percussion instruments,
especially unpitched instruments, to find just the right way
to fit into the character of the music. The percussionists
I have talked with often describe themselves as "tinker-
ers" who are willing to explore a whole range of things that
make sound. Unlike other orchestral musicians, percussionists often collect a wide range of "found" instruments,

from brake drums to snare drums to rocks and pinecones and everything in between.

Another important point is that every time a percussionist plays a note, he or she is a soloist. This is a great responsibility. Percussionists cannot hide in a section of players. Therefore, they cannot be intimated by having to play a solo loud cymbal crash on cue. It is probably unnecessary to add that these musicians have to have an infallible sense of rhythm. Imagine those Mahler hammer strokes coming a bar too early.

Why is a music concert featuring one or two performers often called a recital?

When this question was asked of me, my first response was, "I never thought of that." When I posed the question to faculty member after faculty member, I got exactly the same response! We all know what a recital is, but for such a common word, none of us knew why it was used.

Finding the answer took some research, but an answer there is.

To understand the context, it helps to remember that the modern concept of a public classical music concert did not develop until the mid-nineteenth century. For example, in Beethoven's time a concert might begin with the first movement of a new Beethoven symphony. This could be followed by a concerto movement or two, then a reading of poetry or a dramatic recitation. When this spoken-word part of the concert concluded, a solo piano piece by a different composer might be played, followed by a piece of chamber music, another symphony movement, or what have you. Then the second movement of the Beethoven symphony might be played, after which there could be more poetry, music, or other aural arts. Because there was so much of the spoken word among the music, these concerts were called recitals.

This format started changing around the time of Liszt. In fact, he was one of the first performers to present a concert solely of his own music. This way of presenting music was so novel that it created quite a stir. Liszt, too, called his concerts recitals even though he dispensed with the poetry readings. This became known as a solo recital, to show that it was a presentation of the work of only one person. The terminology stuck.

Today a recital can mean all types of things but usually involves a small number of musicians—perhaps a solo pianist, a singer with accompanist, or a cello and piano. These performances sometimes take place in modestly sized recital halls, sometimes in a major symphony space. But the atmosphere is generally more intimate than a big orchestral concert even when it takes place in a big hall.

The word "recital" is primarily used in classical music and dance. While it could work for any genre of music, it has not made the leap. I have never heard of a jazz, folk, or rock recital except at colleges, where students are usually required to perform a "senior recital" regardless of the style of music.

It is interesting that there are some musicians who are working to make classical music more accessible and enjoyable to audiences. I have seen concerts paired with poets and even painters. This is regarded as cutting edge, but in fact they are returning to a format popular almost two hundred years ago.

I notice that not all musicians in the orchestra play the same amount of time. Some even walk off the stage for

*entire pieces. Even within a piece, the playing time is not
equal. Is this discrepancy reflected in the players' pay?*
Orchestra managers have proposed all sorts of ways to
make their ensembles more cost effective, but I have never
heard of anyone advocating a "pay by note" system. It would
certainly be labor intensive to count all those individual
parts. (And would a C♯ be worth more than a basic C♮?)

There are two basic formulas for paying orchestral
musicians; salary and "per service." A salaried musician is
exactly what it implies. The musician is paid a set amount
per year in return for a set number of "services." A service is defined as a concert, a rehearsal, recording ses-
sion, school appearance, or any of various other activities.
A per-service musician is paid a set amount for each service performed.

However, within each service the musicians are basically paid the same amount, and it is not dependent upon
how many notes or how many minutes they perform.
Regardless of the length of time musicians perform, they
still are an important part of the performance. They have
to be at the concert and rehearsals the same amount of
time (unless they are excused for pieces in which they do
not appear), and they have to spend the same amount of
time perfecting their skill and learning their part.

There are some differences in pay within the orchestra, but pay is *not* based on how much the musician performs. For example, the principal of each section gets
paid more, and certain solo instruments, such as contrabassoon or English horn, are paid more than a section
violin. But the discrepancies are never about time spent
playing.

What many people don't think about is that musicians love playing. Most musicians would rather play

than just sit there. So if there ever was a movement to pay musicians by how much they perform, it might actually make more sense to have it a reverse scale; the more you play, the less you make, because you're having so much fun.

Let's hope we never explore such a system.

6

The Instruments of the Orchestra

THE COMPOSER WRITES THE MUSIC and shares it with the conductor. The conductor studies the music and shares it with the musicians of the orchestra. The musicians learn to play the music on their instruments. Thus, the composer, conductor, musicians, and instruments are all equal partners in bringing the music to life.

The instruments of the orchestra are a varied lot and have remained largely unchanged in design, makeup, and construction for the past hundred years. In this age of digital design and manufacture, it is amazing that so many of the instruments in the modern orchestra are still made by hand or, in the case of some of the finer stringed instruments, were made by hand, decades, even centuries ago.

In this chapter we will explore some of the lesser-known facts (and myths) about the instruments played in the classical music repertoire.

Before getting to the questions, it might be helpful to lay out the basic families of instruments in the orchestra. There are essentially four instrument families: strings, woodwinds, brass, and percussion. The string family consists of (from highest to lowest) violins, violas, cellos, double basses, and sometimes harp. In the woodwind family, we have flute, clarinet, oboe, bassoon, and sometimes saxophone. The brass family is made up of trumpet, French horn (also known simply as horn), trombone, and tuba. The percussion family consists of snare drum, bass drum, tympani, chimes, marimba, glockenspiel, and a whole bunch of noisemakers too numerous to mention. Surprising to most people is that the piano is a percussion instrument, too; it produces sounds by hitting strings with a hammer.

Now on to the questions!

Were "catgut" strings truly made of the guts of cats? Do some people still use them? How does it affect the timbre?

It is still in common usage to say violin strings are made from catgut, but in fact, strings were never made from the intestines of cats. That would be disgusting. Instead, violin strings were originally made from the stretched, dried, and twisted intestines of sheep (or occasionally goats, horses, or donkeys)—that is still pretty disgusting, but it's true. Strings made from real catgut would be much too short and weak for use on bowed instruments, plus they have the annoying habit of making a "meow" sound when plucked. It's been speculated the word "catgut" may have been an abbreviation for "cattle gut" or could be derived from "kit," an early word for a small fiddle.

Since the nineteenth century, violin strings have been made from a variety of materials: various types of steel, nylon, silk, and, yes, real animal gut wrapped in aluminum, silver, or even gold. Today the lower three strings of a violin are made of metal wrapped around a nylon or gut string. The top string, which is too thin to wind, can still be made of gut, but this is a matter of preference.

For any player of a stringed instrument, the decision about what kind of string to use is a question of personal taste. The string player weighs the desired sound, the need to stay in tune, the durability of the material, and perhaps cost. In the United States for the past two decades, the fashion has been to favor wrapped synthetic strings; they are much easier to play and are quicker to break in. The one exception is when a performer is playing a "period instrument," based on a design from the seventeenth or early eighteenth century (if not an authentic vintage instrument). In those cases, gut is always used.

Why are there different colors of strings on a harp?

This question actually has two separate answers. When you look at a harp you will see four or five different colors of strings. From the standpoint of the audience facing the orchestra, it will often appear that the longest harp strings are one color, the middle strings another color, and the shortest strings, still another. That is because the strings are constructed from three different materials. The middle strings are often made of gut, which tend to appear yellowish. The highest strings are nylon, a lunar white. The lower strings are under much more pressure than the others because of their length. They are fashioned from wound metal to maximize their strength and appear bronze, silver, or copper in color. Thus, the first reason the colors differ is a function of the varied materials necessitated by the harp's extremely wide pitch range.

However, if you look closely you will see that some strings, regardless of what they are made of, are red and others are black or dark blue. These strings function much like the black keys on the piano in that they help the performer keep track of where they are. There are forty-seven or forty-eight strings on a harp, and the harpist needs to have some way of knowing which string is which as he or she navigates them. This color-coding system evolved for that purpose. Every C is red and every F is black or blue.

An interesting question: why are the notes F and C singled out for color? I could not find a definitive rationale for this, but I will make a guess, and you can use it as a conversation starter with the stranger next to you the next time you go to a concert. You can be pretty sure they don't know the answer and have never even pondered it. (We will ignore, for now, the fact that they probably have no interest in the answer.)

The fact that C is one of the colored strings possibly relates to the famous middle C on the grand staff and the piano. After that decision was made, another string halfway between all the Cs was possibly deemed helpful. That would be either F or G. F was the lucky winner.

All this color on the strings is unique to the harp in the string instrument family. Since the other instruments of the family have only four strings, they don't need this system.

Musicians tend to rave about their vintage instruments. With modern manufacturing techniques and today's technologies, why can't we replicate or even improve on those instruments?

To answer this question, I spoke with a variety of musicians; while all honored, even worshiped, their older instruments, all felt that great instruments were being made today as well. The general belief is that many of today's finest instruments will become legendary instruments in the future. But it takes time.

This actually makes sense. If you were to visit an instrument museum you would see that the many old instruments in the collection are no longer playable. These were fine instruments in their day but have fallen into disrepair or can no longer be fixed. For intrepid musical travelers, there are many great instrument collections upon which their eyes may feast: to name a few, London's Victoria and Albert Museum, the Smithsonian National Museum of American History in Washington, DC, the Musical Instruments Museum in Brussels, and the Musical Instrument Museum in Phoenix, Arizona (founded in 2010).

This would argue that there is a bit of "self-selection" going on with the great vintage instruments. They were recognized in their day as being quality instruments and have been lovingly tended to for centuries.

To maintain an instrument in top working order takes a great deal of time and money. Probably only instruments that have great tone and playability would be deemed worthy of the trouble. Instruments that are just OK or worse at some point are deemed to not be worth the time and expense of such scrupulous maintenance.

Conversely, once an instrument becomes both valued and valuable, the amount of maintenance it receives assures it will retain its worth and even become more valuable.

Further, instruments, especially stringed instruments, are like a fine homemade soup. They are often better the second day. Instruments get better the more they are played. The wood breaks in: it gets used to vibrating in certain ways and becomes more resonant and responsive to what it is expected to do. But it had to start off good for it to become excellent.

Musicians sometimes describe a modern instrument as "stiff." This means it needs time to breathe, break in, and mature. I think it is safe to assume that some of the instruments being created today will self-select over time, just like instruments of the past. They will be honored and revered in the next century just as instruments from past centuries are admired today.

A bit of a side note: The same logic can be applied to compositions. People often ask me why there is no great music being written today when the music of the past was *all* great. Sorry, but the music of the past was not all great. The same self-selection process is in play with music. Thus, we know the music of Ludwig van Beethoven but not the music of his contemporary Elias Grumsky. And we can hum Beethoven's "Ode to Joy" but are hard pressed to hum the Horn Concerto no.1 of his contemporary Giovanni Punto. And he was a real composer.

I have heard that oboists must make their own reeds. What does this reed-making involve and why are there no commercial reeds?

For the oboist (and the bassoonist), learning to play the instrument is literally only half the story. The other half is learning to make quality reeds. Though commercial reeds are available, most top professionals will use only ones they've crafted themselves.

The bassoon and oboe are called double-reed instruments because, well, they have two reeds that vibrate against each other. (The clarinet and the saxophone have only a single reed.) To be accurate, the double-reed instruments have two parts of the *same* reed vibrating against each other. But still, the two reeds working together create the sound.

The oboist has to create and sculpt the reed by hand from bamboo, but not just any bamboo. Bamboo from different parts of the world possesses different characteristics, and even those characteristics can change from year to year, not unlike wines and for many of the same reasons. It is generally agreed that bamboo from the south of France boasts the best material for making oboe reeds.

Once the oboist has acquired the desired bamboo, he or she has to craft it into a playable reed using knives and other tools. An oboist working at a "reed desk" looks more like a jeweler repairing a fine watch than a musician preparing for a performance.

The reed-making process is one that takes years of study and practice, and even for the most seasoned professionals it is a painstaking and often frustrating endeavor. A professional oboist with a major symphony orchestra often spends upwards of fifteen hours a week just on making reeds, as it takes somewhere around three hours to craft one. This is before the oboist practices even a single note. On top of that, reeds are so temperamental that often only one in three rises to the level of being used in a professional performance. So what makes a good reed?

A good reed

- plays in tune
- has a nice tone
- can play from *pianissimo* to double *forte*
- won't tire the player prematurely
- will retain its tone for more than a couple of days

Even after a reed is made and perfected, it is a temporary work of art.

After all, bamboo is a vegetable. Saliva contains enzymes that to some extent "digest" the reed and over time (sometimes as little as a few days), the fiber in the reed loses its resilience and stops vibrating properly. For most oboe players, even the best reed will last only a week or two—or less! A change in the weather can make a reed work on one day and barely vibrate the next. We begin to understand why oboists have a reputation, perhaps unfairly, of being some of the more high-strung, obsessive members of the orchestra.

Over the past few decades there have been attempts to create synthetic reeds that can produce a beautiful tone and won't degrade like bamboo. Thus far, they have not been widely accepted by professional oboists, with the exception of basic "beginner reeds" for students. Many professional oboists still think they sound awful.

Clearly, oboists have quite an intimate relationship with their reeds before they are even played. And I have touched only the tip of the iceberg here. If this topic interests you, I recommend searching "how to make an oboe reed" on YouTube. There are excellent videos that show this fascinating topic in detail. For the rest of us, it is simply enough to know that not everyone has the patience to be an oboist.

You explained that the oboe is used to tune the orchestra because the oboe reed can be made to reproduce the agreed-upon pitch. But do tell, how does it do so?
What a great question that is! It is during that delicate and time-consuming process of reed making, just described,

that the oboist determines the optimal pitch at which the reed will resonate. The length of the reed determines the pitch. If A is deemed to be at 440 vibrations per second, the reed would be made seventy millimeters long. If A is set at 442, the length would be only sixty-eight millimeters. The shorter the reed, the higher the pitch.

However, that is only part of the story. Contrary to popular belief, the oboe is the most unstable of the woodwind instruments. The small double reed and bore of the instrument enable the pitch to be altered using only the mouth—that is, the embouchure, the manner in which a wind player's mouth and lips are placed—and the air itself. Using the same fingering, one can play a half step higher or lower and everything in between. If the oboist moves his or her mouth slightly up or down or changes where the lips are placed on the reed or blows harder or softer, the pitch will noticeably change.

This is why the oboist still needs to use a tuning fork or, more commonly these days, an electronic tuner to assure the pitch is accurate, as was explained in Chapter 2.

Since electric instruments and electronic instruments and keyboards have been with us for many decades, why haven't these instruments worked their way into orchestras?

Well, they have and they haven't. It depends on what type of orchestra we are talking about and what repertoire is being played. In a traditional symphony orchestra it is true that both electric and electronic instruments are still rare, except in some contemporary works and film scores. While there are certainly exceptions where a composer included a part for a specific instrument (e.g., electric guitar, theremin, synthesizer, bass guitar), the general custom has been to exclude them from the instrumentation. This is not just a matter of orchestras being conservative. Instead, it is a matter of convention.

Composers tend to think of the orchestra as an instrument with a specific and defined palette of sounds. When they sit down to write, they know what sounds they can get from an orchestra and often can hear those sounds in their mind. Further, there are so many possible sounds that an orchestra can make (by combining colors) that most composers feel they have everything they need to express what they are trying to express. Only when a composer feels the need to expand (through amplified voices, electronic instruments, or unusual acoustic instruments like the banjo and mandolin) will he or she expand the palette to include these instruments. Notable recent examples are *The Dharma at Big Sur* for electric violin and orchestra by John Adams; Nico Muhly's *Seeing Is Believing* for the same combination of instruments; *Muse of the Missouri* for banjo and orchestra by Stephen Hartke; *Reeling* and many other electronic-enhanced scores by Julia Wolfe, who won the 2015 Pulitzer Prize in music; and as far back as 1945, Miklós Rósza's atmospheric score for the Alfred Hitchcock film *Spellbound*, which made memorable use of the theremin.

Besides artistic concerns that tend to favor the traditional makeup of orchestras, there are practical concerns. Composers write for an orchestra and know what colors they have to work with, and they can assume this will be constant across the world. Varying from the standard will create complications and additional expenses for an orchestra (and its management) and might result in fewer performances of a composer's work. As it is, performances of contemporary music, particularly after the premiere has occurred, are hard enough to achieve without this additional possible disincentive.

The extensiveness of available sounds plus the practical concerns of breaking the mold keep the instruments of symphony orchestras fairly constant. While you might find it surprising that instruments created back in the 1950s are not yet standard orchestra instruments, consider the saxophone. It was invented by Belgian instrument manufacturer Adolphe Sax in 1840 and is still infrequently used. Two of the most distinctive examples of its use in the standard repertoire are in Ravel's *Boléro* and the same composer's orchestration of Mussorgsky's *Pictures at an Exhibition*, but these are exceptions.

However, the same is not true of nonsymphonic orchestras. Most movie orchestras and popular music orchestras (such as you might see accompanying a singer like Michael Bublé) utilize electronics today. There are several reasons for this. First, the style of music may call for instruments like a drum set, electric guitar, bass guitar, piano, or synth. In more popular styles we expect to hear these instruments, and they sound perfectly normal in that context.

In the case of movie music, unusual instruments might be added for special effects or to create a certain mood. I have seen saws, mandolins, harmonicas, accordions, and every sort of electronic and percussion gear on soundstages.

Lastly and unfortunately, electronics are more and more being used to reduce the number of musicians necessary for live performances. For example, two or three electronic keyboards, one or two violins, one cello, a few brass and wind players, electric guitar and bass, and two percussionists can create a substantial amount of sound, which can be used for musicals, musical revues, and vocal concerts by popular artists.

The bottom line is that we are not likely to see new instruments becoming a regular part of *symphony* orchestras. There are just too many artistic and practical forces working against it. Likewise, we are likely to see more and more use of these instruments in nonsymphonic orchestras for both musical and economic reasons.

I went to a concert that featured the saxophone in a contemporary classical piece of music. The program notes said that in the past twenty years the range of the instrument has expanded exponentially even though the instrument itself has not changed. How can this be? Is this true of all wind instruments?

Indeed, this truly seems impossible, but in fact the range of the saxophone has increased from two and a half octaves to about four octaves in the past few decades, even though few substantive changes have been made to the instrument. To understand this, think about athletes such as runners. Today's common speeds would have won races a half-century ago. While running shoes have certainly improved, they cannot account for such dramatic change. Rather, a better understanding of the running process, more scientific training methods, and ever higher athletic standards have been the major contributors to the increase in speed.

So, too, with the saxophonist. While a few minor modifications have been made to the instrument, its mouthpiece, and its reeds, the most influential change has been in the player's technique. The player has quite a bit of control over the sounds produced by means of what is called voicing. Voicing is the flexibility and control over the mouth, throat, tissue, and tongue. These factors strongly affect the resonating chamber in the head and the air in the passageways. It is through the manipulation of voicing that a saxophonist can control the range and sounds produced. You can get a basic feel for this idea by saying different vowel sounds or simply by whistling.

The role of the vocal tract was not fully understood nor was it fully developed by early saxophonists. Today there are commonly accepted methods to develop the vocal tract. These methods for controlling voicing and extending the upper register surfaced in the mid-twentieth century. But they are so standard today that teachers begin to develop these skills even in very young players.

While the range of all wind instruments has expanded in recent years because of the development of voicing techniques, the expansion of range is most pronounced in the saxophone. This is probably due to the fact that the saxophone is relatively young in relation to other wind instruments and is still progressing and developing. Players are still exploring the acoustical limitations of the instrument and the physical limitations of the body. It will be interesting to see how far they will go.

What is a "harmonic" in a string piece? Why are they written?

Creating harmonics is a very important playing technique for all string players, from guitarists to violinists. How harmonics work is fairly straightforward. But fair warning: it is actually a little hard to believe for many people.

To understand the science of harmonics, you have to trust that things are happening during a performance that you can't readily see or hear. If you are willing to suspend belief, it will all make more sense.

Let's start with a string that is vibrating. If you pluck a string that is stretched between two points, it vibrates up and down, like the image in Figure 6.1. This vibrating string creates a sound wave in the surrounding air that produces the pitch we hear. For example, if the string is vibrating up and down at 440 times per second, it creates a disturbance in the air (a sound wave) that is also vibrating 440 times per second. When that wave hits our ears, our brains interpret it as the pitch A.

Also notice in Figure 6.1 that if you wanted to stop the vibration, the most effective place to do this would be to put your finger at the point of the greatest vibration, which is at the middle of the string, and push down. This becomes an important feature of understanding harmonics (we return to this idea a bit later).

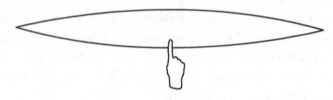

FIGURE 6.1 The fundamental movement of a vibrating string and the most effective place to stop the vibration.

So far so good. Most people can readily understand and accept this basic concept. Now things get funky. A split second after the string starts vibrating in the main up-and-down way, it also begins to vibrate simultaneously in other ways. Figure 6.2 shows the original vibration but also a secondary and tertiary vibration.

FIGURE 6.2 Once put in motion the vibrating string divides and starts experiencing secondary vibrations, each producing additional but generally softer pitches.

While not interfering with the original, the string divides itself in half, and each half vibrates twice as fast. To continue our description from above, if the original vibration was 440 times per second, the secondary vibration is twice as fast, or 880 per second. Our ears hear this vibration as the pitch A one octave above the original but not as loud as the fundamental vibration of 440. This secondary pitch is called a harmonic.

Then the string divides into thirds while continuing to vibrate in the original and in halves. These segments of the string are vibrating in a ratio that produces a pitch that is five notes higher. If the original pitch was A, there is now also the pitch E (A–B–C–D–E).

I have shown only three splits of the string, but this process continues with the string splitting itself into more and more segments and thus producing more and more different pitches.

So when we hear a pitch that we think is just one pitch, we are almost always hearing an entire spectrum of pitches. Some are louder and some are softer than others, based on the shape and construction of the instrument. Basically, this is what makes two violins sound different from one another and different also from a guitar. This same principle more or less applies to understanding why a trumpet sounds so different from a cello even when they're playing the same pitch. Now let's get back to playing harmonics. Remember that if we want to stop the basic vibration, we push down in the middle of the string. In Figure 6.3 you can see that if a musician carefully touches the middle of the string, the primary vibration can be stopped without interfering with the secondary one. When this happens, the listener hears the upper pitches without the primary one. The result is an ethereal-sounding pitch very different from the original. This is called playing a harmonic.

Notice that if the musician carefully touches the string at the point where it divides into thirds, the first two

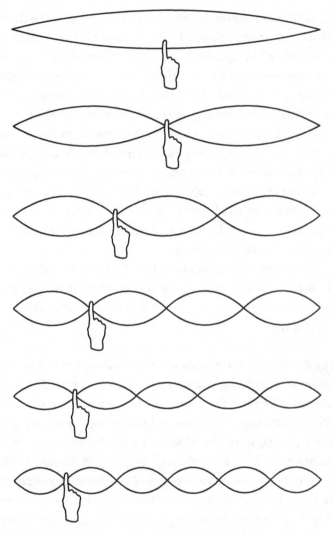

FIGURE 6.3 The most effective place to stop a larger vibration often does not interfere with the smaller vibrations.

vibrations can be stopped without interfering with the third. Again, the listener would hear only this vibration and the ones higher. This creates a completely different pitch (E) but one possessing that same ethereal sound. This process can continue with more and more pitches being produced by mathematically knowing where on the string to touch.

Playing harmonics takes practice but is an important technique for string players to master. Many contemporary composers write harmonics into the score to achieve exactly that otherworldly sound they are after. Sometimes it is written in to allow the performer to play a pitch in a passage and avoid an awkward or perhaps physically impossible hand movement.

Once you hear a harmonic being played, you will come to easily recognize this unique sound. Until then, you will just have to take my word that this crazy phenomenon is happening.

I understand that pianos used by students at conservatories are exchanged every seven years or so. The reason must be that they have arrived at the end of their life expectancy. However, why are organs seemingly more prestigious the older they are? And aren't violinists ecstatic about playing an ancient Stradivarius from the late seventeenth or early eighteenth century? At first glance it appears that there is a double standard here. Yes, it is true that string players praise their well-worn instruments, whereas you rarely hear of a pianist aching to acquire an antique keyboard. But once you think past the surface, you can see that organs, pianos, and stringed instruments are fundamentally different.

First of all, stringed instruments have very few moving parts compared to organs and pianos. Besides the vibration of the soundboards, the only moving parts of a stringed instrument are the tuning pegs, and those are moved only to tune the instrument, not as part of the performance.

With organs and pianos, there are countless moving parts, even during a performance: keys, hammers, dampers, and pedals. During a typical keyboard performance these parts are constantly in motion and often under quite a bit of repeated stress and activity. Pianos and organs need constant maintenance and, even with that, they simply wear out.

High-quality pianos can be rebuilt and new parts inserted as long as the soundboard remains intact. Still, eventually they will need an overhaul and it is often less expensive, at least more cost effective in the long run, to buy a new instrument.

Stringed instruments, on the other hand, tend to improve with age as the wood settles in and resonates more freely. But these instruments, especially the vintage variety, need constant maintenance. They need a controlled temperature and humidity. They need to be played. The strings need to be replaced, and the bow maintained. However, because they do not have all those moving parts, they can last much longer than their keyboard cousins.

There is another factor at play: the string family instruments have not changed much over time. Thus, playing a violin from a century or two ago is not much different from playing a modern instrument. A composer writing for violin today can assume the same range and abilities that an instrument of two hundred years ago had.

The organ and piano, in contrast, have evolved and developed. There are more keys on a piano, for example, than there were a hundred years ago. Pianos are made today (especially in the United States) to project brilliantly in large concert venues rather than in the smaller halls and private chambers so frequently used in western Europe over the past several centuries. Organs have new ranks and features. Thus, unless organists or pianists are attempting to perform in a historically accurate manner, they will often prefer the instruments of today. Further, contemporary composers will always write music to exploit and expand the capabilities of the instrument. Thus much of today's piano and organ music could not even be played on a historic instrument.

The bottom line: whether an instrument becomes prized as "vintage" is often in direct proportion to how many moving parts it features, how significantly its family of instruments has changed over time, how well the instrument was originally constructed, and how well it has been maintained.

Why is it that a lot of music written for the harpsichord is performed today on the piano? Even on classical music radio stations, you don't hear much solo harpsichord.
Most people think that classical music is timeless and therefore immune to changes in popular taste. This is not true. Over time, performance practices with regard to even the most famous pieces of music are altered as to the number of instruments used to perform the work and the kinds of instruments employed, in addition to matters of tempo,

dynamics, phrasing, and musical style. The fact that we so rarely hear harpsichords on the radio today is a perfect example of musical traditions changing.

It is also an example of another belief that proliferated in classical music circles: the idea that music was constantly evolving into higher and higher forms. For hundreds of years many people believed that new music should make old music obsolete. This was especially true during the nineteenth century, wherein the mantra was that new is better; everything new is an improvement on the past. When the modern piano was invented and perfected, it took off like a rocket. It was felt to be the most perfect instrument ever built, and everything that came before it was just its primitive precursor. By the end of Mozart's life, for example, the harpsichord had all but disappeared, and no one even cared. This was kind of like what happened to eight-track tapes of the 1970s.

To show you how far that went, it is said that in 1809 a tough winter left the staff of the Paris Conservatory desperately searching for firewood with which to heat the building. They ended up burning the remaining magnificent harpsichords that had not already been vandalized. Thus began the "dark ages" of the harpsichord. It was all but forgotten or studied only as a historical relic for more than a hundred years.

Fortunately, even though the harpsichord itself was considered old fashioned, it was recognized that much great music had been written for the instrument, including works by Jean-Philippe Rameau, William Byrd, Louis and François Couperin, Domenico Scarlatti, George Frideric Handel, Johann Froberger, Girolamo Frescobaldi, and Johann Sebastian Bach, among many others. In the common thinking of the day, if the music sounded great on harpsichord, it stood to reason that it would sound even more terrific on the piano. Unfortunately, much of the delicacy and color of the music was lost when played on the louder, more bombastic modern instrument, but over time our ears adjusted. Thus, a more than two-hundred-year tradition on the harpsichord disappeared almost overnight.

Fortunately, the harpsichord was resurrected in the first half of the twentieth century by the Polish keyboard virtuoso and teacher Wanda Landowska, who became a rock star of the harpsichord, first in Paris in the 1920s and 1930s and later in the United States, where she settled after fleeing the Nazi regime, in 1941. While she loved the *idea* of the harpsichord, she, too, had become accustomed to hearing original harpsichord music performed on piano. Thus she had a harpsichord that was built to look like a piano and that had a bigger sound than an authentic harpsichord but was still a plucked instrument.

Over the course of the twentieth century, this renewed interest in the harpsichord prompted construction of historically accurate reproductions of the instruments in the mid century. It was only a matter of time before music lovers noticed pieces written for these instruments sounded quite fabulous when played on the instruments (or close facsimiles) for which they were composed. This also coincided with the authentic performance practice movement then sweeping continental Europe, the United Kingdom, and the United States, a movement that continues to this day.

Today the harpsichord is becoming more popular, and you do hear it frequently on classical stations, especially as part of period instruments baroque ensembles, such as the English Concert, the Academy of Ancient Music, Amsterdam Baroque, Bach Collegium Japan, and Philharmonia Baroque. But it still has a long way to go. It is arguable that the modern piano simply "cuts through" more brilliantly and, with a smoother, easier-on-the-ears timbre, is therefore featured more prominently in solo repertoire both on the classical airwaves and in the concert hall. Finally, I think we are still overcoming the performance traditions going back more than a hundred years before Landowska, Ralph Kirkpatrick, Igor Kipnis, and other modern harpsichord pioneers broke through in the twentieth century. This simply takes time but hopefully will happen.

On various occasions, I have seen some unusual instruments used in the orchestra. For example, I have seen performances using contrabass clarinet, basset horn, bass flute, contrabass flute, contrabassoon, or flugelhorn. Where does the musician obtain the instrument to play in the concert? Do most professional musicians have a collection of instruments related to their primary instrument (e.g., C flute, alto flute, bass flute)? Do orchestras own these unusual instruments and lend them to the musicians for a particular concert? Is there an "unusual instruments" rental business?

The answer to this question is "all of the above." First of all, many professional musicians own more than one instrument (with the possible exception of pianists and harpists). For example, most clarinetists would own at least B♭ and A clarinets; both are frequently called for in performances. I know many professional violinists who own two violins and use them for different types of music or ensembles.

However, when you get to some of the more unusual instruments, the answer becomes "it depends." For example, you mention the contrabass clarinet. This instrument is called for perhaps once or twice during the course of an entire season. In major orchestras or in major metropolitan areas, an orchestra will designate a clarinetist on the roster as a sort of "utility player" in addition to the regular first and second clarinet positions. The musician will be expected to own (or be able to easily acquire) and play, as needed, the A, B♭, bass, and E♭ clarinets, as well as the contrabass. However, in smaller cities or in orchestras with lower budgets, you would be unlikely to find a person who owns so many different instruments. In that case, the orchestra might own the instruments or rent them from another nearby ensemble or university.

There are also less common instruments, such as the basset horns called for in such Mozart works as the Serenade no. 10 for winds, the opera *La Clemenza di Tito*, and the Requiem. Another rare instrument, the Wagner tuba, is a valved brass instrument Wagner himself designed for use in the Ring cycle, apparently as a kind of hybrid or bridge between horns and trombones. Wagner tubas were also frequently employed by such composers as Richard Strauss, Arnold Schoenberg, and in modern times, David Bell in his scores for the TV series *Star Trek: Deep Space Nine* (as well as in many film scores). An orchestra would not expect its staff musicians to own these instruments for the few occasions they are used. The orchestra would own or rent these instruments as needed.

When the score calls for a specific instrument outside the normal configuration, the orchestra will often hire an outside musician who is an expert on that particular instrument and owns one. Examples of this I have seen are mandolin, lute, banjo, harmonica, theremin, and musical saw. Yes, the musical saw. It's the kind of saw you would find in a hardware store and is typically played while the "sawist" is seated, the tool's handle squeezed between his or her legs. The sharp end of the saw is held with one hand; the instrument is bowed with the other. Several years ago, I actually saw a major American orchestra feature a saw soloist.

So to answer your question directly, in most cases, the musician will own the instrument that is needed. In cases where a regular member of the orchestra is expected to play a highly unusual instrument, the orchestra will usually provide it, either from its own collection or through a rental.

How many instruments does a major orchestra own? How about a less well funded regional or local orchestra? What about college orchestras?

Almost all professional orchestras will own (or supply through rentals) the percussion, timpani, and any keyboard instruments. Major orchestras go further. I checked with the Los Angeles Philharmonic, and the management feels that it is pretty typical in owning percussion, timpani, and keyboard instruments, as well as a set of four Wagner tubas, a contrabass clarinet, bass flute, bass trumpet, and basset horn. The LA Phil also owns some fabulous stringed instruments donated or purchased over the years, including several Stradivarius violins.

School orchestras always provide the percussion and keyboard instruments. Beyond that, they depend on students owning instruments or rent or borrow them as needed. There is quite a network among orchestras, conductors, players, and orchestra managers at all levels (collegiate

through professional). Lending and renting between organizations is common.

This demonstrates an aspect of programming that is
often not realized. The music director and the rest of the
artistic team must take into account the availability of
instruments when putting together the music programming for a season. Even further, the team will need to
take into account the logistics of utilizing these additional
instruments. The music director must ask fundamental
questions, such as if the musicians are going to double, will
they fit on the stage?

This is just another example of how complex an organ-
ism the modern symphony orchestra has become.

*I heard the other day how happy players became when
valves were invented for the horn. The poor players
before that time must have had a hard life, able to get
only four notes on a bugle, for example. But why does
the horn have rotary valves instead of the "piston" kind
found on most other brass instruments? Is there an
engineering reason, like no space? Or does it have to do
with sound?*

Before we get to the question of the piston valve, let's
address the first part of the question. Unlike the bugle,
early horns produced more than four pitches. Horns are
made from substantially longer pipes than are bugles. This
extra length gives the horn a lower fundamental pitch,
resulting in more usable overtones. Plus, early performers
could expand the basic natural tones through changing
crooks, even during a performance.

In Vienna in 1814, two piston valves were added to
the so-called natural horn. However this did not result in

a happy day for the performers; not all of them believed at the time the added valves marked an improvement. Indeed, for the better part of fifty years there existed two camps: natural horn and valve horn players. Both thought their instrument was the only way to go.

The natural horn players actually became quite proficient. Brahms usually wrote for natural horn. But the horn began growing in importance in the orchestra in the nineteenth century, and it became imperative for a player to produce all the instrument's pitches with equal purity and strength. To ensure this could occur (notwithstanding the occasional horn "clam," or whopping error) necessitated four valves.

Regarding the question of piston vs. rotary: there are horns with piston valves. These are called Wiener (pronounced "*Vee*-ner") horns. These Viennese horns are the exception; the rotary valve allows the horn player smoother transitions between notes. Rotary valves also produce a darker sound with more projection, both of which are important to the characteristic horn sound in a modern orchestra.

I recently saw a drawing of a euphonium that showed an instrument with two bells. Additionally, Meredith Willson mentions a double-bell euphonium in **The Music Man.** *What is going on with the two bells? I can't imagine the amount of air that would be necessary for splitting the vibration column to have two simultaneous tones produced, one for each bell. Plus, I have never actually seen one of these instruments, though I attend many concerts. Do they really exist, or are they like the unicorn?*

The double-bell euphonium may not be as mythical as the unicorn, but it certainly is almost as elusive. The double-bell euphonium is an instrument that has a second bell that makes a sound much like a trombone or horn. The two sounds are not made at the same time. Instead there is a valve on the horn that is used to switch between the two bells as desired. The second bell is almost always used for special effects.

The double-bell euphonium was never very popular because the second bell, which was naturally made of brass, made the instrument very heavy to carry and hold while playing. Since the player tended to use the primary bell most of the time, the extra load wasn't worth the effort. Thus, you probably will not see one anytime soon. They have not been produced since the 1960s.

During a US Marine Band concert, the famous euphonium soloist Arthur W. Lehman is said to have explained the best reason for having that second bell is to hold his white gloves when he is not wearing them.

I recently heard someone say that keyboard instruments cannot play in tune with an orchestra because of equal temperament? Is this true? Can you explain this?
This is technically true. I will *attempt* to explain it.

If you play a keyboard instrument, like the piano or organ, you have little control over the actual pitch being produced by the instrument. Essentially if you push the C key, you will hear a C pitch provided the instrument is in tune. If you push the F♯ key, you will hear F♯.

For orchestral instruments, especially strings, as well as for singers, it is quite a different story. The violinist, for example, can make slight changes to where he or she places a finger on the instrument and make subtle but significant changes in pitch. And they do that all the time.

One of the main reasons to alter the pitch is to make it more expressive within the context of the key of the composition. For an example of this, sing out loud or in your head a scale using do–re–mi–fa–sol–la–ti and hold that ti pitch for several seconds. It will feel as if it is pulling you upward to resolve to do. To render this sensation even more powerful, the performer can raise the pitch of ti ever so slightly; this makes that upward pulling effect even stronger. It would evoke a similar response in someone simply listening to the ascending scale.

Now (stick with me on this), understand that if the scale you sang in your head was the scale of C major, the note you held and raised was B. However, if the scale you sang in your head was G major, the B note would be the mi and would not be raised but played straight on. In other words, the pitch of B would be altered depending on the scale (or key signature) in which the composition was written.

This is the power of instruments for which pitches can vary. A keyboard instrument does not afford such flexibility. Any key that is depressed produces a specific pitch, regardless of the scale or key.

Originally, instruments were designed to play in certain keys, or they accommodated alterations to allow different keys to be featured. The problem was that you were confined to a specific key unless you switched instruments. It made key changes quite hard.

The answer was to devise equal temperament, a tuning system in which the octave is divided into twelve semitones of equal size; that is, the distance between every pitch is exactly the same. The distance between D and D$\sharp$ is the same as the distance between G and G$\sharp$ regardless of the particular key signature or scale being used. This was definitely a musical compromise but had the upside of making the piano, harpsichord, and organ keyboard possible. However, when a keyboard plays with an instrument that is not tied to equal temperament, the fireworks begin.

Nonkeyboard instrumentalists deal with this all the time. For instance, in duo repertoire (piano plus another instrument) the intonation the nonkeyboard player is accustomed to using while performing in an orchestra, string quartet, or wind quintet must be altered to sound in tune with the piano.

This phenomenon goes beyond instruments. This is always an issue when vocalists or especially choirs sing with piano accompaniment. That is why so many choirs prefer to sing a cappella, or without instrumental accompaniment.

So why do we have this compromise? The real advantage of equal temperament is the ability of keyboardists to move outside the limitations of a given key. Without equal temperament, modulations from one key to another on a piano would be impossible.

As an aside, I received a call from one crusty listener to my *Ask the Dean* show who wanted to know who should get the "blame" for nontonal music. He thought the blame should go to Wagner because he modulated—changed keys—so frequently. I explained that the true culprit was the piano. If the piano had not been invented, musicians would be forced to stay within one key where they belong.

But I digress. Like any compromise, equal temperament has its pros and cons as well as its detractors and supporters. But it has certainly caught on, so I would say the benefits outweigh the disadvantages.

In view of our America's diminishing manufacturing capabilities, I was wondering if that also applies to orchestral instruments? How many are made and assembled in the United States?
There is an organization called the National Association of Music Merchants, or NAMM, which monitors the entire musical instrument industry. They report that total US musical instrument manufacturing has, indeed, declined in recent years. Asia, especially China, has expanded its manufacturing of pianos, wind, string, and percussion instruments dramatically, with giant automated factories.

However, the picture is not as black and white as the question suggests. It is perhaps more accurate to say the industry has changed. The instruments made in Asia are those that are, for the most part, mass-produced. These large, automated factories can produce extremely high-quality instruments at a price that would not be possible with the older hand-produced methods. The upside: entry-level and medium-level instruments of a very high quality, usually pegged at a price point that beginners and amateurs can afford. I am always shocked when I visit today's music stores and realize how inexpensively a young or beginning musician can purchase a relatively high quality instrument. This leads to a better experience and, therefore, I believe, allows more people to be eager participants in all kinds of music making.

However, this picture changes with higher-level and professional-grade instruments. These are still made by hand, in many cases, and still very often in the United

States. Steinway and Sons has created a line of pianos called the Boston, made in China to Steinway specifications, and they are extremely good. However, the fabled company's professional and concert lines of pianos, those with the Steinway moniker, are still crafted by hand in their New York factory.

Likewise, the Martin Guitar company makes mass-produced instruments with high-tech computers but uses a good section of its Pennsylvania factory for making its custom line of handmade instruments. Further, private makers of traditional stringed instruments still work more as artisans than as producers. The artisan segment remains strong in the United States, as well as in Europe and the United Kingdom.

Therefore, while it would be safe to say that *total* manufacturing of traditional instruments has declined in the United States, this may not be the best measure for the health of the industry. It may be the best of both worlds: prices have dropped or stayed the same for quality instruments. And the quality of mass-produced instruments has substantially improved in many cases. This means more people have access to quality instruments.

Thus we are creating a more musical society, a stepped-up need for music teachers, and a demand for the highest quality instruments, many of which are manufactured in the United States.

I've just become acquainted with a group that plays Renaissance-era music on Renaissance instruments. I can visualize an evolution from older to more modern instruments: sackbut to trombone, shawm to oboe, recorders to flutes, and so on. I see also that some of the older instruments (the krummhorn, for example) have exhibited a graceful extinction. How do modern builders of ancient instruments know what to build with these modern reproductions? There can't be a large body of historical information on their construction, can there? Some people think of Renaissance instruments as ancestors of modern instruments, but musical scholars think of them more as early model cars with slightly different designs. The shawm is not the ancestor of the oboe but instead is the Renaissance version of the oboe. The sackbut is very little changed from the Renaissance; in fact, Italians always called it the trombone. The krummhorn, a double-reed wind instrument with a narrow bore that produces a buzzing kind of sound, is not extinct but lives on as an organ stop. Let's appreciate and celebrate these instruments for what they *are* rather than as primitive or inferior versions of what we have today.

Modern builders make these reproductions by hand. They copy surviving instruments in museums or other collections, follow the lead of Renaissance paintings or stained-glass window depictions of the instruments, and can also rely on some surviving written descriptions and scale drawings. From these varied sources, they know quite a bit about these early instruments and work hard to make as accurate a reproduction as possible.

The real challenge comes in knowing *how* the instruments were played. We can make an exact replica of a viola da gamba bow, but we don't know how it was held. For this, musicologists have to rely on a variety of investigative tools. A sort of CSI: Florence.

In studying early artifacts, such as paintings and drawings, we now know that most violinists stood during performances. It appears bows were held in what would be regarded today as an awkward position, and we even can look at singers and determine that they tensed up while performing, which likely produced a more strident tone than what we expect to hear in a modern performance.

Of course there is one major problem with this approach. One has to assume the artist was accurate in capturing what the musician was doing. Unfortunately this was not always the case. Therefore, a researcher has to find multiple examples of a particular playing behavior and try to form a consensus.

Interestingly this problem of artisans' not being perfectly accurate when depicting musicians continues today. You don't have to watch TV very long before you can see a model or actor "playing" an instrument, be it a guitar, violin, or piano, in a way that is impossible or at least implausible. Years ago I had the opportunity to speak with a commercial editor who had produced a commercial that showed violinists playing their instruments backwards. I asked how this could happen. He said that it was filmed correctly, but from a "visual composition standpoint" it looked better if he digitally flipped it, so the tip of the bow came into the frame from the right of the screen instead of the left. It drove me crazy every time the commercial came on TV, but the editor thought I was being uppity by questioning his artistic license.

In the same way, Harpo Marx once said that he initially learned to play the harp with the instrument sitting on his left shoulder instead of his right. He taught himself to play and took his cues from a statue of an angel in the Marxes' home when he was growing up, a statue that had been made incorrectly.

I recently read of a Stradivarius violin that was shattered when a violinist fell. Are such valuable instruments insured? If so, by whom? How much are the premiums?

Instruments of the vintage and quality of a Stradivarius will sell for several million dollars. But even more "common" professional-caliber instruments will often cost as much as the average house. Obviously, this constitutes a major investment for any musician, even a highly successful soloist. The purchase is usually financed more like a house mortgage than a traditional loan. But even world-class musicians are frequently the beneficiaries of long-term loans of precious instruments by a foundation, an individual collector, or even a private company that owns the musical treasure.

This level of value and financing requires that the instrument be insured for its monetary value. Professional-grade instruments are insured in several ways. Perhaps the most common method is as a rider on the musician's home-owner's insurance. This covers the replacement cost of the instrument even when it is being used outside the home, such as during a concert.

Another very common method is through the musicians' union. Since the instrument is not only a major investment for the musician but is also their method of making a living, the union recognizes the fundamental need for insurance and provides insurance as a service to the members. These methods are excellent and adequate for most instruments.

For instruments at the extreme high end, such as a so-called golden period Stradivarius (crafted by Cremona's Antonio Stradivari between the years 1700 and 1720 and including cellos and violas as well as violins), there are independent companies, private foundations, or sometimes the talent agency representing the artist that can arrange insurance.

A Los Angeles area businessman and philanthropist purchased a golden period Strad in 2006. He purchased it for approximately five million dollars. Eight years later, it was appraised at ten million. He believes the insurance premium he pays—just under twenty thousand dollars a year—is a bargain. But then the instrument is so recognizable, so precious, a thief could never resell it or have it repaired. Though it lives primarily in a vault at the Walt Disney Concert Hall, along with the LA Philharmonic's own impressive collection of Stradivarius and other great instruments, when it's at the owner's home, he doesn't worry too much about climate control. "If you're comfortable, the violin is comfortable; after all, it's lived for three hundred years."

In general, premiums vary widely and are dependent on the type of instrument and, importantly, how and where it is going to be used. An artist who travels internationally throughout the year will pay more than the musician who never takes the instrument far from home.

There are also very specific rules attached to some of these policies. Most musicians with very expensive instruments will not let them out of their sight. Once I was driving a world-class soloist from USC to the airport and, without thinking, opened my trunk for her violin. This offer was refused; her insurance policy specifies the instrument cannot travel in the trunk of a car. Nor can such an instrument be checked as a piece of baggage on an airplane. This is no big deal for a violinist or violist, but for the cellist it means purchasing a second seat on the plane. While this is an added expense, at least the cellist nabs double the drinks and tiny packages of peanuts from the flight attendants.

Most musicians are extremely careful with their instruments and treat them like family. This makes sense. Musicians have a very personal relationship with their specific instrument, and each has its own personality. While an instrument may be insured for its appraised value, in most cases the instruments could not be replaced at any price. This is especially and literally true for vintage instruments. Like a painting by a Renaissance artist, if it is lost or destroyed, it is lost forever.

If an old violin, such as a Stradivarius, Amati, or Guarneri, is damaged, can it ever be repaired to its original condition?

It is always sad when there is a report of a precious instrument being damaged. This often happens after someone who does not even understand its fragility, which makes the story doubly sad, has stolen the instrument. Whether these instruments can be repaired naturally depends on how badly they are damaged. Today's violin makers and restorers are excellent craftspeople, but they can do only so much.

The first issue is whether the actual wood has been damaged. It is the wood of the top and the bottom of the instrument that resonate with the pitches being played. It is the wood (and its finish) that gives an instrument its characteristic sound. If the wood is damaged by cracking or breaking, it is very unlikely the instrument will be able to be restored to its original condition.

Conversely, if the damage lies primarily on the fingerboard, sound post, head, or tuning pegs, it is very likely that a repair can be done successfully, and the instrument returned to its original condition.

But all of this begs the question of when a Stradivarius (or any other instrument) ceases to be a Stradivarius. Bridges, neck shims, chin rests, and some hardware are replaced as part of routine maintenance of instruments. However, once other parts are replaced, it becomes more complicated. One rule of thumb is that if nonmaintenance parts are repaired, it remains a Stradivarius, but if these parts (or too many of these parts) are replaced, it becomes, well, "not quite" a Stradivarius.

The bottom line—well, it actually comes down to a pair of bottom lines: if the instrument still plays beautifully after a repair, it remains valuable to the musician as a special instrument, but it may lose some of its value to a collector or its price on the market. So as with most things in music, the answer as to whether an instrument can be returned to its original condition depends on the definition of "original condition" (whether musical or physical), how badly the instrument was damaged, where the damage occurred, and whether you are concerned with collector's value or musical value.

Aside from those concerns the issue is crystal clear.

Do all woodwind instruments use two reeds?

No. Some woodwind instruments use one, some use two, and one uses none. So utilizing a reed is not a defining characteristic of a woodwind instrument. Surprisingly, not all woodwind instruments are even made of wood.

The instruments of the woodwind family and their reed status are as follows:

flute: no reed
clarinet: single reed

saxophone: single reed
oboe: double reed
bassoon: double reed

Whether an instrument features one reed or two makes a big difference in the sound, as well as in how the instrument is played. The double reeds require the player to create a more direct and focused column of air. Double-reed players also need to provide more pressure than their single-reed counterparts, which is why double-reed players often claim they work harder (physically) than single-reed players. However, it is not that simple. The double reeds have an easier time with articulation because both reeds vibrate, whereas on the single reeds, that reed hits right up against the hard mouthpiece; the player must use his or her tongue to aid articulation. This can be quite exhausting, and this is why single reed players insist *they* work harder!

While the oboists, bassoonists, clarinetists, and saxophonists are arguing about who bears the heavier burden, flutists remain above the fray. They not only don't use reeds, but their instruments are made of metal. Entry-level flutes that are used by beginners are often made of silver-plated nickel or brass. Professional-grade flutes are made of solid silver, gold, or even platinum.

The reason the flute remains in the woodwind family is historical precedent. The flute evolved out of the recorder family, and recorders were and still are made of wood. As time went on, metal replaced the wood because it provided better resonance and projection, but the flute's rightful place in the woodwind family remained.

I am confused about period instruments. I have heard that Yo-Yo Ma plays a Stradivarius cello. Is that a period

instrument? If it is, why isn't it called that? If it isn't,
what is the difference between his cello and a cello played
in an orchestra called a period-instrument orchestra?
You are confused for a very good reason. As usual in music,
the term is more of a "guideline" than a hard and fast rule.
There are actually several different scenarios that would
earn an instrument the right to be considered period, or
"authentic." First, it could be an old instrument that has
not been altered to align with modern-style accommodations. Second, it could be an accurate reproduction of an
old instrument. Third, this could refer to playing on a modern instrument but in a style and state of mind and with
performance practices that mimic the playing of a true
period instrument.

In the most common usage the term "period instruments" refers to instruments from the baroque or earlier
periods or accurate reproductions of these instruments. This
reference is important because baroque instruments, like the
cello, were made differently than those of today. The baroque
cello fingerboard had a wedge underneath it and sat at a more
perpendicular angle to the soundboard. This allowed for
internal resonance that was well suited for light playing. The
instrument also normally used gut strings, which produce a
lighter sound than a modern instrument's strings. Baroque
players also use a different type of bow, one that emphasizes
a difference in articulation between up and down, an articulation that is central to the true baroque style.

Period instruments do not have the big, resonant sound
that you expect to hear in a modern symphony orchestra.
They just were not intended to be used that way.

So, what about Yo-Yo Ma's instrument? He plays
an instrument from the baroque era and yet he sounds

"modern." You could go as far as saying he probably defines the modern cello sound.

I am pretty sure that Yo-Yo Ma's Strad at some point had its fingerboard wedge removed, fingerboard replaced and/or its angle changed, and metal strings added. Add to that configuration a new bow and a tremendously powerful, persuasive, and virtuosic player, and you end up with a three-hundred-year-old cello that is not a period instrument.

In some ways this might remind you of the old gag that there is a museum that owns the original ax of the American folk hero and frontiersman Daniel Boone—but it's on its eighth head and ninth handle! However, it not quite the same for instruments. The shape of the body and original wood, which is what truly gives an instrument its tone, is still intact. Therefore, the fundamental resonance and balance and sound quality of the period instrument are still there.

How does a percussionist make the cannon sounds in Tchaikovsky's 1812 Overture?

This is a perplexing problem for conductors. Tchaikovsky designated in the score that actual cannon should make the large booms. Thus, in many ways, he condemned the piece to being performed outdoors. This didn't bother him because he reportedly really didn't care much for the overture and would probably be shocked and disappointed to learn that it is one of his most frequently performed pieces today.

When the piece is performed outdoors, as it is so often during American Independence Day concerts, real cannon are often used, deployed with electronic triggers to fire at the exact right moment. When the piece is performed indoors or without the budget for real cannon, the conductor has to get creative. In most cases the percussionists simply use the largest and most resonant bass drum available, and as one conductor told me, they just "go at it."

There are some even more creative solutions to this quandary. When the overture is performed inside a concert hall, the cannon sounds can be computer-generated or rendered by firing a shotgun into a barrel backstage. The cost for this particular solution can be high; the orchestra must hire a fire marshal or law enforcement officer to stand guard backstage for safety reasons.

Perhaps the most creative and inclusive solution happened when Maestro Harvey Felder, conducting the Tacoma Symphony in Washington State, handed out paper lunch bags and gestured to the audience when to fill them with air and then pop them right on cue. It resulted in a big mess and considerable chaos, but reportedly a great time was had by all.

The 1812 Overture also calls for church bells to be rung, and Tchaikovsky originally intended for local churches to get involved. You can imagine the logistical complexity, and today this is almost never done. Instead, the percussionists play random notes on the chimes, striking them as hard and loud as they can. Again, this scenario provides opportunities for creative solutions. Several years ago I attended a concert where the maestro requested the audience members to pull out their key rings. He turned to the audience at the appropriate point in the music and indicated for us to jingle them as fast and loud as we could. It was an outdoor concert where thousands of people were sitting on the grass, and the effect was actually quite effective.

*Given the fact that the physical stature of people liv-
ing in the time of Haydn and Mozart was considerably
smaller than now, I presume the size of their hands was
proportionally smaller. Therefore, were the keys on
keyboard instruments narrower?*

Yes, they were, and no, they weren't. The actual size of keys
on keyboard instruments was not (and is not) standardized. During the era of Haydn and Mozart's early compositions, the keyboard instrument of choice would have been
the harpsichord. Many examples of harpsichords from this
time reveal considerable variability in the size of the keys.

The usual way of comparing keyboards is by measuring
the size of one octave. For the past three hundred years the
most common measurement for the octave has remained
at about 164 or 165 millimeters. Since this number is not
a required standard, however, instruments can be found
throughout history with octaves ranging from as little as
125 to170 millimeters. Some of this variability was based
on individual instrument maker's preferences and beliefs,
on mechanical considerations, or to suit certain needs.

The reality that people—and their hands—come
in many different sizes, not just in the past but today as
well, has resulted in a number of attempts to accommodate musicians with smaller hands. As recently as the
1970s, some pianos were built and marketed with a 15/
16 size (152 mm octave span) and the 7/8 DS Standard
(140 mm octave span). There was even a device proposed
in the United States by pianist Hannah Reiman that would
allow existing pianos to be modified with interchangeable
keyboards of varying sizes. There have also been numerous attempts to market pianos with smaller keyboards for
children.

An industry standard was actually agreed upon in the late 1940s, but no current manufacturer makes a piano to that standard. Instead, there are differences in key size as well as in the distance between the keys among all the major piano manufacturers.

To be sure, these differences are minute. But a skilled artist can feel the difference between models. Interestingly, today many pianos made in Asia have the largest and widest keyboards, even though the population there is, on average, shorter than in most Western nations.

Which helps us answer the original question. Keyboards have varied in size and continue to vary, but not because of the physical size of a particular culture or individuals of an earlier historical time. They vary by manufacturer or piano maker.

Talking to faculty about this question also revealed something about classical musicians' humor. In my discussions I had to endure some variation of the following joke three separate times: *Since piano keys are all the same size, which key is the most important? Answer: The one that unlocks the keyboard cover.*

I know that the lid of the grand piano is lifted for concerts to help project the sound toward the audience. This makes sense in a proscenium theater. But when the theater is "in the round" (i.e., the audience surrounds the musician), why don't they remove the lid during a piano concerto to allow the sound to disperse in all directions? They generally do this, after all, when the piano is playing as part of the orchestra.

It is true that the lid works to project the sound toward the audience. But it also provides more control and focus of the sound, precisely because it forces the sound to be more directional. In concertos, the piano part needs to respond to shifting sonic textures in the orchestra. Therefore the performer needs the lid up to retain this added element of control. When the piano part is just part of the orchestral texture (not in a piano concerto) removing the lid makes it easier for the conductor and pianist to see each other. Also, the piano blends easier (without dominating) precisely because the sound is less directional.

The lid performs another role besides just projection. It allows the pianist to hear the instrument more clearly, because it reflects a more accurate projection of overtones back to the player. It would be a major adjustment for a solo performer to play without the lid.

Here is an interesting tidbit: At the Steinway Museum in New York there is a piano that was constructed with two "lids": one on top that opens upwards and one underneath that opens down to project even *more* sound toward the audience. The piano never really caught on for two reasons. First, while this configuration does project more sound toward the audience, it does it in a way that the pianist cannot readily hear. This makes it difficult for the performer to judge the sound being made. Secondly, this instrument really looks somewhat ominous; I think it might scare the audience.

I notice at some orchestra concerts that percussionists sometimes play while holding their head flat against the big drums. It looks like they may be listening or tuning, but no action seems to directly follow their head bowing. Do you know what is going on?

Those big drums are the timpani, or kettledrums. They come in four basic sizes.

Each size is capable of being tuned in the interval of a fifth. In other words, if the lowest note is A, it can go from A to E, or five notes.

The timpanist is indeed tuning the drum. The reason you don't see any motion is that the drums are tuned with a foot pedal. The percussionist pushes the pedal down, much like a gas pedal on a car, the drumhead is tightened, and the pitch rises. Pulling the pedal back has the opposite effect.

The timpanist's face is close to the head because he or she is listening to the pitch while hitting it lightly (so it is not audible). It has to be in tune for the next entrance. Composers actually have to allow time in the score for the timpanist to retune.

This practice has been around for a long time. Berlioz was perhaps the most famous writer of timpani parts. He was a timpanist himself and expanded the instrument's capabilities. In *Symphonie fantastique* he called for two pairs of timpani, cymbals, suspended cymbal, tenor drum, bass drum, and bells. In his Requiem he requires an astonishing sixteen timpani (ten players), plus two bass drums, ten pairs of cymbals, and four tam-tams.

So don't worry, those percussionists are not dozing off during performances. They are just tuning.

Why don't the "standard" orchestral stringed instruments (violin, viola, etc.) have frets like stringed instruments outside the orchestra?

The answer to this has nothing to do with whether the instrument is played in an orchestra or not. Instead, it has much to do with how the sound is created.

First, let's examine what a fret is and what it accomplishes. A fret is the small piece of gut, bone, ivory, wood, or metal fixed to the fingerboard of an instrument to help place the pitch. The most common example of an instrument with frets is the guitar.

When the performer depresses the string, he or she depresses it behind the fret. This causes the string to rest on the actual metal (or other material) and it is from the point of the fret that the string will vibrate. This is very different from a nonfretted instrument, where the performer is depressing the string directly on the fingerboard and the string vibrates from that point.

There are advantages and disadvantages to both methods. The first difference is related to how the string is actually vibrated when playing. The sound of an orchestral string instrument is most frequently produced by a bow being pulled across the string. With fretted instruments, plucking the string produces the sound. The difference comes into play when the musician is trying to sustain a tone. With a bow, the sound can be sustained almost indefinitely. However, with a plucked instrument the note lasts only as long as the string can vibrate after the initial pluck. Holding a string down against a metal fret allows it to vibrate much longer than if it were held down by a finger, which is much less firm and has the tendency to move. This difference can be heard if you listen to a note plucked on a violin (called pizzicato) as opposed to a guitar. The violin sound is much more of a plunk than a tone.

While the fret adds to the sustaining power and brilliance of a tone, it also comes with limitations that nonfretted instruments do not have. Since the frets on most instruments are fixed, the performer is confined to using the equal temperament system discussed earlier in this chapter. Not so with nonfretted instruments. The performer can slightly

190 | who knew?

alter individual pitches to add to their expressive power. Secondly, by using the finger instead of a fret to stop the string, the performer can wiggle his or her finger slightly to produce a vibrato sound much like the human voice. Adding vibrato results in a more "lyric" sounding instrument, which is especially important when playing a melodic line.

Would the average concertgoer notice if the members of an orchestra traded in their very fine (and hugely expensive) instruments for student-quality instruments? Would trained musicians and critics notice such a substitution?

The quick answer is yes to both of these questions. Student-quality instruments, although much better in quality than just a few decades ago, still lack the tone, sustaining power, and resonance of more expensive instruments. They are also harder to control in terms of pitch, dynamics, and expressive quality. While trained musicians can do remarkable things with a good student-quality instrument, they would be limited. I have to believe that if a professional orchestra switched to student instruments, the average audience member would be able to quickly tell that something was wrong. I have never heard of this being done, but it would be an interesting experiment. (It would be sort of the converse of violinist Joshua Bell's famous experiment in 2007: playing, unrecognized, as a busker in the Washington, DC, Metro system. Interestingly, the listeners who gave him their most rapt attention were little children, particularly an attentive three-year old. In forty-five minutes, Bell collected thirty-two dollars. Of the more than a thousand people that passed through the station, six stopped to listen.)

However, if we change the question slightly and ask about modern professional-quality instruments, I think the answer might be different. There have been studies in which a Stradivarius is electronically compared to a new high-quality instrument, and there was little difference. Further, there have been blind listening tests between great instruments and good instruments, with few listeners being able to tell the difference. I don't doubt these results, but there is so much more that goes into a high-quality performance than the tone of the instrument.

Musicians talk about finding "their" instrument. There is karma between musician and instrument that is really hard to explain. When an instrument is "right," it seems to be working *with* the musician as a sort of partner. This can alter from night to night as weather conditions change, but there is nothing better than the feeling of having your instrument working with you. This allows musicians to soar, not just play their best. It's this type of partnership that ultimately makes an instrument great. In contrast, a merely good-quality instrument might just go "along for the ride," and a cheaper instrument might work against what you are trying to do.

Ultimately this partnership is what the audience members will hear. They would not so much hear a difference in tone as perhaps a difference in the flow, the musicality, and the expression of the music. These differences might be subtle but still perceptible. It might be the difference between hearing a performance that is enjoyable and one that leaves you with goose bumps.

It is important to remember, however, that the most critical variable in any performance is still the person playing the instrument. I would always choose to listen to a great musician on a lousy instrument than a lousy musician on a great instrument. To a certain degree a trained musician can overcome the limitations of an instrument. An extreme example is the famous episode when the then fourteen-year-old violinist Midori was performing the fifth movement of Leonard Bernstein's Serenade, with Lenny himself conducting. It was her solo debut with the Boston Symphony at Tanglewood. In the middle of a solo passage the E string on her violin broke. She calmly traded her three-quarter-size violin for the concertmaster's full-size instrument and continued, without missing a beat, to play in tune. Mind you, this meant every pitch had to be created differently from the way she had practiced the piece for untold hours. A moment later, another string broke, and she had to turn to the associate concertmaster for yet another instrument trade. While these were all undoubtedly very fine instruments, they were different in size and tone, but the always intrepid Midori was able to continue with a world-class performance.

The opposite is not true. I will not name names to protect the innocent, but I have suffered through many a performance where a fine instrument was played by a less than high-quality musician with very unsatisfying results.

7

The Music

FINALLY WE GET TO THE heart of the matter. We have explored the people involved with music and their instruments. Now it is time to explore the music itself. If you want to know about the history or form of a particular piece of music or, for that matter, almost anything about a specific piece of music, you can find a plethora of information online or in a variety of music history or music appreciation books. In this chapter, we will explore more general questions about classical music and some of the accepted conventions and oddities of this beloved art form.

Most classical announcers and concert programs list the key in which a piece is written. What possible use is this information to the average listener or concert-goer? Is it given to somehow enhance the listener's enjoyment?

This practice of having the key as part of the name (as in the Symphony in C by Georges Bizet) is so commonplace that few people even question it. You are absolutely correct that knowing in what key signature a symphony or other piece is being performed makes no difference to average listeners today, except perhaps to help them accurately remember the precise piece they heard for future reference or to purchase it.

194 | WHO KNEW?

But it wasn't always this way. Before the universal adoption of equal temperament in the mid-nineteenth century, individual keys actually sounded different from one another. The unequal-tempered tuning systems of the times resulted in chords that sounded more "in tune" in the keys more closely related to C. As you modulated to keys farther away from C, you would hear the tension increase. As the piece moved back to the home key of C, the tension would relax.[1]

Besides this difference in perceived harmonic tension, certain instruments would gravitate toward particular keys. Until around the year 1800 (natural) trumpets were commonly constructed to play in only the keys of C and D. If you liked pieces with trumpets, you knew you would only hear them in one of those keys. Likewise, flutes of the day tended to favor keys with sharps.

Since the keys sounded different from one another, there emerged commonly held beliefs of the affects associated with each key. From the baroque through classical periods there were elaborate descriptions for various keys. These ranged from majestic, regal and pure for C major (good for creating light in Haydn's *Creation*), heroic for E♭ (also the Trinity, with the symbolism of its three flats), amorous love for A major, rustic and pastoral for F major (as in Beethoven's Sixth Symphony), peasantlike for G major.

1. This is a very general description of this phenomenon. A more accurate description would require some basic music theory explanations that are outside the scope of this book. For more information, see Ross Duffin's *How Equal Temperament Ruined Harmony (and Why You Should Care)!* (New York: Norton, 2007).

Even now, as we discussed earlier, many composers have distinct preferences for certain keys. Chopin tended to write in keys with lots of sharps and flats because he felt those keys lay more comfortably under the hands. A noted eighteenth-century German poet and writer on music, Christian Friedrich Daniel Schubart, laid out his views on the characteristics of individual tonalities in an 1806 book about musical aesthetics. He believed key signatures with sharps worked best in music depicting great passion; flat keys expressed more serene feelings. (As a composer himself, he presumably used those sharp keys to write music during his ten-year prison stint in the forbidding fortress of Hohenasperg; his apparent crime: insulting the mistress of the duke of Württemberg. Beethoven, Franz Schubert, and Robert Schumann were all familiar with Schubart's writings on the characteristics of certain keys, but they didn't always agree with him.

Today, the key designation is simply a part of the title. It is almost like someone's last name. There may be many Ashleys in the world, but further identifying someone as Ashley Jones separates a specific Ashley from all the others. Likewise, there are many symphonies, but fewer examples of the Symphony no. 243 in A♭ Minor.

Why is the opus number given when describing a piece of music? What possible use can this be to the average listener?

Opus numbers indicate the order in which a composer's output was created. Therefore, unlike the key designation of a piece of music, the opus number does generally tell a story in addition to being part of the formal name of a piece of music. In most cases, the opus number will indicate when during the course of a composer's career a specific piece was written. This isn't foolproof—some composers designate an opus number when the piece is finished, some when it is first performed, others link it to the publication date—but the opus number will usually indicate when in a composer's life the piece was written: early, middle, or late period.

Like visual artists, great composers follow an artistic progression. Early Beethoven compositions sound very different from late Beethoven. I think hearing the difference adds to a listener's enjoyment and perhaps builds a deeper appreciation for what the composer accomplished.

You may wonder why the numbers given to a composition (such as Haydn's Symphony no. 104) are not enough. For example, one would assume that Beethoven's Symphony no. 6, the "Pastoral," was completed after his Fifth Symphony. One would also assume that between such major works he would have written some other compositions. But he was actually working on both symphonies at exactly the same time, and they were premiered at the same marathon Viennese concert in the winter of 1808. Their opus numbers, 67 and 68, respectively, make this clear. Nothing was composed (or at least completed) between these two major works.

Of course, some composers make things difficult. César Franck and Béla Bartók stopped adding opus numbers to their compositions halfway through their career. Sergei Prokofiev was one of the worst offenders. He provided an opus number before he wrote the piece and would sometimes add a new number if he later revised it. Other numbering systems were entirely the work of a later publisher or cataloguer—in the case of Mozart, it was the Austrian musicologist and botanist Ludwig von Köchel. During his all too brief stay on this planet, Mozart brought us such an abundance of musical riches that it required a tome of a thousand-odd pages, Köchel's thematic catalogue, just to number them chronologically and give them what are popularly called K (for Köchel) numbers. The catalogue was first published in 1862, more than seventy years after Mozart's death at the age of thirty-five.

I hear things played by a trio, quartet, or quintet. I thought this simply meant the number of performers, but I am starting to suspect it is not that simple.

You are right that there is sometimes more to this type of group designation than simply the number of players. Sometime the title describes (or implies) the instrumentation as well. The most basic chamber groups are the piano trio, the string quartet, the woodwind quintet, and the brass quintet. To further confound the issue, these names are sometimes shortened in regular conversation to simply a trio, quartet, or quintet. Other times, an established ensemble formally adopts just the numerical designation as part of the group's name, as with the Turtle Island Quartet or the Calder Quartet.

Though it seems logical to assume a piano trio is made up of three pianists, not so; instead, it is generally composed of a piano, violin, and cello. A string quartet is likewise not composed of four violinists or four cellists, but specifically two violins, viola, and cello. Likewise, a woodwind quintet typically consists of flute, clarinet, oboe, bassoon, and horn; the brass quintet has two trumpets, horn, trombone, and tuba.

While these formations are the most common, you can find every possible combination you can think of. (String trios are popular, for example, usually consisting of violin, viola and cello, but there could also be two violins and cello, etc.) Truly any three instruments playing together are a trio, just as any four instruments in an ensemble make a quartet.

So the real question becomes how did these basic formations become so dominant? And why do they persist today? Why don't we see standard quintets of violin, bassoon, snare drum, horn, and bass?

There are two reasons for the popularity of these basic combinations. First of all, they form a well-balanced ensemble in terms of overall volume and pitch range (from high to low). In addition, these instruments offer ample varieties of tone color with which the composer can work to create an interesting piece of music.

Because these combinations of instruments are so popular among composers, a great deal of music has been written specifically for them. This wealth of literature leads to the second reason these groups remain popular. Since there is so much great music written for these groups, groups of musicians come together as ensembles to perform and record the music. Once these ensembles form, they seek out new music, and composers are inclined to write (or to be commissioned) for the particular instrumentation. Thus, the cycle continues. As an aside, one faculty member I spoke with offered another advantage of keeping these ensembles intact, namely, the brass players don't have to put up with string players, and vice versa.

In the second half of the twentieth century we start seeing even more flexibility of instrumentation. Many chamber ensembles now include percussion or instruments of mixed "families." Another contemporary phenomenon is the appearance of groups of changeable size and instrumentation. Ensembles whose very names seem to reflect their flexibility (and lack of conformity) include X-Tet, yMusic, eighth blackbird, and ICE (the International Contemporary Ensemble). While none of these have become standardized, they have prompted composers to create hundreds of new and exciting works to enrich the chamber music repertoire.

I always thought composers notated with precise markings in the score how they wanted a piece performed. Yet I have several recordings of Antonio Vivaldi's **Four Seasons** *and they sound very different from each other: different speeds, different phrasing, even different instances of ritardando, those passages where the music gradually slows down. Is the conductor ignoring the composer's wishes?*

Every conductor with whom I spoke about this was adamant: his or her main task is to bring the composer's artwork to life in just the way it was intended. True, this sometimes means "reinterpreting" a composition in a way more meaningful to a new era of listeners—but always remaining fundamentally true to the composer's wishes. As one conductor said: "No way! The conductor never ignores the composer's wishes!"

That being said, even when the composer was meticulous about notating the score, there is clearly room for interpretation. Musical notation can never represent every nuance of what was in the composer's head. This was especially true in the past. It is not a coincidence that your example of diverse interpretations involves Vivaldi. In the baroque period, when Vivaldi lived, and even the early classical era, there are relatively few markings. The conductor has to have a strong working knowledge of performance practices in earlier times: What were the tempi, how loud was a fortissimo, how soft a pianissimo? This becomes more complicated when the musicians are using contemporary instruments. These modern instruments have a much wider dynamic range than the instruments of Vivaldi's time. In this scenario the conductor has the unenviable task of restricting the musicians from using the complete dynamic and expressive range available to them.

During the romantic era, expressive markings grew more detailed and more voluminous. In addition, through letters, chronicles, and published reviews, we can bank on more authoritative accounts of how the works were performed.

Today, we often have an even clearer idea of what the composer intended. Parts and scores are prepared electronically; we no longer have to interpret handwritten notation. Plus, we often have recordings of the premiere, at which the composer is often involved as conductor, soloist, or perhaps just providing counsel during rehearsals.

So is there no interpretive role for the conductor with contemporary music? On the contrary: there is still plenty of wiggle room. For example, a given conductor might try to get a performance to be even closer to what she feels the composer was trying to express but couldn't, for some reason, achieve. It could be that the musicians were not good enough, that the original conductor was not good enough, that there was insufficient rehearsal time, or simply that it never quite gelled.

It is clear that a conductor would never *deliberately* try to do something against the composer's wishes. Still, performances of the same work will vary with conductors.

With older music there is still some debate about what constitutes an authoritative interpretation. In more contemporary music it is a matter of trying harder to get to the ideal that was in the composer's head.

Composers mark musical scores with words like "largo," "allegretto," "allegro," "presto," and so forth, to denote the proper tempo of a piece. Is there a standard metronomic interpretation of those words, and do conductors "obey" the composers' instructions in this regard? Yes, there are definitely standard metronome markings indicating tempi such as largo (slow), moderato (at moderate tempo), allegro (fast), and so on, but these interpretations themselves are open to interpretation. (Sorry you asked?)

Tempo is designated as the number of beats per minute, or BPM. As you specify, it is measured by use of a metronome, either electronic or mechanical. However, rather than a specific number of beats per minute assigned to each tempo marking, a *range* of beats per minute is suggested. For example, allegro is usually considered to be 120 to 168 beats per minute. However, I have known conductors to interpret allegro as much slower: 105 BPM.

Before the invention in around 1815 of the clockwork-driven metronome by German engineer Johann Nepomuk Maelzel (who borrowed some features from an earlier Dutch inventor), these vague tempo designations were the only way to describe the intended speed of a composition. Needless to say, they were open to interpretation by both the composer who wrote them and the artist who performed them. It would be as if someone asked you to walk "quickly," which could mean something very different to you than to another person. Is a quick walk the same as a slow run? Is walking quickly the same as walking briskly?

As the metronome came into common use, these tempo designations were assigned the ranges of interpretation described above. As time went on, especially in the twentieth and twenty-first centuries, composers tended to be more and more specific about such markings.

Most conductors feel it is their responsibility to stick to the composer's markings to the best of their ensemble's abilities. Again, this is open to interpretation. Many years ago I heard a radio broadcast by commentator Karl Haas, in which he compared all the recording of Ravel's *Boléro*. The recordings ranged from a quick twelve minutes to over eighteen. Most recordings clocked in at about fifteen minutes, which would put the tempo at about 72 BPM.

Through this comparison, Mr. Haas was trying to determine the "best" speed for *Boléro*. Ultimately, he could not decide. This is not surprising. Ravel himself was unsure. In his own copy of the score, the printed metronome marking is 76 BPM, but he crossed it out and wrote 66 instead.

For a very interesting discussion of Beethoven and his tempo markings, you might want to check out a Radiolab podcast called "Speed Beet." In this program, Beethoven's own tempo indications are contrasted with the speed at which the pieces are usually performed today. What makes this podcast memorable is the opportunity to hear multiple performances of the same pieces of music—by the same musicians—at wildly different tempos. It also offers us ample evidence Beethoven was a speed demon, at least as far as metronome tempos were concerned.

Incidentally, it was because of his friendship with Maelzel that Beethoven became the first composer to notate precise metronome rates, in beats per minutes, in his musical scores. Since he was near the end of his career when, around 1817, he began to work with Maelzel's machine, he added tempo markings to his earlier symphonies retroactively.

When a composer states that a symphony is in a specific key, what does that mean? Does it mean that some percentage (say, 90%) of the piece will restrict itself to the eight notes that occur in the scale that makes up the key? Does it also mean that it must start and end on the key note?

As I explained in an earlier answer, the designation of the key in the title of a piece is one way to differentiate one composition from another. It does not come with specific rules or restrictions that the composer must follow. There are no enforcement officers who break down composers' doors in the middle of the night and arrest them for modulating to G♭ minor (although I have heard pieces that made me wish such officers existed).

However, there are some historic traditions which have shifted over time. In the classical period and before, a composer would usually start and end in the same key. For example, if Haydn started a symphony in C major, he would almost certainly end it in C major. He would most likely emphasize the notes of the C major scale, especially those that best establish the key (the first, fourth, fifth, and seventh notes) but would not restrict himself to that. He would feel free to introduce notes not in the C major scale and even wander into other keys for parts of the symphony. One convention of the day was to start in a key, have a middle section in another key (or wander through several keys), and then return to the home key for the end. There would often be relationships between the keys of the individual movements.

These conventions changed during the romantic era. Composers would usually start in the key that was in the title but would feel very free to move to other keys and stay there if they desired or move on to new keys. There was no longer the convention to return to the home key at the end, though it was still the norm in a classic four-movement symphony. Basically the key of a symphony became much less important as composers pushed the limits of what the ear would tolerate.

The practice of de-emphasizing the key continued and grew in the twentieth century to the point that naming a symphony by its key today is the exception rather than the rule.

Composers before Beethoven were composing symphonies in abundance (Mozart wrote 41, Haydn, 106), while after Beethoven, almost all the major composers stopped at or before 9. Examples are Brahms (4), Schubert (9), Schumann (4), Dvorak (9), Bruckner (9), and Mahler (9—plus a little of a 10th). I read years ago that Mahler was so scared of no. 9 that his symphony no. 10 was never finished, and he worked on it in secret. The unfinished score was found after his death. Is this true? In your opinion is no. 9 cursed after Beethoven?

I don't know about a curse, but things certainly changed for composers during the time of Beethoven. Prior to Beethoven, symphonies were much shorter and tended to follow an accepted form. For example, first movements were constructed in a very formalized manner, with an opening section, or "exposition"; a middle, "development" section; and a return to the first section, or "recapitulation." The second, third, and fourth movements followed in a fairly predictable manner. Thus it is understandable that earlier composers were able to crank out quite a few symphonies.

This changed with Beethoven. He broke with many of the conventions of the day and set the stage for works that grew in several ways: the size of the orchestra, a work's sheer length, and its complexity. Compare the last movement of Mozart's Forty-first Symphony, the "Jupiter," with the "Ode to Joy" movement of Beethoven's final symphony (the ninth) to see how dramatically symphonic form changed within one generation. So yes, composers tended to write fewer symphonies and make them much more highly personal. While it took them longer to compose each piece, it was also more difficult to get performances of these larger works because of the expanded musical forces need to mount a performance. Also, since these symphonies took longer to compose, the corresponding cost of a commission went up. All these factors meant the days of writing eighty or a hundred symphonies in a lifetime were largely over.

But is there some kind of curse about writing more than nine symphonies? Would it be like the curse of the first person to break Babe Ruth's career home run record? Some composers thought so. One of these was Mahler.

According to Mahler's widow, the composer was very superstitious about a "ninth symphony," which tended all too frequently in the romantic era to be a composer's swan song. He had reason to worry. After all, Beethoven, Schubert, Bruckner, and Dvorak all died after completing their ninth symphony. Others composers never even reached that number.

He decided to outsmart fate. After his Eighth Symphony, he composed another symphony but didn't call it a symphony and certainly did not number it. This is much like hotels that number the thirteenth floor as the fourteenth because of superstition. He named his symphony *Das Lied von der Erde*, "The Song of the Earth." Scored for two vocal soloists and a very large orchestra, this shattering six-movement work is clearly a symphony in scope, in depth—in all but name. Hedging his bets, perhaps, Mahler named the achingly beautiful last movement *Der Abschied*, "The Farewell."

The plan seemed to work. Mahler finished *Das Lied* and was feeling fine. He felt so confident that he had beaten the Beethoven Curse that he embarked on another symphony, actually being so bold as to number it nine.

Having finished the massive ninth, with its own deeply poignant final movement, which many commentators have described as another brand of farewell, Mahler launched his Symphony no. 10. But it was not to be. He died with much of the work incomplete. Only the first movement was largely finished. Mahler left enough fragments and drafts that a cobbled-together tenth symphony was able to be reconstructed—but not until 1960. And even the reconstructor himself, Deryck Cooke, acknowledges there's very little actual music of Mahler after the first movement.

So is there a curse? If there is, Shostakovich beat it by composing fifteen symphonies. An even more prolific twentieth-century symphonist was the American composer of Armenian heritage, Alan Hovhaness. He wrote sixty-seven, more than thirty of them following his sixtieth birthday. But few other modern composers have even come near writing nine. For me, I am not taking any chances. I'm sticking with writing books instead of symphonies.

The second movement of Tchaikovsky's Sixth Symphony sounds like a waltz but I can never seem to tap my foot to it like a regular waltz? Can anyone? Am I just a klutz?
I have no way of knowing if you are a klutz on the dance floor, but I *do* know that you are a very perceptive listener. This is the famous waltz that is not quite a waltz.

Most waltzes are in triple time. In other words, there are three beats per measure. This would be counted as **1**-2-3, **1**-2-3, **1**-2-3, with an accent on the first beat. This underlying pulse makes the music flow, thus lending itself to dancing something as elegant as a waltz.

In the second movement of his Symphony no. 6, Tchaikovsky uses an extremely uncommon underlying pulse with five beats per measure. However, he places the accents on beats 1 and 3, resulting in a pattern of **1**-2-**3**-4-5, **1**-2-**3**-4-5, **1**-2-**3**-4-5. It is impossible to dance a waltz to this (at least without consuming a significant amount of alcohol), and that is why you cannot tap your foot to it. As I say, this pattern of five beats per measure is very rare in music. It just does not seem to move naturally.

Then why does it *sound* like a waltz? Tchaikovsky, a genius at creating memorable melodies, floats a beautifully flowing tune over this irregular pattern. The listener attends to the melody and does not even notice the awkward underlying pulse. It is truly an amazing musical phenomenon.

How old is the twelve-tone scale? Did scales arise independently in different parts of the world?

The twelve-tone scale, what is commonly called the chromatic scale, divides the octave into twelve equal parts. Most people readily accept that this is what defines an octave because of the prevalence of the piano. But dividing the octave into twelve equal parts—equal temperament—is just one way to accomplish this.

The ancient Greeks recognized and wrote about the many ways to divide the octave. For them dividing the octave into parts was a matter of calculating mathematical ratios between certain notes. Around 530 BC, Pythagoras, an early student of the vibration of strings, created scales based on having a perfect three-to-two ratio between the upper and lower notes of a fifth. This worked well but changed depending on what note you started your calculations with.

It wasn't until the late 1500s that theorists divided the octave into twelve equal parts. This led to the creation of the keyboard and equal temperament (discussed elsewhere). Since that time, the twelve-note division has become so ingrained in Western music that our ears are hesitant to accept anything else.

The second part of the question is interesting. The octave seems to be fairly universal. Music of all cultures recognizes and uses it. But how the octave is divided has evolved very differently in different cultures. When it is divided into numbers that are different than twelve (the division most of us are used to), the result is pitches that are not in the same relationship to the octave as in Western music. The obvious result: music from other cultures will sometimes sound "out of tune" to us. It is not. It is just a different way of dividing up the pie, so to speak. Imagine an apple pie that was divided, not into the six or eight equal parts we are accustomed to seeing, but instead into seven (or nine or five) unequal parts. It would look unusual to us. The same is true with music. If the octave (the pie) is divided into some number of unequal parts, the individual pieces (the pitches) will sound funny to our ears. The pie is still a pie and the pieces still taste good, but we need to adjust our expectations to be able to appreciate them.

Could you kindly tell me why the 1812 Overture, a piece written by a Russian composer that celebrates the Russian victory over the French in the early 1800s, has come to be associated with American Independence? After all, there are actual American composers— Bernstein, Copland, Gershwin, and John Philip Sousa, who composed those rousing marches, to name just a few alternatives. Why don't these composers get celebrated on the Fourth of July?

I can answer this question in one word: Cannon! None of the American composers wrote a piece with cannon (we've already addressed how orchestra players create these explosive effects in Chapter 6). A bit of history: the overture was premiered in 1882 to mark the consecration of the Moscow Cathedral of Christ the Savior. The cathedral, in turn, was built, as you say, to commemorate Napoleon's retreat from Russia in 1812. We also alluded to the fact that Tchaikovsky wasn't particularly enamored of this piece. He said it was "very loud and noisy." But people like loud and noisy, and over time it became one of his most popular and frequently performed works.

How it became associated with our Independence Day celebrations is actually quite interesting and a fairly recent development. To understand it, we need to go back to the early 1970s, during the long tenure of Arthur Fiedler as conductor of the Boston Pops (he led that orchestra from 1930 until his death at the age of 84 in 1979). Fiedler was a master showman with a flair for knowing what the public liked. As the Boston Pops were going to be telecast as part of the 1974 July Fourth celebrations, he wanted something very special that would make an impact on the television audience. He programmed the *1812* Overture for this outdoor concert, complete with cannon, bell choirs, and fireworks. There was a huge television audience watching, and the public loved it.

The timing could not have been better. Music directors and orchestra managers across the country were in the process of planning for the bicentennial celebrations of 1976. Each needed something big, special, out of the ordinary, and well, spectacular. What they saw on TV that night was just what the doctor ordered.

For the bicentennial celebrations across the county two years later the *1812* Overture with all the trimmings—cannon, chimes, fireworks—was scheduled at outdoor concert venues around the country. A "tradition" was created overnight, and it continues today.

I agree that we have much more appropriate works by American composers. I have always wondered why the Charles Ives work *Three Places in New England*, with its wonderfully quirky marching band section, isn't the no. 1 piece for Fourth of July concerts. Some American pieces are often played on the first half of the concert, Copland's *Appalachian Spring* and Sousa's *Stars and Stripes Forever*, for example. But we could probably do better.

However, we also have to remember that for a large part of the audience on the Fourth of July, this is the only symphonic concert they will attend all year. If any concert has to border on "entertainment," this is it. So until some-one writes a louder and noisier piece with more cannon than the *1812*, I think the best thing to do is accept the illogical pairing and sit back and enjoy the music.

Last fall I heard on my local classical music station a live broadcast of a concert where the orchestra played a Simon and Garfunkel piece. Does playing a piece of music by an orchestra make it "classical"? If a hip-hop piece of today were orchestrated, would it, too, be cat-egorized as classical? I guess my bottom-line question is, what makes any piece of music classical?

You hit on a very interesting point, one that most people don't quite understand. I meet many people who think that anything played by an orchestra, even anything by a solo violin, is "classical." This is not the case. In your hypothet-ical instance the hip-hop piece would not be classical, but neither was the Simon and Garfunkel song.

Whether something is classical or not has little to do with orchestration. A solo piano piece by Mozart is just as classical as his symphonies, just as a Haydn string quar-tet is classical. The classical period—think Haydn, Mozart, early Beethoven—is characterized by music that is grace-ful, symmetrical, and orderly. The melody is always clearly audible against a structured accompaniment. The harmo-nies follow an organized pattern. This music is classic in design, thus the name which attached to an era. People sometimes call this music "Classical" with a capital *C* to distinguish it from other "art music."

The always-small-letter version of "classical" denotes *all* art music from at least the time of Johann Sebastian

Bach (1685–1750) through composers of today. This is admittedly a loose term; for some it includes music of the Renaissance as well, even medieval offerings. While using "classical" this way is not technically correct, it is common usage. We all do it.

However, many people call anything performed by an orchestra—or more accurately, by a string section—classical. If the basic music term is not "art music," this is inaccurate, though a common enough error. Orchestras themselves add to the confusion by performing "pops concerts." That's what you probably heard on the radio. Thus, if the local orchestra plays a piece by the Beatles or a hit from a Broadway musical, it seems to indicate that it music be classical music.

A similar type of misnomer occurs with the term "opera." Often, anything sung by a voice with a vibrato is considered opera.

All of this *is* confusing. I was in a meeting of deans from some of the major music schools around the country, and we got into a debate about how to define classical music. While we were all pretty sure of what we meant by "classical," we could not agree on a definition. Nor could we even agree whether certain compositions on the fringes of such a style would or would not be categorized as "classical." So you are not alone in your bewilderment.

Obviously the word "classical," with a small *c*, can be quite broadly defined. Still, there are clearly pieces of music, like pop songs, that would not fit into this classification, even if they were played by the Berlin Philharmonic.

This discussion on musical terminology touches only the tip of the iceberg on the topic of how to classify music. The whole idea of classification of music is falling apart before our eyes, anyway. I think partly because of the iPod, the whole idea of genre is dissolving. I see it in our students. They may play a "classical" instrument, but their musical tastes—and their playlists—are very diverse. Likewise, so-called classical, or serious, composers are taking leads from everywhere and incorporating new musical streams and influences into their compositions. This often includes elements of popular music from their own culture. Just as Debussy and Ravel incorporated Asian elements into their music and just as Bartók and Kodaly reflected the profound influence of Hungarian folk tunes they collected in the fields and meadows, today's young composers are finding inspiration in electronic dance music, hip-hop, and other popular forms.

I don't know where this is all going, but the classifications we have been using for hundreds of years are becoming too vague to be of much value. Even a word that was once fairly descriptive, like jazz, is getting murky. The lines that used to divide genres of music are constantly moving, becoming less clearly differentiated.

What will emerge to take the place of our current classifications is unclear. The streaming music service Spotify has just announced that it will no longer classify music by genre because listeners have ceased to identify music that way. They hope that new classifications will emerge from how their listeners use music today. It will be fascinating to see where this leads.

I've often wondered what the difference is between a Magnificat, a setting of the Jubilate, a requiem, and a mass. I know they're all types of religious choral music, but there must be some distinction between them.

These forms are all based on specific religious texts of the Catholic Church. Therefore, more than anything else, the text dictates the form. The first two (Magnificat and Jubilate) are very focused. The last two (mass and requiem) are broader. A mass and requiem are usually much longer and more complex works as well. And, yes, they are all choral forms.

The Magnificat is based on texts from the Canticle of the Blessed Virgin Mary, found in the Gospel of Luke, 1:46–55. In the Roman Catholic Church it is sung daily as the climax of the evening Vespers service. Many, many composers have set it to music. In addition to its liturgical use, musical settings appear frequently in Advent or Christmas concerts.

The next form, Jubilate, means "sing joyfully" and is the opening line of Psalm 100. So a choral piece set to Psalm 100 is a Jubilate. There are at least as many settings of this as there are Magnificat settings!

The Mass is the Roman Catholic communion service. The liturgical texts divide into those that are said (or sung) everyday, known as the Ordinary, and those that are specific to a particular day (such as Christmas or Easter), known as the Proper. In musical terms, "mass" almost always refers to settings, by one composer, of the Ordinary (Kyrie, Gloria, Credo, Sanctus-Benedictus, and Agnus Dei).

A requiem is a funeral mass. It retains all the elements of the Mass's Ordinary, except for the Gloria and Credo, which because of their joyful nature are considered improper in a funereal setting. There are also added sections from the Proper texts, such as the introit ("Requiem aeternam") and the sequence (the Dies Irae). Composers, such as Fauré, sometimes omit the Dies Irae ("day of wrath") in their musical settings to sustain a musical mood of comfort and calm.

It is important to remember that these terms do not dictate musical form or musical genre. For example, Bernstein's *Mass* is very different from Beethoven's Mass in C, despite the fact they use many of the same texts. There are also Masses written in musical styles such as rock and roll, gospel, and country.

What is the origin of the "fa-la-las" sung in so much music? When they use the words "fa-la-la," are they singing the notes fa and la (as in do–re–mi–fa–sol–la–ti–do)? This seems like such an easy question that it really should have an easy answer. Unfortunately the answer is quite complex. In fact, one of the faculty members of the Thornton School teaches an entire semester graduate course on just this topic. Here is a concise answer to a complex question.

First of all, let's get the easy part over with. Singing the fa-la-las as refrain syllables has nothing to do with the solfeggio (or solfège) syllables of do, re, mi, fa, sol, la, ti, do. So we can discount that theory completely. So where did they come from?

The fa-la-las that are sung as refrain syllables are part of a long tradition that dates back at least to the High Middle Ages, or the time of the Fourth Crusade (circa 1200). The fa-la-las are just the best known of many different syllable series that were used in refrains called *dorelots*. Besides the fa-la-las, other common syllables were tra-la-la, ture-lure-lure, fa-la-diddle-diddle, and dilly-dilly.

These dorelots were part of a musical genre called the pastourelle. (Though essentially French and rural, the tradition also flourished in post-Renaissance Italy as the *pastorella*.) Now as boring as all this sounds, pastourel-les were songs that were *always* about a gallant knight meet-ing a shepherdess in the woods. Before your mind takes you to inappropriate places, you should know that the basic theme of this meeting is that the knight speaks fancy city language and the shepherdess speaks country talk or even makes animal sounds. The dorelots reflect the shepherdess speaking in birdsong or animal sounds, nonsense syllables, or half-words that have meaning. The use of animal sounds would often signify her supposedly "animal" nature and the rustic nature of the song itself. The dorelot can also be the sound of a flute she plays or a rustic bagpipe.

In these songs, the shepherdess was often named Mary or Marion, with a boyfriend named Robin. In typical medi-eval fashion, Mary was sometimes associated with the Virgin Mary or with the human soul.

The animal and woodsy nature of the theme was recog-nized in its time as being erotic. Today, the pastourelle is quite the research topic in feminist studies because of the symbolism given to the female character. As Adam Knight Gilbert, an associate professor at USC Thornton and the director of the Thornton Early Music Program, says of the pastourelle: "The tension between love, infidelity, rape, voyeurism, and the plays between high and low class and language have been rehearsed many times since the genre was first preserved in the twelfth century." So this ques-tion really hit on a hot topic today that was a different type of hot topic eight hundred years ago.

A number of compositions are based upon "traditional" or "folk" melodies. Is there a difference between tradi-tional music and folk music?

From the eighteenth century and earlier, folk music was considered to be rural and collectively written or at least so old and obscure in origin that there's no way to know if any one musician should get the credit for composing a song or piece. One often finds multiple versions, all of them legitimate, of folk melodies; after all, they were passed along from musician to musician and town to town over many years. Think about how a sentence changes during a game of telephone. This is a shortcut example of how songs were transformed when passed on through the aural tradition, meaning without notation but rather through hearing the songs.

A traditional tune can have a more urban and identifiable origin. A song could get into popular culture so that it is known that *somebody* wrote it but no one may know exactly who. In the case of a traditional melody there is usually one "right" version or multiple versions with minor variations.

An important factor in all this is the distinction between notated music and the so-called aural tradition. Folk music is not generally assumed to have been composed by literate musicians and was therefore not officially written down at the time of its creation. Traditional music was generally notated. Many of the melodies that are now considered traditional come from art music of the sixteenth or seventeenth centuries. Often a composer would write a catchy melody in a piece. That melody or a snippet of it might be set to a text, used, and reused for a myriad of purposes. These melodies often boasted multiple texts over the years. Because the melody can be traced back to an individual, however altered it was by countless others, it would be deemed traditional.

Obviously there is a subtle yet clear difference between traditional and folk melodies. Composers who use these melodies are usually very careful to differentiate how a given melody came to them.

Composers often write a single-movement work and call it an introduction, prelude, elegy, nocturne, improvisation, or any one of a multitude of other descriptive words. Does each of these titles imply a specific musical form, as do the titles of larger works such as symphonies and concertos?

The titles composers give to these sorts of single-movement works are often chosen to match the emotion or mood the composer is aiming to convey. For example, a quiet, peaceful, contemplative piece might be called a nocturne (defined as a musical composition of a dreamy character) but could also be called "An Evening in the Woods (with Robin and Marion?)." Other times the composer will choose the title, such as prelude or introduction, to describe the function the piece might play in a concert or theater work.

Regardless of the use, none of these terms designates a specific musical form. Instead, they imply that the piece will be a single movement composition that is not as long as a symphony or concerto.

Basically the composer has free rein to use any of these terms and will not be called to task for an inappropriate use as long as the piece kinda, sorta sounds like its title.

From time to time I hear that a certain piece, frequently by Haydn or Mozart, is deemed witty. But I can't find the joke. Is this explainable?

I was working on this question while visiting with my daughter. I read it to her and she said, "Wow, what an insightful question. It's like the third movement of Beethoven's Piano Sonata no. 14 in C♯ minor (the *Moonlight*, op. 27, no. 2). I can't get through playing that without completely breaking up with laughter."

If you have ever heard that piece you will understand why I stared at her in disbelief thinking she was kidding. When I realized that she wasn't, I started thinking, "Did I help raise this child? Could I be accused of some sort of musical child abuse?"

I—and probably most, if not all, listeners—find nothing funny in that piece of music. Yet she did. When I questioned her about it, she explained that she feels it is "so over the top stereotypically Beethoven that I think he wrote it as a parody on his own style. He couldn't have been serious." Thus, she finds it funny, and Beethoven probably turns over in his grave every time she laughs. Interestingly, now I can't hear the piece without getting a smile on my face because I see where she is coming from.

I tell this story to point out that descriptions of music, of any type, are completely subjective. You should not worry about trying to discover what other people say they hear. That being said, I know that announcers on classical music stations or conductors speaking from the podium often make these types of comments. This highlights a problem we have had from time immemorial: using words to describe music. If it could be adequately done, we wouldn't need the music. As the poet Heinrich Heine said, "Where words leave off, music begins."

When describing music, I think some words are better than others. For example, "whimsical" or "lighthearted" could more accurately describe some music by Haydn than "humorous" or "witty," but I might be splitting hairs. Still, it points out that often people are very casual in the words they use to describe music.

If you want to listen for jokes in music, you will find these only in specific pieces. The Toy Symphony of Haydn (now believed to have been written by Leopold Mozart) comes to mind. So do the Ives Second Symphony and the works of P. D. Q. Bach and Victor Borge.

So when you hear these comments, it might be too much to expect that you'll be doubling over with laughter at this "witty" music (unless you were raised in the Cutietta household). Instead, listen for how these pieces sound lighter than air: cheery, fun, sprightly, or buoyant. I think you will hear that.

Has there always been a divide between classical and popular music?

Throughout the centuries, music has often been divided into two broad categories. But these categories have not always been defined as "classical" and "popular."

During the Renaissance there was sacred and secular music. Sacred music was usually considered more uplifting. Secular music was considered more functional and utilitarian, as it was often used for dancing, singing, and entertainment.

During the classical period there was the music of the court and the music of the people. The music of the court was considered more sophisticated. One could argue that this roughly translated along the lines of what today would be classical and popular.

During the romantic era, with the emergence of a middle class, there came to be these differentiated categories of popular and concert music. While concerts were not as cleanly delineated between the two genres as they are today, this is when the bifurcation really took root.

During the twentieth century things started getting murky. Many classical music lovers did not embrace the so-called classical music that was being composed, especially after 1950. In that era, many composers throughout Europe and America were writing atonal or serial music, based not on conventional harmonies but on the twelve-tone principles formulated by Arnold Schoenberg in the early 1920s, in which "the structural hierarchies provided by the tonal (key signature) system were largely abandoned." Because of this, we saw classical music itself divided into two broad categories, classical and contemporary. Many audience members refused (and continue to refuse) to accept contemporary music in classical concerts. I recently witnessed at least a quarter of the audience at a classical music concert walk out on a piece by a composer as mainstream as Philip Glass. That is how clear-cut this division has become.

What this means is that the division most people think is clear (classical and popular) is anything but. Today it seems that if there is a bipolar division, it is much more between acoustic and amplified music than classical and popular.

For many music lovers, if the music is performed in a concert auditorium, like the Walt Disney Concert Hall in Los Angeles or Severance Hall in Cleveland, they will accept it as long as it is not amplified (and not contemporary!).

I often hear people say they went to a classical music concert only to learn it was an orchestra playing film music or arrangements of songs from musicals. Conversely they attend a classical music concert with contemporary works involving electronics or other amplification, and they don't feel they heard classical music. Today these divisions are all but useless except at the most basic levels. Probe any of them and you will see them fall apart rather quickly.

The bottom line is that there are so many styles of music that the brain simply looks for an organizing principle to make sense of it. The way we organize anything is to create categories. So whether they are accurate or not, we need to organize all the genres of music. We always start with big categories, and "popular" and "classical" work just fine. Until, of course, you try to decide into which category jazz, gospel, bluegrass, or electronic art music is supposed to fit.

I'm always intrigued when a classical radio announcer confidently talks about a given composition's popularity hundreds of years before Billboard's *Top 100 list was ever published. How do musicologists determine the success of a piece before media revenues and concert ticket sales were precisely tabulated?*

If we go back in time, we may not have had the *Billboard* Top 100 to tell us which pieces were the most popular, but we can still make somewhat intelligent guesses about which pieces made the greatest impact in their day.

In earlier times, how widely a composer's works were distributed during his (or her) lifetime is regarded as an indication of the popularity of the work. For example, many of the magnificent choral works of Josquin des Prez (ca. 1440–1521) were published around the end of the six-teenth century. We can assume that these were printed because they were able to be sold. Thus, we know there was a demand throughout Europe for his music and can deduce that his compositions were popular in their time and afterward. Another way of determining popularity (or validating the sales numbers) is by reading the writing of contemporaries who mention or discuss the works of certain composers and how they were received. For example, the sixteenth-century theologian Martin Luther dubbed Josquin his favorite composer.

Examining statistics can determine popularity. Researchers count how many printings or editions a work underwent or perhaps how long an early opera remained in the repertory of major companies. From this, popularity can be inferred. Another way to determine popularity is to try to compute the income of a composer. This has been done for Mozart and other figures.

Gradually, during the twentieth century, increasingly accurate statistics, showing numbers of performances, sound recordings, and the like, were compiled and published. For example, the old Schwann record catalogs were a pretty reliable source for how many times a work (one still in print anyway) was recorded and by whom.

Recently some researchers have turned to measuring the "column inches" devoted to composers and individual works in musicology textbooks and scholarly journals. (Presumably this also measures historical impact.) I think that's arguably another way to infer popularity. Of course, then we have the problem of a self-fulfilling prophecy: if everyone knows a piece is popular, we have to write about it, which makes it appear more popular.

At the end of the day, these radio announcers are just trying to make your listening more enjoyable and provide the listener with some context. As you can see, we do have a general idea of which composers and compositions were popular, but not in the systematic way we can determine popularity today.

Can you explain how it happens that a "lost" work, often from the seventeenth or eighteenth century, can be discovered in a library or archive? Are there piles of unsorted manuscripts just left about in heaps that no one has gotten around to cataloguing for the last few hundred years?

It does seem almost inconceivable, but the simple answer to this question is "yes, there are piles of unsorted manuscripts that no one has catalogued." Even though the works of composers have been raked over very thoroughly, there are still plenty of unpublished works, even by major composers, lying around in archives, still in manuscript form. But you should not think you can simply saunter into such an archive and easily stumble onto such a piece.

In the past, many composers who are famous today were working musicians. Those attached to a royal or noble court, such as Haydn at Esterháza, would be expected to produce large quantities of music, and many of these compositions remained unsigned. A good example of this are the ballets recently identified in a Czech archive. These were pieces produced anonymously, for functional purposes in the Viennese theaters, where they gave two or three ballets a night as interludes in other entertainment, such as spoken plays or operas.

It took a knowledgeable person to know the importance of these random manuscripts. This researcher determined that some of the scores were by the renowned eighteenth-century Bohemian composer Christoph Willibald Gluck, long in the service of the Hapsburg Court in Vienna. He was sure of this attribution (1) because court payment records show that Gluck was responsible for composing the ballet music for the season they were produced; (2) because he had compiled a thorough catalogue of ballet titles from a manuscript theater chronicle, newspaper accounts, and diaries; and 3) because, in some cases, movements from these the ballets show up in Gluck's later Parisian operas.

Sometimes the works are known but who composed them is unclear. This was the case with some early symphonies attributed to Wolfgang Amadeus Mozart that are now believed to be the work of his father, Leopold; the manuscript bears only the last name. In such cases a definitive answer becomes possible only when new evidence is found, such as an original (not a copy) in the composer's own hand. At other times a new technology can be revealing, such as new methods to date the ink or the manuscript paper.

While these manuscripts might have previously been known to exist, when one of these methods allows them to be attributed to a composer such as Mozart, they often make the news as being newly "discovered."

More often than not, the music discovered is not regarded as a major component of a composer's output. The music could have been composed for a special occasion, such as a coronation, and discarded because it was intended for only that specific occasion. Very often the composer would dismantle these pieces, reusing them in later works, as did Gluck.

Thus, there is still possibly a large quantity of music composed by famous (and not so famous) composers still to be found; but uncovering a hitherto unknown major work? Unlikely. Further, it is less likely an untrained person would even recognize something like this were it to be found.

The bottom line is that you probably shouldn't expect to visit a European archive or antique store and discover Beethoven's Tenth Symphony.

When we are listening to a particular composer's mass for voices, we hear the wonderful soloists and choruses, but we don't hear a clergy section. Were these masses written with the intent to be heard in churches as part of a regular Sunday mass or just to be performed in concert halls for the sheer enjoyment of them?

The simple answer to this question is that if the mass was composed before the turn of the twentieth century, it was probably intended to be part of a church service, at least initially. Only in the twentieth century were masses composed primarily for the concert hall. But like most things in classical music there are exceptions and some complications.

Let's look at the Mass in more detail. The Roman Catholic Mass consists of two sets of texts. One, called the Proper, changes every day in accordance with the church calendar. The other, called the Ordinary, is the same for every mass and consists of the Kyrie, Gloria, Credo, Sanctus-Benedictus, and Agnus Dei.

These texts were originally spoken or sung. If they were sung, for what was called a high mass, Gregorian chant or newly composed music was used. During this time composers wrote single compositions for each text so there would be volumes of Kyries, Glorias, and Credos that could be mixed and matched as desired. In the late Middle Ages the composer Guillaume de Machaut was the first to compose pieces on each of the five texts. These pieces created a unified musical composition in terms of style, harmony, and other musical conventions. This started the tradition of composers creating a unified collection of pieces utilizing the Ordinary texts. This has remained the norm.

Settings of the Mass were composed throughout the baroque and classical eras, becoming longer, more popular, and in some cases (the Verdi Requiem, for sure, and even masses by Beethoven, Mozart, and Haydn) downright operatic in style. While some of these operas . . . I mean, masses . . . seem today to be well suited for the concert stage, they were originally intended to be part of a liturgical service. In fact, in many regions, church officials forbade these compositions from being performed *outside* the church.

As I said, these works were greatly loved by everyone. That is, everyone except the Austrian emperor. He passed reforms prohibiting the church from presenting music that was deemed "too operatic." Composers such as Haydn, who had written many of these popular masses, were forced to stop composing liturgical music.

When Austria got a new emperor in 1796, he relaxed the restrictions. This opened the door for composers to return to writing operatic masses. They responded by writing longer and more elaborate masses lasting up to forty minutes in length, which became the norm for the next hundred years.

It is unclear where the idea of a mass performed as a concert piece originated, but it may have been with

Beethoven. Beethoven was commissioned to write a mass (his Mass in C Major) for a service intended to celebrate the wife of Prince Esterházy. Unfortunately the prince didn't like the music, and Beethoven received no further commissions from the prince. Not to be deterred, Beethoven removed the Latin text from the composition, substituted a German text, and that enabled its performance as a thinly disguised concert piece.

This must have been successful because several years later he was commissioned to write his mighty Missa Solemnis for the coronation of the archbishop. Unfortunately he did not finish it in time for the ceremony. He also added the word "O" before "miserere" in the Gloria. This automatically rendered the piece unusable in worship, as the Roman Catholic Church did not allow changes to the liturgical text.

This simple change cleared the way for Beethoven to have his Missa Solemnis performed in concert. It may be that it was here that the idea of a concert mass came to be. It still was the exception; with only the requiems of Verdi, Berlioz, and Dvorak (as well as lesser composers) getting this treatment. All other masses were for liturgical use, even the elaborate works of Anton Bruckner. (An interesting aside: Bach's B Minor Mass, arguably the most famous of all masses, was performed as a concert piece in the mid-nineteenth century.)

In the twentieth century the idea of the concert mass really took hold, and the full-fledged musical mass intended for liturgical use all but disappeared. Today, when we hear a composer's mass it is usually in a concert setting; so as you pointed out, we are not hearing the entire liturgy but instead only the choral and soloist parts.

Hearing a mass in a concert hall is a different experience from hearing it as a support of the liturgy. Recently I heard Schubert's Mass in G performed in a church as part of the Sunday morning service. The sections of the mass were sung at their appropriate places in the service, with the other parts of the service, from sermon to Offertory, spoken and interspersed. It was actually a completely different experience (as it should be) from the many performances I have heard of this piece in a concert setting.

By the way, composers often set Proper texts, too. These are called motets.

How does classical music acquire a nationalistic character that is easily recognized? Is it because composers tend to be mentored by their countrymen, which perpetuates and reinforces certain melodic and harmonic patterns? Or do they subconsciously imitate the folk music they grew up with?

First of all, not all classical music has a nationalistic character per se, as in attempting to reflect the musical spirit of a specific country or region such as Russia, China, Spain, or the United States. This type of nationalism is intentional and deliberate and is probably a fairly small percentage of a country's overall output. On the other hand, it is true that very often you can guess what country the composer is from. This second type of nationalism is not consciously created by the composer.

To be a nationalistic composer in the first sense is somewhat easy to explain. Often the composer has made the conscious decision to represent or celebrate a certain nation (frequently his or her homeland). In this case the composer calls on folk tunes or melodies from that country and uses melodic harmonies and rhythms that would be found in that region or as part of that culture. Sibelius's *Finlandia*, Dvorak's *New World* Symphony, and Copland's *Appalachian Spring* are prime examples of this type of composition. Such pieces were often written during great periods of nationalistic pride and can be quite inspirational.

The second type of nationalism, if you want to call it that, is more complex. Here, the influence of the culture or country in which the composer was raised manifests itself in the music. But the results can be subtle. The composer is not consciously adding this ingredient to the musical mix.

To understand this, we have to remember only that we all grow up in a culture and we share its aesthetic values and musical vocabulary. We also hear the rhythms and inflection of our native language. These become ingrained.

We grow up with these conventions, and it is almost impossible to discount them. However, these influences can be diminished. Classical composers often study at great institutions throughout the world, and there is a melding of cultures and styles that takes place in these schools. Still, basic musical instincts are arranged from birth, and we never completely lose them.

An old saying is that Mozart wrote great music because he was a genius, but he wrote symphonies because he was born in Europe, not Asia. There is much truth to that.

I recently attended a concert of Renaissance music, and a whole fleet of questions came to mind about this music from so long ago. I've seen examples of medieval music preserved in cathedrals. Do modern players of ancient music read the old stuff in original form? Do they understand it well enough to play it as it may have originally sounded, the way a jazz combo knows and produces the music without its being written out? Do they rewrite the ancient music in modern notation and then play what they read? It is silly, I suppose, to ask how close to the original music the modern performances are, but I will ask anyway.

While this question is about very early music, it actually could be asked of all music written prior to the twentieth century. It was only after Edison invented the phonograph that we could actually know for sure how music from an earlier period would sound, even if we had the notation.

As an extreme example of this, let's leave the classical world for a moment. If we found the printed music to an early rock and roll song, let's say "Johnny B. Goode," but we did not have a recording of it, what are the chances that anyone would perform it with the characteristic wailing guitar sounds that makes the song unique and of its era?

This is essentially the case with all music written prior to the development of recording. However, this challenge is even more pronounced in music from the medieval and Renaissance periods because both the notation and the instruments were so different from what we have today.

Modern performers of medieval and Renaissance music have to be more than skilled on their instrument. They need to be well read on the most current research regarding performance practice from these eras. Performers today sometimes perform from old notation and sometimes from modern editions. Professional ensembles often make the modern editions themselves by studying the originals.

Your analogy to jazz is actually very apt. Much early music was performed with a high reliance on improvisation. Performers today improvise and reconstruct how

they think pieces may have sounded in their original setting. As you can imagine, this takes a great deal of scholarly knowledge about the styles and customs of the period.
No one wants to hear a John Coltrane–inspired improvisation in the middle of a Renaissance song.

Not only would the notes that are improvised be differ-
ent, but also the very "feel" of the music would be altered.
Scholars know that people beat time differently in the
Renaissance, with accents on somewhat different pulses.
Knowing that fact helps them reconstruct the appropriate
flow and feel of the song.

Still, one Renaissance specialist told me that even
though every new piece of research he reads brings him
closer and closer to the original sound he seeks, actually
capturing that sound is still elusive. Even if the performer
does re-create the original sound, how could anyone
be sure?

Clearly, playing early music is definitely a case of con-
jecture, but that is certainly some of the fun and fascination of trying to master it. Simply put, that is what playing
early music is all about.

*I recently attended a concert at the Hollywood Bowl,
where it was explained that Stalin was very threatened by the music of Dmitri Shostakovich. I understand
how someone could be threatened by vocal music, but how
can someone be threatened by orchestral music? How
could it possibly carry political power?*
It has always amazed me, too, how threatened some people, especially those in authority, are by the sheer power
of music. At its best, music clearly has the power to excite
and stir the soul, and politicians often use this to their

advantage. All you have to do is look at the care given to the music played at rallies for presidential candidates to understand how seriously it is taken.

But using music to stir up and excite a crowd seems an easier concept to comprehend than music as some subversive power. Still, that was the common belief not too long ago.

Throughout the nineteenth century and into the twentieth, many writers discussed and debated the power of instrumental music to convey meaning. Some believed instrumental music carried specific meaning through the actual pitches.

There are also many people in the general population who believe that all classical music has a narrative, or a story to tell. Works such as Berlioz's *Symphonie fantastique* and Smetana's *Moldau* are examples of music with a literal storyline, or program, provided by the composer. The success of these types of pieces led many people to think all music must tell a story. Political leaders worry that people will find a story in the music that is not in keeping with a certain political stance—*their* political stance. I recently had lunch with a world-famous contemporary composer. I was surprised to hear to him talk about his fascination with the narratives people tend to create in their head while listening to his music. This is a very powerful side of music and obviously can be threatening to those in power.

Related to this, leaders worry about the power music has because it speaks directly to the emotions (which it does). They worry that certain music might stir up the "wrong" emotions and people could be incited to action or go out of control.

In the case of Shostakovich, he had to contend with the explicit expectation in the USSR that art should communicate directly and *simply* to the common person. Any art that smacked of elitism or ties to Western high art culture was suspect and dangerous at worst; at best, it was a poor model for the proper Soviet attitude and lifestyle. Most painfully for the composer, the Communist Party denounced his opera *Lady Macbeth of Mtsensk* in 1936 for its allegedly sympathetic portrayal of a murderess and for its perceived amorality. It was banned in the Soviet Union for almost thirty years.

We can find many unofficial examples of musical propaganda today; besides the aforementioned use of music at political rallies, music is also used in church services, TV commercials, and movies. In other parts of the world it can still be constrained by official policy. One country that I visit frequently has a requirement that there must be a composition by a native composer on every classical concert. Further, the piece of music must evoke 'positive" emotions; summoning up negative emotions will not lead to good.

In a nutshell, music has the power to stir the soul. We all know and love that about it. But to a politician or a regime trying to hold onto power, this can be quite a threat. As a musician I must admit that I love that.

Does truly pure music exist? Isn't all music somewhat thematic in the mind of the composer or is at least interpreted that way by the listener?

This wonderful question has been asked for ages, and each new generation seems to answer it somewhat differently.

All music is about *something*. Music expresses human feelings, human conditions, human experiences. Said another way, all music takes us to a place that can't be touched by words. If words could take us there, there'd be no reason to write the music. We could just talk about it.

I think we can agree that all music is at least a reflection or an expression, if very rarely a literal self-portrait, of the composer. Composers tend to approach a piece with an idea of something they want to convey. What that might be is often intangible, but the feeling is there just the same. This is ultimately what motivates a composer to write (aside from the commission dollars) and what inspires the audience to listen.

In the end, it's this mystery that music possesses that draws us to it.

I just finished reading a new biography of Charles Ives. Seeking an answer to this question was a major theme of his entire life. He believed strongly that many pieces of music are (and should be) thematic. You have only to look at the titles of many of his pieces to see this. He also felt that pure music existed but was elusive. Ives went so far as to say that music didn't need to be performed. In fact, he went further and suggested that some music *shouldn't* be performed because the performance inserted, artificially, the performers between the music and the listener. In his mind, pure music did indeed exist, but the music we actually hear is an imitation or someone's interpretation of that pure music.

That gets heavy pretty quickly. Most people don't ponder the issue to that extent. Still, it shows the depth of the issues implied in this question. I think most of believe on some level that music, especially great music, is always the product of human emotion. The creative process most often starts with some sort of thematic element, whether conscious or not, in the mind of the composer.

My wife is an alto in a local choir, and I have heard her practice the alto part for Beethoven's Ninth Symphony. It is my contention it would hardly stand on its own as a song. Yet in The Music Man, where Meredith Willson has the Buffalo Bills sing an old standard ("Good Night, Ladies") while the ladies of the town sing "Pick a Little, Talk a Little" or has them sing "Lida Rose" while Marian sings "Will I Ever Tell You?," we have four parts that do stand up on their own.

Several questions come from this observation: Did the four songs exist independently, or did Meredith Willson carefully craft all four from scratch to go well together? Is it a simple matter of putting them in the same key or is it just magical?

While the effect that is created by this compositional device is certainly magical, the actual crafting of melodies that can fit together is not. Instead, it is the result of careful craftsmanship and problem solving on the part of the composer. To understand why some melodies have this effect, as in *The Music Man*, and others do not, as in Beethoven's Ninth, it is helpful to understand a bit about choral harmony.

There are two fundamental ways to create harmony. The easiest way to think about this is that one is horizontal, the other, vertical.

To understand horizontal harmony, try to picture a melody that travels along, in a horizontal way, with the notes rising and falling. One effective way to try this is to picture what the notes of the melody would look like on the printed page if they were connected with a line. You would end up with a line graph that shows the contour of the melody. With a melody like this, there is no harmony; only one note sounds at any moment in time.

If we added a second melody to the page and connected the scrawled notes of that tune, we would end up with a graph showing two interweaving lines, two melodic contours that intersect at various points. And at each point along the graph we have two notes sounding: we get harmony.

This is exactly what is happening in these songs. However, while any two melodies together create harmony, it may not be terribly pleasing harmony. Writing two interesting melodies that harmonize with one another is quite a challenge. Writing three or four melodies that work together is an even bigger challenge. This type of harmony is called polyphonic, which means "many voices."

A second type of harmony is more vertical. In this type of harmony the parts all move together to create block chords. If we were plotting this, we would draw a series of vertical lines to connect the pitches of the individual parts. This type of harmony is homophonic ("one voice"). In choral music, this results in the words of each part being sung at the same time, much as in a church anthem or hymn.

A really obvious example of these two types of harmony can be found in the "Hallelujah" chorus from Handel's *Messiah*, where the composer alternates between the two types of harmony. For example, when the choir sings "Hallelujah," they all sing together. This is homophonic. But when you reach the words "and he shall reign," the parts split into four voices, soprano, alto, tenor, and bass lines, and the words are no longer chugging along at the exact same pace; rather, they're staggered. This is polyphonic.

Which takes us back to the original question. In polyphonic music the individual parts are interesting and can

stand on their own. But in homophonic music the individual parts, being secondary to the unified whole, are not
usually all that interesting. This is why his wife practicing
the alto part of the Ninth is not all that interesting.

So the individual melodies in *The Music Man* didn't just
happen to fit together, any more than the individual lines
of the "Hallelujah" chorus just happened to blend. These
added melodies ("Pick a Little, Talk a Little") were metic-
ulously created to be a perfect fit as counterpoint to the
original melody.

What compositional techniques or tricks do composers use to make music sound spooky? For example, A Night on Bald Mountain *or some film scores?*

There are many instances where a composer wants to make
music sound spooky or dark or even evil. The effect can
range from subtle moments in Mozart's *Don Giovanni* to
the over-the-top scratching violins of the classic Bernard
Herrmann film score for *Psycho*.

Composers seemed drawn to the darker sounds of
the lower register and the minor mode, as well as to that
"devil in music," the tritone (the interval from C to F♯, for
example) to evoke feelings of spookiness or scary images.
You can hear examples of this throughout history. There
are terrifying moments in the requiems of Mozart, Berlioz,
and Verdi. In the late sixteenth and early seventeenth centuries, Don Carlo Gesualdo wrote hauntingly weird, highly
chromatic, and forward-looking harmonies in his sets of
madrigals. Of course, it didn't hurt his fear factor one bit
that he ended up murdering his wife and her lover on the
spot, upon discovering them "in the act" at the Palazzo San
Severo in Naples.

Dissonance, the combining of pitches that clash with one another, is another technique that can evoke goose-bumps. Richard Strauss's *Salome* uses extreme disso-nance to express terror and madness. The scene involving Salome as she becomes maniacally obsessed (even sexually obsessed) with John the Baptist's head, bestowed upon her on a platter by Herod, contains some of the harshest, most clangorous dissonances and textures conceived up to that point in the history of music. It is truly terrifying, and one can understand why so many houses in conservative early twentieth-century Europe banned the opera.

Benjamin Britten was able to express horror and dark-ness brilliantly as well. The *Serenade for Tenor, Horn and Strings* is a powerful example: the tenor sings a "fire and brimstone" text to the same haunting melodic line repeated over and over (as a passacaglia) while the orchestra plays a fugue underneath. The two musics have little to do with one another, and the results are quite splendidly frighten-ing. Even eerier is the aria from Britten's *Rape of Lucretia* entitled "Within this frail crucible of light." The gentle rocking tune, almost a lullaby, juxtaposes similar slight dissonances. It is sung by Tarquinius, prince of Rome, as he spies upon his sleeping prey, about to spring forward and rape her.

Movie composers take these sorts of musical effects even farther. They use techniques that, in a concert hall, would send the audiences running for the doors but in a movie are delightfully effective.

There are specific techniques that are used in film scores but rarely in concert music. In addition to dis-sonance, film and television composers use clusters of pitches. This would be the equivalent of pressing your entire arm down over a section of the piano. These composers will also include aleatoric, or improvisatory, sections or assign the musicians to play a series of pitches as fast as they can, which produces a very unsettling feeling in the listener (as well as the musician). Brass players often see an inverted triangle in their scores; this means to sound the lowest possible note and play it loud. These pitches often sound guttural, almost animal. Conversely, string players are often asked to play the highest notes of which they are capable, which, as in *Psycho*, can sound pretty squeaky . . . and pretty scary.

Film and TV composers also call on some techniques explored in the musique concrète era of concert music in the mid-twentieth century. A main technique in this style is to record instruments, especially percussion instruments, and then play them back very slowly, even backwards, as part of the orchestration.

In film music there is also a technique that has nothing to do with the composition of the score but instead involves juxtaposing music in unexpected contexts. This can be chilling, too.

An example of this is hearing a simple music box tune just before or while someone is being murdered or a peaceful lullaby played during scenes of great violence. For me, an excellent example of this technique can be found in the movie *Platoon*, where Barber's *Adagio for Strings*, one of the most peaceful and comforting works ever composed, accompanies a horrible battle scene, filled with pain, suffering, and death. The effect is downright terrifying.

Leroy Anderson's typewriter song, as recorded by the Boston Pops, fascinates me. Was an actual typewriter

***used? And was it by any chance supplemented by bell
and carriage-return sound effects?***

"The Typewriter" was written to be performed on an
actual typewriter. The performer hits the keys according
to printed notation. The typewriter (I suppose the soloist
would be called simply the typist?) is nearly always amplified and is often placed in the location where a soloist
would stand for a concerto, in front of the first violins. The
typewriter part is shown in standard rhythm notation but
specific keys (the typewriter kind) are not designated.

Tapping the keys in rhythm is not that hard, but the
carriage return and bell can be problematic. Therefore,
these are often performed with a ratchet and bell from the
percussion section to perfect the timing of the ensemble.

I have seen this piece performed with a celebrity "playing" the typewriter part. In this case someone in the percussion section played the typing sound on some sort of
woodblock, too. But Anderson intended it to be played on
a typewriter.

Of course, this begs the question: how long will it be
until no one in the audience knows what a typewriter is or
what it sounds like? Believe it or not, instrumental rental
houses are starting to stock typewriters for performances
of this very piece because they are becoming so hard to find.

While I type the answer to this question, I am paying attention to the sound of the keys on my computer. It
sounds nothing like a manual typewriter, of course, and
there is no bell or carriage return. I can see that today's
young people will soon be hard pressed to relate in any way
to this fun and novel piece of music. Sadly, I have to believe
this is one work that, as time goes on, will see fewer and
fewer performances.

What is twelve-tone music? What about the other tones? How does a composer choose which twelve tones to use? Why use only twelve? When did twelve-tone music become popular?

This might in some ways be my favorite of all the questions that have ever been asked on the radio show. It reminds those of us who are professional musicians how casually we use terms, assuming everyone else knows what we are talking about. We hardly ever stop to think how ridiculous some of those terms must sound to the untrained listener.

This whole idea of writing music using twelve tones goes back to the first part of the twentieth century. Composers were trying to break away from confinement by tonality, or being restricted to writing in a certain key or tonal center. But they were having difficulty doing so. The idea of a key signature for music is so ingrained in our psyche that it was proving hard to shake the temptation to revert to favoring a specific pitch as the tonal center. Yet Wagner's *Tristan und Isolde*, Mahler's Ninth and (unfinished) Tenth symphonies, and Arnold Schoenberg's Second String Quartet (1905), in which a soprano hauntingly sings, "I feel air from another planet," had pushed the confines of conventional tonality to the breaking point. Something had to give.

It was felt that a daring new technique was needed, basically a new type of music theory that would enable composers to leave behind the "restraints" of the past. The best way to ensure this was to use all the available notes *equally*. The system that arose, formulated by Schoenberg in the early 1920s, was one in which each individual pitch had to be used before any pitch could be repeated. Paradoxically, like the fugues of Johann Sebastian Bach, it actually was a throwback: an extremely structured way of crafting music.

The part of the question that is so interesting to me is what one considers "every note." I would assume many people, if asked how many pitches there are, would think of a piano keyboard and say there are 88 notes; after all, that is the number of keys on a piano. As logical as this seems, it is not the case. In Western music, there are indeed just twelve that repeat over and over: A A♯, B, C, C♯, D, D♯, E, F, F♯, G, G♯.

In twelve-tone compositions, also called serial music, the composer avoids repeating a given pitch until all the others have been used. Thus, all the pitches in this "series" are treated equally. If all are treated equally, no single pitch takes precedence or becomes the tonal center. Also, the pitches used can be in any octave. So every note on the piano keyboard could be utilized.

Again, all this elaborate structure is designed to avoid the pull of tonal gravity. Twelve different pitches repeated in a series: that's serial, or twelve-tone, music.

Regarding the question "When did this get popular?" I would answer by saying most of us are still waiting.

While the philosophy and theory behind this writing style is fascinating, as well as immensely challenging for the composer, at the end of the day it really seems a strange and rather clinical method of writing music. It accentuates the intellectual, theoretical, and mathematical aspects of the art form while ignoring the psychological and emotional needs of the listeners. Having said that, many stunning and even affecting works have been written using Schoenberg's twelve tone technique as a basis, including the violin concerto of Schoenberg's pupil Alban Berg, the mature orchestral scores of Pierre Boulez, and what Boulez himself described as "faceted crystal": the uncanny, brief, and texturally compelling orchestral works of Anton Webern, another Schoenberg protégé.

Yet I think tonality serves a very special function for the listener. It sets up strong musical expectations. The listener's response comes when those expectations are met, not met, or met in a delayed fashion. When tonality is abandoned the tonal expectations disappear.

For this reason, strict serial music never caught on with the general public. While, as I say, there are undeniably some great pieces in this style, I am not sure we would ever say this style was "popular." It was used in the first half to middle of the twentieth century. Today, serial writing is one of many techniques composers have at their disposal to say what they want to say in music.

What is considered the fastest music ever composed? Was it Rossini?!

You would think this would be an easy question. But believe it or not, there is no precise definition of what is "fast" in music. Usually, "fast" means the speed of the beats or the tempo of the piece as a whole. This is measured in terms of how many beats there are per minute. I have seen a number of markings of 200 beats per minute. However, marching bands often work at 240-plus beats per minute.

Once a tempo reaches 200 beats per minute, players, conductors, and listeners tend to perceive the beat as being every other beat or even every measure. This creates the conundrum: what are we measuring when we talk about speed? Are we measuring the actual, notated beat or the perceived beat? There is no good answer to this.

To leave music for a moment, if you are on a straight stretch of highway, traveling in your Ferrari F12 Berlinetta at ninety miles an hour, your perception of how fast you are going would be very different from what it would be if you were on a roller coaster, whipping into tight turns at forty miles an hour, or on a turbulence-free airplane traveling at five hundred miles an hour. You might actually consider the forty-mile-per-hour roller coaster the fastest experience.

Likewise with music. We often *perceive* a composition as fast based on how many notes are played per beat, not how many beats there are per minute. A perfect example of this is Rimsky-Korsakov's *Flight of the Bumblebee*. There are so many notes per beat that performers and conductors sometimes have to slow down the beat to make it playable. Yet the listener would still think this music was fast.

As you can see, this is probably an unanswerable question. The "simple" ones often are.

What makes for a good melodic line? Why do some melodies, be they Bach's Toccata and Fugue in D Minor, Beethoven's "Ode to Joy," Mendelssohn's Italian Symphony, Deep Purple's "Smoke on the Water," or the Beach Boys' "Barbara Ann" stick in our heads? Clearly it is not just a matter of quality.

If I could answer this, I would be writing melodies instead of books. Naturally there is no absolute answer to this question. That is good. Wouldn't it be terrible if music (any part of music) could be reduced to a foolproof formula?

You are not the first to ask this question. This exact question has been asked and researched in the music psychology literature, where the subject is the focus of whole chapters in textbooks. What the research tends to show is that while no one can actually predict what makes a good melody, there are some basic considerations. A good melody

- must have some basic rhythmic and tonal patterns that are recognizable to the listener
- must conform to the basic rules of Western music (that tonal pull, a sense of tension and release)
- must have a contour or shape that is interesting or attractive
- has a balance of simplicity and complexity with regard to its tonal, rhythmic, and harmonic structure
- must break all of the above rules but just enough to be interesting, not alienating

Even with these guidelines a melody remains a very personal thing. What is a "good melody" for a child is possibly not a good melody for an adult. (Anyone remember the PBS *Barney* theme? Alas, yes.) A good melody for the untrained ear might not be compelling for the trained ear. Finally, a good melody for 1929 might not make it today.

The best answer I can come up with is that certain melodies balance these guidelines perfectly right, and the result is not just attractive but even addictive. I have always found this fascinating: did you ever notice that the melodies that get good and stuck in your head are often not all that good? Or at least, not all that likable? The question mentions "Barbara Ann" as a case in point, but just go to a wedding and hear everyone singing "YMCA" or crooning "Sweet Caroline" (uh-uh-uh), and you will realize these melodies resonate with huge numbers of people. These are melodies everyone knows and you can hardly keep from singing them, but they are hardly great melodies. Or are they?

It seems as if music, when added to film, aids in the evocation of a stronger emotional experience for the audience. How long did it take filmmakers to realize the *power of music? When was music introduced in film?* *Moreover, when did film scoring become the norm?*

It is true that music is now such an important part of any film that it would seem awkward to watch a film that did not have music. In fact, we're so accustomed to a score that the lack of a score in a film or TV production is often used to tremendously eerie effect. That is because films have *always* had music to accompany them. Music was a part of films as far back as the Lumière brothers' film experiments in Paris in the 1890s.

In the early days of silent films, music was provided by a piano or organ and had a functional role as well. The music masked the sound of the noisy early projectors. It didn't take long for filmmakers to realize that the keyboard player could help stir up the audience's emotions, from excitement to sadness, triumph to tragedy, carefreeness to worry.

At first the music, whether performed by piano in smaller towns or theaters or by orchestras in larger cities, was lifted from the classics. The music of Beethoven, Tchaikovsky, and Wagner were considered especially dramatic and effective for this purpose.

In 1908, Saint-Saens was the first major composer to write an original score for a movie. This launched a trend, which started slowly at first, for composers of concert music to write for film. Soon this list would include Honegger, Milhaud, Shostakovich, Copland, Leonard Bernstein, and many more.

The classic D. W. Griffith movie *Birth of a Nation*, released in 1915, boasted two scores, one based on familiar classical works by Beethoven, Wagner, Weber, and Suppé;

the other was an original score by Joseph Carl Breil, a lyric tenor and stage director and one of the first American composers to write specifically for the medium of film. By the 1920s this practice was commonplace.

Still, the technology of the time did not allow the music to be coordinated and synchronized with the film. It wasn't precisely what we call film scoring today. The movies were all silent, and the music roughly mirrored the movie's action and timing.

Everything changed for music in 1927 with the introduction of talkies. After the release of *The Jazz Singer*, the new technology allowed for better synchronizing of music to film. Thus, the modern art of film scoring was born, with pioneers being Alfred Newman, Max Steiner, Erich Korngold, Miklós Rózsa, and David Raksin. In 1933, Steiner wrote a score for *King Kong* that was so powerful and so enhanced the movie that there was little doubt in anyone's mind: film music was here to stay.

When did music start?

The simple answer to this is "a long time ago." Recently a forty-thousand-year-old flute, believed to be the oldest musical instrument we know of, was found. It is almost certain that music is older, much older, than that, as certainly singing, dancing, and drumming preceded the making of instruments.

We have evidence that music has been around for as long as we have recorded history. Early cave drawings depict dancing, early rhythm instruments such as shakers and drums, and even some early flutes. It also shows that every culture, past and present, primitive to advanced, has had music as a part of it. So while we cannot answer definitively when music started, it is accepted that music has been a part of the human experience for much of human existence.

A related question is not *when* did music start but *how* did it start? While it is impossible to prove how music was created, scholars theorize that it happened in one of three ways: functional uses, human evolution, or divine creation.

As for the last theory, the Old Testament credits Jubal, also known as Yuval or Yubal, a descendent of Cain, as "the father of all who play the harp and flute"—thus the creator of music. Greek mythology attributes music's creation to several gods and goddesses: these include Athena (creator of the song), Pan (creator of reed instruments), and Hermes (creator of the flute and lyre). In the Hindu tradition, Brahma, the supreme spirit of the universe, invented music, and for the Chinese, Emperor Fu Xi gets the credit for "inventing" music. Xi was a busy man. When he wasn't busy inventing music, he also taught mankind the use of fishing nets, the breeding of silk worms, the taming of wild animals, and most significantly, the basis of the Chinese written language, the eight trigrams.

Functional theories on the origins of music argue that early man imitated nature in the form of birdsongs and the rhythms of crickets. Or it is possible that music simply grew out of our earliest need to communicate. Music used for communication might have been mating calls, songs, or beats to coordinate group work, impassioned speech to express emotions, or drum patterns to tell stories and send out warnings over distances.

Lastly, the evolution theories argue that as the brain developed, it gradually learned to recognize and organize visual and aural patterns. As these skills developed, the brain responded by demanding more and more things in which to find patterns. The brain derived pleasure from finding patterns in abstract work, and thus both visual and aural art forms emerged.

Regardless of where it came from, it is clear that music is a uniquely human phenomenon and has been a part of the human experience for a very, very long time.

When did the term "classical music" begin? When did we start calling this style of music classical?

The term "classical" or variations on the word started cropping up in relation to Mozart and some of his contemporaries in the late eighteenth century. In 1797 Mozart's early biographer Franz Xaver Niemetschek referred to the "classical content" in Mozart's works and compared his musical forms and styles to writings and visual art from classical antiquity. Mozart's music, like the great classical literary works, could be listened to over and over for continued enjoyment.

At this time, there were other uses of the term "classical" as well. The highly elaborate French styles of the era of Louis XIV, including literature, drama, sculpture, and furniture design, were sometimes referred to as classical.

However, despite my asking many of the music professors of the Thornton School, none knew exactly when "classical" began to refer to all art music. Some speculated that its use to describe the "refinement and class" of Louis XIV–era arts imparted a certain cachet, or ring, to it. It seems the term's first use in reference to an entire musical era appeared in the 1830s, describing the "classical" period from J. S. Bach to Beethoven as a golden age. Once established, the term just stuck.

Positing the mid-nineteenth century for the establishment of this word is plausible. With the rise of the middle class at that time—and with no fancy cars to show off one's high level of sophistication to others—being seen at classical music concerts was the next best thing.

Where did the names do, re, mi come from?

This is the only place in the book that I am going to provide two equally plausible answers and let you decide which you want to believe. The first answer is that Maria von Trapp and Julie Andrews co-created them for the movie *The Sound of Music*. From the royalties from this song alone, they both comfortably retired.

The second answer is that in the eleventh century, Guido d'Arezzo, an Italian monk who was a formidable music theorist, was trying to teach his young choristers to learn melodies. He came up with a method that was based on a popular hymn of the day. The Latin text of this hymn was

> Ut queant laxis
> Resonare fibris
> Mira gestorum
> Famuli tuorum,
> Solve poluti
> Labii reatum,
> Sancte Iohannes.

Which translates roughly to this:

That thy servants
may freely sing forth
the wonders

of thy deeds,
remove all stain of guilt
from their unclean lips,
O Saint John.

The really interesting and useful part of this hymn was
that the melody was created in such a way that each line
started on the next higher note of the scale. If we place ourselves in the key of C, this would mean that the first line
started on C, the second line on D, the third line on E, and
so on. The other useful part of the hymn was that everyone
already knew it.

Guido had his choir practice singing just the first syllable of each word on the appropriate pitch. Thus they sang
the scale using Ut, re, mi, fa, sol, la; somewhat later added
the syllable "si" from the initials of Saint John found at the
end of the hymn (*j*'s were *i*'s in Latin).

Once Guido's choir could sing these syllables on the
designated pitches, he had them mix it up, singing them in
a different order to practice. He obviously felt that "When
you know the notes to sing . . . You can sing most anything!"

But the medieval monk had another trick up his
sleeve. Literally. To communicate what he wanted from
the choir, Guido assigned different pitch syllables to
the different knuckles and joints of his left hand. He
would point to the different parts of his hand and the
choir would sing the appropriate syllable and pitch.
This became such a popular method for teaching singing that for centuries to come, every serious textbook
on Western music features the obligatory drawing of
Guido's left hand. Even today, a thousand years later, our
students in the Thornton School study Guido's left hand.

(Be honest: the Maria and Julie answer is sounding more plausible every minute, right?)

When the system came into English-speaking countries, two changes were made: "ut" became "do," to make it easier to sing and hold a pitch; and "si" was changed to "ti" so that each syllable could start on a different consonant.

The official name for this system of learning to sing is *solfège*, derived from the syllables sol and fa. A modern adaptation of both the syllables and the use of hands to communicate the pitches can be found in what is called the Kodály method of music teaching, named for Hungarian composer Zoltán Kodály. Today, many children around the world learn to sing from this method, which has its roots in an ingenious and emphatically low-tech teaching tool developed by an eleventh-century monk.

How does a surviving composer complete a deceased composer's work? For example, Mozart, Schumann, and Schubert all wrote works that could not be completed within their lifetime but were finished by others after they passed away. Who decides which surviving composer or composition student will finish the job? Or does the first person that wishes to do so simply take charge?

When a composer passes away, it is not unusual for there to be works that are left incomplete. Perhaps the composer was actively working on the piece when he or she died. The movie *Amadeus* showed this scenario, which probably happens in real life more frequently when the composer dies young; Schubert was just thirty-one, Mozart was thirty-five, Schumann, forty-six. The second scenario is one in which composers leave fragments or sketches of works from earlier in their career, sketches they had hoped at some point to return to.

Typically, no one is "selected" to complete a composition unless there is a business or financial agreement in place. This might happen today with a film score. Otherwise, it is certainly the exception. For most concert music the reconstructions are done by highly trained composers or musicologists (or both working together), perhaps a close assistant to the deceased composer (as was the case of Frederick Delius's "amanuensis," Eric Fenby, who completed *A Song of Summer*, the Third Violin Sonata, and many other unfinished works). This means that there is a great deal of knowledge of and admiration for the music brought to bear on the project.

While anyone could conceivably examine an unfinished work in an archive and attempt to finish it, that rarely happens. The person must first be respected as a scholar or expert on the composer's music. Even then, all efforts are going to be highly scrutinized and critiqued by others, possibly for years or decades to come. The scrutiny can get nasty.

The reconstruction is rarely made up of completely new music by the surviving composer. When a living composer or musicologist tackles the reconstruction of an unfinished work, existing sketches for the missing sections certainly help to guide the process. However, the number of sketches and their level of completeness determine how much "original" music is necessary to complete the job.

There are some instances, though rare, where a piece is completed with no sketches to rely on. In these sorts of situations, the surviving composer must analyze and understand the compositional style of the deceased composer in a very intimate way.

Finishing another composer's work is tedious and can be quite stressful. Most composers would undertake the task only as a labor of love and out of deep respect for the deceased.

Here we get another glimpse into classical musicians' humor. When I asked this question of the faculty, I often had to endure some variation of the following joke: "Do you know why the living composer who is finishing another composer's work has to compose quickly? Because the dead one is spending all his time *decomposing*."

I recently went to a concert where the program indicated that the piece was in four movements. But the work was performed without a pause between the movements. If the piece is continuous, how can there be movements? Even further, if a piece can be performed with the movements hooked together, what is the purpose of movements? I always thought they were to give the players a chance to rest and, if necessary, retune.

Musical compositions got longer from the baroque era through the romantic era. One of the forces behind extending pieces was the use of texts in music. In choral music, the idea of the Mass came into being. Here the entire composition is unified by the text of the Ordinary of the Catholic Mass. But there are many other ways the composition is held together, or unified:

Utilizing consistent key relationships between sections, a homogeneous orchestral ensemble and voicings, similar compositional style, and recurring musical themes brought together the different sections of the Mass. The same was true of operas and cantatas. The text provided the overarching structure of the composition, and the composer leaned on other methods to unify the piece. Thus, a composition could be created that was extended in length but could hold a listener's attention and be perceived as a complete entity in itself, even with multiple movements.

The same was not true of instrumental music. Without the unifying power of a text, it proved harder to compose works of increased length and have them be perceived as a whole.

Early music would often use dance forms for structure. A group of dances grouped together formed a suite. This was common in the music and time of Bach. While each dance was a brief work unto itself, composers sought a sense of unity. Therefore they utilized many of the same compositional principles that were being used to unify the different sections of a mass, cantata or opera. Composers utilized common themes, key signatures, key relationships, and instrumentation choices. All these elements were subject to systematic variation.

As composers grew tired of being confined by concrete forms like dances, they sought more abstract ways to arrange disparate pieces of music into a whole. In the classical period, individual movements that had some relation to each other started to appear and be accepted. Even though the composers were no longer tied to antiquated forms like French court dances, the earlier ideas of how to create unity with the dances carried over into the new forms.

Eventually the full-blown symphonic form emerged. Its development can be traced from the eighteenth-century opera sinfonia (overture) structure: a fast movement, a slow movement, and another fast, dancelike movement.

So movements emerged as an abstract means of unifying a large-scale work. They were not created to give musicians a rest or allow audience members to clear their throats, although these are definitely appreciated even in our own day.

As the question implies, sometimes the composer avoids any break between movements. This can be done to add even more unity to the piece or to offer a dramatic *attack* into the next movement or because the composer simply feels that the two movements flow together. In that case, the orchestra musicians are alerted on the printed score to the start of a new movement with the words "without pause"; the audience won't know the difference unless the music changes dramatically.

Thus, movements are just one of many compositional devices a composer has at his or her disposal when creating a large-scale work. If the composer feels a break between movements will spoil the mood or rob the music of dramatic punctuation or a sense of momentum, there will be no such break.

Why do so many symphonies end with a loud flourish instead of fading away softly? Is it to wake up the audience so they will clap?

Let's start with the obvious. Every composer loves applause, and some popular composers and arrangers will often write a big Hollywood ending or insert a dramatic key change or deceptive cadence to get applause at the end. But writing for applause probably does not carry over to the concert composer.

To support this premise you have only to look at music written over the last hundred years, especially music being written today. I know of no statistics on this, but it seems to me that if we look at twentieth- and twenty-first-century symphonic music, just as many pieces end with a soft, sometimes very soft, ending as end with a loud flourish.

Also, having a "big ending" is not the only way to get applause. I have been to many concerts where the piece ended very quietly but intensely, and after a moment of silence the audience broke into wild applause. The oft-mentioned Mahler Ninth Symphony has this kind of ending.

Still, I understand the spirit of the question. When most people refer to symphonies, they are thinking of those from the romantic era and prior. In these, the big ending *was* often driven by public taste and social attitudes. The romantic era was one that prized over-the-top emotionality and grandeur. And for the first time in the history of music, there were instruments that were capable of producing this volume of sound in concert halls where it would powerfully resonate. Composers tend to exploit these capabilities to the delight of audiences, whether then or today.

If we go back earlier, to the classical and baroque eras, composers tended to prize intellectual stimulation over naked emotional response. While many pieces did end with a fast and furious finale, it was not uncommon for an opera, oratorio, or similar dramatic work to end quietly.

The big ending was characteristic of much romantic music, and it is the romantic-era symphony that most people associate with such a grand finale. But that doesn't mean all symphonies end with a bang. Before and after, quiet, even somber, endings can be readily found.

Is it possible that classical music will ever "go out of style"?

I hope not, because then there would be no one to buy this book. There are probably some other reasons this would be bad, but that is the prime one.

This question stimulated a very lively discussion among faculty members of the Thornton School. The first part of the discussion was that this seemingly simple question could be interpreted in at least three different ways.

If the question refers specifically to music of the classical era—for example, the music of Mozart—it is certainly possible that it will go out of style. In fact, it already *is* out of style. I don't know of any serious composers that are composing in the style of Mozart any more than they wear wigs in the style of Mozart.

It is important to understand that this is not a value judgment. It certainly doesn't mean that this is anything less than glorious music. It simply means that it is not in the style of today.

If we interpret this question in two other ways, we get different answers. First: will classical music, the music of Haydn and Mozart's era, eventually be considered so old-fashioned that it will stop being played? I think that's possible—again, no value judgment intended. Musicians will probably always love playing this music. But just as certain works from the Renaissance sound somewhat odd to us today, it's possible that in two hundred years, Mozart's music could fall out of the mainstream and off the roster of orchestra concerts. In fact, it would be amazing if that doesn't happen. However, there are certainly people who would argue that it has already passed the test of time and therefore will last forever. I am not sure that is what will happen.

Before I start getting all the hate mail, let me stress one more time that this is not a value judgment. I think classical music will always be attractive to musicians because it is just so wonderful to play. I am not as sure we will go to Disney Hall in the year 2210 and hear Mozart, at least as much Mozart.

Now let's interpret her question the way she probably meant it: will *art music* ever go out of style? In this case there was strong agreement that, barring some awful environmental or political event, art music will continue and flourish.

Certain musicians will always strive to create great music and will distinguish functional music (music for entertainment, creating moods, religious ceremonies, etc.) from music that exists simply for its own inherent beauty and expressive power. This striving for great music is a part of being human. It will always be shared among a minority of the people, almost by definition, but will not only live on; it will continue and flourish.

In order to flourish, art music will need to reflect its era and continue to change and evolve. This is what will keep it alive. As this happens, some older music will drop off concert programs, but that's how the art form renews itself. We should celebrate every time we hear a new piece of art music being performed. Sure, some of this new music will be good, some will be awful, and some will be great. But that is what will keep music vibrant.

Classical music, or art music, will not go out of style because if it is truly vibrant, it will reflect the society of its time and fill a human need.

It is precisely the need for this vibrancy—the fact that music must stay alive and current—that I suspect will lead to the results I outlined in the first two interpretations of the question. In two hundred years, think about how much more great music will have been written. Since music takes time to learn, rehearse, and

perform (unlike pictures, which can be hung in museums, the only limitation being wall space), only so much
can be presented before the public. It is only natural that
some music has to move a bit farther back on the shelf to
make room for the new.

8

This and That

THE QUESTIONS FROM LISTENERS COME into the weekly radio show in seemingly random order. It wasn't until I started organizing the hundreds of questions I had received that I began thinking about how they could be grouped. The natural groupings that emerged dictated the titles of the earlier chapters.

There were some great questions, however, that were left over after sorting the others into chapters. These fell into no real discernible categories, so I lumped them all into this final chapter that I call simply "This and That" because "Miscellaneous Questions" sounds too generic and "Questions That Don't Belong" is simply too sad. Enjoy!

I just left a rousing performance of César Franck's Sonata for Violin and Piano in A Major. The second movement ended with an energetic flourish from the soloist, as probably intended by Franck. A few people in the audience applauded, while the rest of the audience glared at them.

Why would composers write something that seems to demand applause if they don't want applause then?
You have hit on one of the myths of our time: the idea that applause is not appropriate between movements. In the case of this piece, most likely Franck not only expected the

audience to clap but would have been disappointed if they had not.

In fact, until the twentieth century clapping was the norm. Beethoven, for example, probably expected that if a movement ended with a flourish, as the first movement of the Fifth Piano Concerto does, the audience would leap to its feet and let the performer and composer know they appreciated the piece.

Brahms reportedly complained when an audience failed to applaud between movements of his compositions, and Mozart wrote that it was a sign the audience loved a piece when they demanded an encore before it was over.

The current practice of not clapping between movements did not really become institutionalized until the 1950s or 1960s. Where this practice originated is open to debate. For example, Wagner was not a fan of audiences interrupting his music with applause, but Wagner was not a fan of too much of anything that others did.

Instead, it seems that the most likely source was Leopold Stokowski in Philadelphia in the 1930s. He supposedly shushed the audience once when they clapped between movements and told them that he thought the practice of clapping was more appropriate to the Middle Ages. It seems that he was actually against *all* clapping in concerts, even at the end of the composition.

The practice truly goes against our common instincts. So often a movement ends with the flourish described above only to be met with an awkward silence by the audience. This is not a feeling that leads to having an aesthetic experience.

The only reasons I have heard given for this practice is that clapping breaks the concentration of the musicians and interrupts the recording of the work. The latter reason may have some validity, and restraint could be in order when the performance is being recorded. However, the idea of concentration doesn't seem to hold much water.

I spoke to several of my faculty members; none of them felt applause would hurt their concentration, and many felt it is time for a change. Emanuel Ax wrote on his blog:

> I really hope we can go back to the feeling that applause should be an emotional response to the music, rather than a regulated social duty. I am always a little taken aback when I hear the first movement of a concerto which is supposed to be full of excitement, passion, and virtuoso display (like the Brahms or Beethoven Concertos), and then hear a rustling of clothing, punctuated by a few coughs; the sheer force of the music calls for a wild audience reaction.

The *LA Times* has several times called for a relaxing of the rules to return applause to a more natural response. Still, it has become such an imbedded convention, in such a short time, that I wonder how it will ever change back to the way it was intended.

However, a warning if you are going to make it your mission to break this convention. You have to be a pretty confident individual to go ahead and applaud. I was at Disney Hall a few weeks back, and a few people insisted on clapping between movements. Oh my, the dagger looks they received! This type of independence is not for the faint of heart.

Last Wednesday, my wife and I went to the opera. There was applause by the audience at the beginning of each act of La Rondine. Then to our surprise the performers

came out to take a bow at the end of each act, not just at
end of the entire performance. I had always been told
that when attending classical music, you clap only at
the end of the entire piece. Was this break in tradition
because **La Rondine** *is considered an operetta, or is*
something else going on? A special idea by the director
or just a coincidence?

Here is yet another question about the mystery of classical
music concerts: to applaud or not to applaud. In this case
the answer is quite simply that the rules are different for
opera than for symphonic music, and that is why you heard
applause when you would not normally expect it.

The reason you heard applause at the beginning of
each act is that oftentimes an opera audience simply likes
the look of the set and production design and applauds its
appearance in each act. Not long ago this seemed to be truly
spontaneous; it was almost a response to the audience's gasp
when the curtains first opened. Unfortunately, it has become
such a convention that clapping even for a ho-hum set seems
to be expected. Too often now the applause is of the polite
variety instead of the truly spontaneous, somewhat like the
mandatory applause after each solo in a jazz concert.

As for the bows at the end of each act, the company
you saw was following a very traditional custom in many
European houses and some bigger US houses: having the
principal singers take bows after each act. Whether to do
this or not is at the discretion of the music director.

This question touches on a bigger, more philosophical
question when it comes to opera. There is a long tradition
of placing a great value on the singer-audience relationship in opera. Bringing the singers to the front of the stage
allows another audience-performer interaction.

As positive as this sounds, not everyone agrees with it, and some fear it can go too far. Tenor Juan Diego Flórez recently received a lot of press for immediately repeating the famous aria in Donizetti's *La fille du régiment* (the one with the nine high Cs) at the Metropolitan Opera in response to the audience's applause. There was discussion in the press that the Met had allowed the tenor to break its policy prohibiting this older practice of repeating arias when the public demanded it.

While I am generally opposed to *anything* that lengthens an opera, I find the current movement to be more relevant and in touch with the audience and thus very positive. While this outburst at the Met was shocking for some, it really is a sign of the times. I see it as an attempt to assure that these great works do not become museum pieces but remain vibrant and responsive to today's audiences.

There is one other point that should be mentioned on this topic, one unique to *La Rondine*. The chorus appears only in act 2. Therefore when this is performed, the chorus is often given a bow at the end of its last act rather than keep it waiting downstairs till the end of the show.

Many years ago, I heard a concert in which Yehudi Menuhin played at least a dozen encores and another in which Andrés Segovia played almost as many. In contrast, I recently heard one of America's best-known pianists stingily give only one. What factors determine how many encores an artist is willing or able to give? Clearly it's not just audience enthusiasm.

After attending concerts for decades, I can honestly say that there seem to be no rules or standards when it comes encores. I talked with two faculty members who are international performing artists, and their answers were quite different, confirming this inconsistency.

The idea of an encore dates back at least to the seventeenth century. In those days the audiences at operas would demand to hear a favorite aria again by shouting "encore," which means "again" in French. In the days before recordings this was the only way for an audience to hear a favorite piece when one hearing was not enough. The opera soloist would oblige, and almost no one seemed to care that the storyline was being interrupted or delayed. In many ways it was the "instant replay" of its day. But not everyone approved of this practice. I have heard that Franz Joseph Haydn, for one, during a performance of his *Creation* in 1799, pleaded with the audience to refrain from requesting encores to keep from distracting from the work's dramatic effect.

Despite the objections of some, the practice grew in popularity and was eventually extended to all soloists, both vocal and instrumental. By the mid-twentieth century the encore was so well established that some audience members felt cheated if they did not get at least one encore from a favorite artist.

Today, encores are not as automatic as they were just a few years ago. There are many reasons for this, and several of these get to the heart of the question.

First of all, it seems that most soloists do have two or three short pieces they keep current in their repertoire specifically for encores. These are short pieces that can be played without added rehearsal time or excessive stress on the performer.

But deciding whether to play an encore or not and, if so, how many, depends on the audience, the type of concert, the venue, the maestro, the soloist, the union rules, and the concert format.

If the concert is a solo concert—in other words, if there is only the soloist (as in a piano recital) or soloist and accompanist (as in a vocal or violin recital)—it seems the encore is almost automatic. The artist prepares an encore and plans to perform it. The only way this would not happen is if the audience applauds so little that the soloist cannot make it back to the stage or if the soloist was having health or other issues and was just happy to be able to finish the concert.

I have been to many recitals where because the audience's response was not particularly enthusiastic, the soloist sang the encore immediately after the first bow. Sometimes you can feel (but not hear) a groan from the audience. But most know to expect it.

When the soloist is performing with an orchestra—for example, in a violin or piano concerto—things get fuzzier. First, the concerto is often programmed in the first half of the concert, and it seems a bit odd to have an encore before the intermission. Plus it creates the somewhat awkward situation of having the entire orchestra sitting on stage during the encore.

Whether the soloist performs an encore in this scenario depends largely on the artist and the type of concert. If the artist is a world-renowned soloist, it can be assumed that many in the audience purchased a ticket primarily to see him or her. If so, they would expect an encore. Also, if the event is a gala concert to open or close a season or celebrate some major event, the encore is likely to happen.

Outside of those scenarios it is usually up to the soloist *and* the artistic director whether or not the encore will happen. Some artists just prefer not to do them. Some artistic directors feel it takes too much attention away from the other musicians of the orchestra. It also depends on the overall length of the concert. Union rules for musicians are very strict. If the concert's length approaches the time limits of the union contract, allowing an encore might force the management to pay overtime to the entire orchestra even though the musicians just sit on the stage during the encore.

This is exactly what happened to one Thornton faculty member. After playing a piano concerto early in his career, the audience's ovation called him back to the stage three times. He did what seemed natural: sat down at the piano and played a short Scarlatti sonata. Upon walking off the stage, beaming, he was shocked to see the executive director of the orchestra looking quite unhappy. He then learned that because of his "outburst," the concert would now go over the time limit, and the entire orchestra would be paid overtime at the union rate. He was never invited to perform with that orchestra again. Despite now having an international reputation, he always defers to the conductor as to whether or not to perform an encore.

Hall acoustics being what they are, the topic must be a major issue with performers. Is it a matter of concern and discussion amongst the faculty? Are there artistic considerations that a conductor must take into account depending on the venue, or are they just "doomed" to whatever acoustics they are given by the gods?

There are definitely changes that an orchestra can make when adjusting to a new hall that may have less-than-desirable acoustics. To help with this process of adjustment, the assistant conductor, who sits in an audience seat during rehearsals, becomes essential. It is this person's ear that the orchestra must trust, because many times it can be extremely difficult to discern the true acoustics of a hall from the stage.

Every hall is different in that regard, different for the musicians and, many times, very different for the conductor. What sounds to the conductor on the podium like a well-balanced orchestra may be something completely different from what's actually heard in the hall.

Depending on what the assistant conductor says, there are easy adjustments that can be made by the musicians instantly. For example, the assistant, finding that the brass generally overpower the strings, may simply tells the conductor to have the brass section take everything down a dynamic. The same is true for any other section in the ensemble. This can often happen within a section as well. Sometimes the violins are strongly heard, yet the hall picks up the lower strings less well. Again, this is something that musicians can modify by adjusting their dynamics, or the volumes at which they play.

Musicians can easily make other adjustments through articulation. For instance, if a hall is very "live" and boomy (like playing in a church), the musicians can make sure to play their notes on the shorter side so as not to sound muffled or "mushy." The opposite works in drier halls; there the players can make sure their shorter notes are "rounder," played with a touch more length. In these cases it is the conductor who makes these determinations on the spot, with the help of the assistant conductors, and instructs the orchestra members how to alter what has already been rehearsed.

There are also physical changes that can be made to the hall. The idea of adjustable acoustics in halls, while somewhat controversial, is quite common. In these halls, curtains, ceiling panels, and even the walls themselves can be moved to best suit the ensemble and type of music being performed.

Even in halls without adjustable acoustics, the actual orchestra or ensemble can be positioned on the stage differently to overcome or take better advantage of the hall's acoustical properties.

Yes, the acoustics of every performance venue are different. Part of being a seasoned musician or conductor is knowing how to alter what you do to make the most of the physical environment handed to you.

Were I to borrow a time machine and go back and pick up Ludwig van Beethoven, escorting him to the early twenty-first century, what would he probably think of

    a.   *the quality of the current orchestra musicians?*
    b.   *the talents of instrumental soloists?*
    c.   *the capabilities of a modern piano?*
    d.   *the various genres of modern music, such as jazz, big band, folk, rock, movies, musicals?*

I first answer your question by posing one of my own: From whom will you borrow a time machine? I would love to be able to go back and experience some famous concerts for myself, so please let me know.

Now let's answer your question. It's pretty safe to say that Beethoven would be pleased by the modern leading symphony orchestras compared to those in Vienna in his day. Today's concert halls are (arguably) better acoustically, the instruments (especially the non-string variety) are far better, and the players are more specialized and better able to devote themselves fully to orchestral playing. All of these factors support the premise that today's performances are most likely better than performances of the past.

That being said, Beethoven would have to get used to different playing techniques and a very different sound from today's instruments. Providing he could adjust, he would most likely be very impressed.

He would also most likely feel that today's soloists are superior to those with whom he worked. Beethoven's music was considered cutting edge and difficult in his day. The musicians would have been struggling to play, understand, and interpret his music. Today, his music is standard repertoire for musicians. Today's soloists benefit from the generations of performers before them who brought these works to life. Second of all, as just noted above, the instruments of today for soloists are better. Even vintage instruments maintained over time have been altered and improved.

The situation is not as clear-cut when we get to the piano. Beethoven would probably be partly pleased with the modern concert grand piano, but he might regret a certain loss in delicacy of tone present in the old Viennese instruments with their wooden bracing, small hammers, leather covers, and availability of various muting effects.

The modern piano, developed well after Beethoven's day, is intended to fill a large hall. Certainly he would like the durability of the modern piano compared to the fragility of the old ones, but I think the jury is still out on whether this would counterbalance the extreme difference in sound.

It is pretty clear that if Beethoven suddenly were confronted with atonal music, jazz, rock, or movie music, it would be hard for him to understand any of it. All great music reflects its time and culture, and Beethoven would not have the cultural context to process our contemporary music. Plus, we accept our music partly because we know what came before. We understand a certain progression. If he were presented with any of today's music, there would be an almost two-hundred-year musical gap for him to have to fill in. That gap would seem impossible to overcome, even for a musical genius like Beethoven.

Relatedly, people speculate as to what Beethoven (or Mozart or any other great composer) would be doing if he were born today. It is often argued that Beethoven and the others, if they lived today, would be pop musicians rather than classical ones. That's a nice idea but doesn't seem very logical. There was certainly a lighter type of music in existence in Beethoven's day (e.g., Italian operas or the folk or popular music heard in restaurants and inns). Beethoven seems to have had disdain for this type of music and seemed very conscious of a distinction between high art and the popular taste. He was not averse to making money with the latter, but he placed the greatest value on the former. He was something of a snob. Of course, since he was a great improviser he might have found jazz to be an interesting challenge.

Of course, all of this is speculation. Please hurry up and borrow that time machine and report back.

Recently, a friend sent me photos taken at a relative's 103rd birthday party, where the former chanteuse was highly praised. The singer doesn't look any older than seventy, and my friend says she has never had cosmetic surgery. This information triggered a look at other, older singers' faces, and sure enough, they all look great! So do fifty-plus years of singing address facial flab in a positive way? If so, perhaps some will be encouraged to take up the musical arts for purely personal reasons!

To get an answer to this question, I had to leave the faculty of the Thornton School and head over to USC's Keck School of Medicine. There I spoke with a well-regarded plastic surgeon, who was very helpful.

A youthful face has smooth skin, a strong jawline, and elevated fat pads—commonly called cherub cheeks. Further, the eyebrows are situated above the orbit, which is the socket in the skull where the eyes sit. You know orbits; they are the spooky holes you see in skulls at Halloween.

As we age, there are changes at multiple tissue levels, including skin, fat, bone, and muscle. We see these changes as wrinkles and drooping, sagging skin around the eyes and the neck and at the jowl. Loss of fat can result in a sallow appearance around the cheeks and eyes. Recent studies have shown that bone loss plays a very significant role in the gaunt appearance of a face. Additionally, loss of normal muscle elasticity can result in neck sagging.

Considering that a vocalist keeps his or her facial muscles, particularly those in the neck, in shape, it is reasonable to assume that maintaining normal muscle tone may prevent sagging of the muscles around the mouth and the neck. Since the muscles are attached to bones and active muscle use can keep bones strong and healthy, it is reasonable to assume that the neck and the lower face may avoid a sagging appearance by "keeping in shape" in accordance with the rigors of being a vocalist.

Before we get too excited about this, it is important to note that these effects might be more pronounced in making a hundred-year-old person look seventy than a fifty-year-old look thirty-five. This is so because most of the effect is probably due more to bone loss in the jaw and cheek and has less to do with reduced muscle sagging and other chronic skin changes that happen with time. The bone-loss phenomenon is more pronounced at increased age, thus the effects of singing are more pronounced later in life.

But don't give up on singing. Regardless of the effect on the face, imagine how helpful it would be for your spirits to sing everyday.

There have been a number of studies on the salutary impact of music instruction on the young. Have there been comparable studies on the potential impact of music instruction on the geriatric generations?

Yes, there have. In fact, many of these are being conducted at the Brain and Creativity Institute at USC, but it is also becoming a major area of study all over the United States and worldwide.

There is now a mounting body of evidence that participating in music, especially reading from notation, can help senior citizens with

- memory
- depression
- mental ability
- physical ability
- social skills

When you think about it, this really should not be a great surprise to anyone. When you consider the mental and coordinative skills that are required for playing music, it would almost be more surprising if the research showed there was no benefit. Keeping the brain and muscles active is key to healthy aging, and playing music involves both to a very intricate degree.

I find interesting the fact that reading from notation is so important. For example, playing songs on the piano that you have known for years, while beneficial, does not have the same effect as learning a new song from reading notation. This points to the complexity of reading notation and suggests that it is the mental exercise that seems to be most beneficial.

I am currently a member of a dissertation committee for a doctoral student in gerontology who is comparing several thousand adult twins, of which one does music and one does not. While her results are not finalized yet, it shows how this type of research is conducted and how extensively some studies are being conducted.

Most of these results revolve around performing music. What is less clear is what effect *listening* to music has on aging. Listening has been shown to help somewhat with memory, but that is more along the lines of reminding someone of a point in her life and helping her to remember it or relive it. While important, it seems that active participation in music is what makes the biggest impact.

I love the whistling in Ennio Morricone's score to* The Good, the Bad, and the Ugly, *and now I associate whistling with the American West. Do other cultures whistle music for enjoyment?

Yes, that is a wonderful use of whistling, but let's not forget Bing Crosby's superb whistling in "White Christmas" during the film *Holiday Inn*, which was supposed to take place in Connecticut. So just from movies, we know whistling covers the entire United States.

But it does go further—in fact, seemingly worldwide and across many diverse cultures. For example, it is common to hear men whistling while working in Bulgaria and Hungary. In Ireland there is a specific art of whistling that is very highly regarded. One faculty member remembers hearing a bicycle man who pedaled around Agra, India, whistling tunes from American movies. There are recordings of whistling by Akan (men) in Ghana and as part of Ngoma performances in Tanzania.

Not all whistling is the same. For example, African whistling is much less melodic than we hear in the West. It sounds almost percussive and has smacking sounds. However, most of the rest of the world sounds pretty similar to what we hear here. In other words, whistlers in Asia do not produce a more nasal sound corresponding to how they alter the singing voice.

Interestingly, in all cultures, including that of the United States, men seem more inclined to whistle than women. I have no idea why this is so.

What considerations go into deciding what music will be played in an orchestral concert? Who makes the decision? How does one concert in a series relate to the season as a whole (if at all)?

The easy answer to this question is that it is ultimately the music director of an orchestra who is responsible for programming an orchestra's season. However, the amount of negotiation and compromise that takes place varies dramatically by organization.

A common procedure has the music director pondering the artistic vision for the season. He or she shares this with a small cohort of colleagues that includes artistic administrators (who are in contact with various artists' managements), the marketing team, and technical staff. When preparing the proposed season, many variables are taken into account.

For starters, a grand scheme for the season is conceived. Each season must start with an exciting opening concert that is "welcoming" and end with a closing concert that is "culminating." Next, any special projects the orchestra is planning or special anniversaries of historical events, specific works, or composers are taken into account. Finally, the season is outlined according to the ebb and flow of a typical season so as to account for pre-holiday concerts that sell well and early January concerts that sell poorly and devise concerts that excite audiences during ticket and renewal times.

After this rough skeleton of the season is complete, decisions are made regarding what soloists to use and how. The music director must be careful not to schedule too many piano concertos but not enough violin or cello concertos (unless the artistic theme for the year overrides such balancing). From there the decision is made as to what soloists to approach for specific concerts and ascertaining their availability on appropriate dates.

Next the real work begins. The music director, as the keeper of the artistic "brand" or "mission" of the orchestra, must fill in the remaining concerts to further this identity. He or she must balance how much music to perform from the many different time periods of music history, including music of today's composers and music of different cultures and countries, and critically, must balance what will challenge and please the players with what will challenge and please the audience.

Finally, each individual concert is crafted, with the size of the venue, the length and flow of each concert, the compatibility of individual pieces, the rehearsal time available and the size of the orchestra for each concert, and a host of other very practical issues all kept in mind.

The goal is for every concert in a season to be a piece of a much larger artistic mosaic that is the entire season. Also, each entire season is part of a larger mosaic that is the overall artistic identity of the orchestra.

After all this work, which is done years in advance of when you actually hear a concert, there are two important next steps. First, the season will be presented to an artistic committee (if there is one) for approval, then it goes for final approval to the budget committee or board of directors. If the season is deemed too expensive or artistically lacking, it is sent back for tweaking or major renovation.

So as one can surmise, putting even a single program together takes a wealth of thought and consideration by many partners. Putting a season together is a Herculean task and is done years in advance. Many music directors will tell you that they know more readily what will be performed on a specific concert two to three years hence than what is being performed next month. That is because their mental and artistic energy is at the service of long-term planning.

Perhaps the best analogy to this whole thing would be what a master chef might do to create a great restaurant. However, add to this that he or she would have to plan every night's dinner two or three years in advance, deciding how the courses would complement one another, planning what ingredients would be available each night, with the goal of creating a splendid dining experience with a unique overriding character and identity for the restaurant.

Is there an optimal age to start music instruction? Can you start too young? Are the teenage years too late?

Once again, this is an easy-sounding question with a complicated answer. In this case the answer depends completely on what is meant by "music instruction." For most people "music instruction" translates to "learning to play an instrument." In that case the answer is yes, a person *can* start too young, and no, the teenage years are not too late. However, if we change "music instruction" to "age-appropriate music instruction," the answer changes completely to no, you cannot start too young, and yes, the teenage years are too late. Let me elaborate.

There is a body of research that indicates that we are all born with an aptitude for music. In other words, all of us have some degree of musical aptitude (commonly called talent) when we are born. However, if this aptitude is not *nurtured* from birth, it does not develop and is lost. Many researchers feel that if one's natural aptitude is not nurtured in the first seven years of life (or for some, nine), it is lost forever. No quantity of lessons or training later will make up for what was lost.

The question then becomes a matter of how to nurture a child's musical aptitude. It does not mean to put a trumpet in the child's crib. Instead, it means providing age-appropriate musical activities for the first years of life, beginning at birth. For infants these activities could be listening, moving, singing, being sung to, and specific structured musical activities. There are several structured programs for children (and usually their parents) that specialize in providing age-appropriate learning. Kindermusic is one example of this type of instruction, but there are many available.

At about age three to five, some instrument training can begin—but again, only if done appropriately. Children of this age usually begin with a string instrument, piano, or guitar. The goal of this instruction is not necessarily to learn to play that particular instrument for life. Instead, the instrument is a vehicle for learning more concrete aspects of music and performance. One of the most popular programs, the Suzuki method, utilizes the violin, cello, or piano. However, even this excellent program was never meant as a way to learn violin, cello, or piano. The full name of the program says it all: the Suzuki Talent Education. The instruments are used to give a child appropriate musical activities that can be transferred to any instrument later. Once a child has the physical skills to try other, more physically challenging instruments, such as the brass instruments, he or she has a great musical foundation that can be transferred.

Unfortunately, if nothing is done prior to, say, the teenage years, it is probably too late for a child to truly excel. It is much like riding a bike or learning a second language. While you can learn to do this later in life, it will never be natural. On the other hand, we live in a society where it is unlikely that anyone will have no childhood music experiences, so some nurturing is probably taking place in every child.

I hope you can see that it is never too early to begin age-appropriate music instruction, but it can be too late (I address this issue in much more detail in an earlier book, *Raising Musical Kids: A Parent's Guide*, published by Oxford University Press).

Is it ever too late to start music lessons? Do you know of anyone who has taken up an instrument at an advanced age—say, after sixty—who has acquired more than just average skills?
As I explained in answering the last question, much will depend on what types of musical experiences the adult had

as a child. Let's assume that the adult had a rich musical childhood but never really worked much with an instrument or, as is often the case, ceased playing an instrument when he or she got to the teenage years.

In this scenario one is never too old to begin to learn or revisit an instrument, with the following caveat. Since playing instruments is a physical endeavor, the natural aging process and its corresponding decreases in ability will certainly interfere with the learning process. Arthritis, especially in the fingers, can really interfere with playing.

The second caveat is that the chances of becoming a world-class performer are stacked against the adult learner simply because the time to do so is limited. A child beginning at age five has twenty to twenty-five years to mature, develop, and progress. An adult beginning at sixty simply doesn't have the same time luxury.

However, I doubt many sixty-year-olds begin playing an instrument with the dream of becoming a world-class performer. Instead, the learning is probably for the enjoyment and rewards it provides to the player. In this case, age should not be much of a stumbling block.

Even if the adult was not exposed to music as a child, learning to play is still possible. Unfortunately, learning to play will be much more difficult, and in my experience, the performance will never flow naturally and musically.

I recently had the wonderful experience of attending an entire piano recital given by a friend who is in his seventies. While he took lessons as a child, he did not return to playing until he retired, when he was sixty-two. The recital was exceptionally well played. Likewise, I attended a string quartet recital given by adults in their seventies. Three of the four musicians began playing their instruments (viola, violin, cello) for the first time in their late fifties and early sixties. They had all played other instruments as kids but had been able to learn these new instruments quite respectably. The fourth musician had played violin her whole life but never professionally.

Clearly, there is no reason (except physical ones) that adults cannot start learning an instrument later in life. This is especially true if they played an instrument in childhood or had rich musical experiences. I believe the rewards of making music will be as great, if not greater, later in life.

While recently watching a YouTube video of someone playing Bach's Fugue BWV 542 on the organ, I was surprised to see in a close-up that some of the keys on a lower keyboard were going up and down by themselves while the fingers of the organist were busy depressing the keys of another keyboard at an upper level. Was this caused by the organist using his feet to play what seem to be even more keys down below, or was it the ghost of Bach helping the organist?

To answer this question, we first need to define some terms.

The first term is "manual." The official term for an organ keyboard is a "manual." In regard to organs, the words "manual" and "keyboard" can be used interchangeably.

There are usually at least two manuals (keyboards) on pipe organs, but they can have many more. The largest organs can have five, six, or even seven manuals. These manuals are "stacked" one on top of another and usually have sixty-one keys each.

The next term is "rank." A rank is a specific set of pipes on the organ with a specific sound, such as brass, strings, flutes, and the like. Every key on a manual has a pipe tuned to a specific pitch, say B♭. If there were an organ with *one* pipe tuned to every key on *one* manual, it would be an organ with one rank and would have 61 pipes. However, what makes the pipe organ so dramatic is that pipes can be made to have different sounds. If the first rank of pipes sounds like trumpets, a second rank can be made to sound like strings. This organ, with two ranks, would have 122 pipes (61 times 2). A third rank could be made to sound like flutes. This organ would have 183 pipes (61 times 3). How many ranks an organ has is often a matter of cost and available space. Ten ranks is not unusual (610 pipes), with the largest organ ever constructed being the Boardwalk Hall Auditorium organ in Atlantic City, New Jersey. This organ contains an astonishing 449 ranks, or 33,114 pipes.

The last term is "stops." Stops are the button-shaped levers that can be seen on each side of the manuals and underneath them. Each stop activates one rank of pipes. If the trumpet stop is pulled out for the first manual, all the keys on that manual will sound like trumpets. If the flute stop is pulled out for the second manual, all the keys on that manual will sound like flutes. Playing on both keyboards will produce a blend of trumpet and flute sounds. Multiple stops can be pulled out at any given time to produce combinations of sounds.

Now we can address the actual question. An organist might have one manual set with a specific combination of stops and another manual with another set of stops to produce exactly the sound that is desired. However, we can go further.

Since there are often more than two manuals on an organ and organists have, at most, two hands, it becomes impossible to take advantage of some of the pitch combinations on the other keyboards. This is why on many organs the manuals can be coupled. In this way, to take a single example, the unique setup of manual no. 1 can be combined with the unique setup of manual no. 3 to produce a totally new sound. When these two manuals are coupled, the actual keys on the coupled manual will move up and down in mirror fashion to what the organist is playing on the other manual.

So while the "ghost of Bach" answer would be much more intriguing and much easier to understand, in fact what you were seeing is the result of manuals being coupled. Of course, if the performance was in a haunted house, then all bets are off.

A friend told me that the phrase "pull out all the stops" had something to do with music. Is this true?

I will "go for broke" on this answer and say your friend was correct. On a pipe organ, every time the organist pulls out a stop, another rank of pipes is added to the sound. If two stops are pulled out, the number of pipes playing (and thus the volume) is doubled. If three stops are pulled out, the sound is tripled; four stops, quadrupled; and so on.

If you pull out *all* the stops on an organ, you activate every single available pipe for each key. It can't get any bigger or louder than this. So when the organist is pushing the limits of the organ sound to its max, he or she pulls out all the stops.

This phrase has morphed into common usage, where it means to go full force or without any limitations.

Do people remember pitches? When somebody announces a piece that I know, the opening phrase pops into

my mind. When the piece actually starts, it turns out that very often the opening note matches the chord in my mind; they are in tune with me. The question is, am I really remembering the pitch, or does my mind immediately pop into tune with whatever I'm hearing?

When I used to teach the class "The Psychology of Music" to graduate students, this was a topic that was always intriguing on many levels. Most people don't think much about this, and when they do, they start realizing just how amazing the brain can be when working with music.

First of all, for the sake of simplicity let's completely ignore the fact that some people have what is commonly called "perfect pitch." Those folks can actually hear a pitch, such as C♯ and know it is a C♯ as readily as the rest of us can see the color red and know it is red. Let's forget about them for the moment.

For the average person, the brain does not necessarily remember actual pitches to a melody. When you think about it, this makes sense. If you hear the tune for "Happy Birthday" or "Jingle Bells," you recognize it as such even though you rarely hear the song performed in the same key from performance to performance. Since you are hearing the song in different keys each time, the actual pitches are different as well. Still, we recognize the song. Think about that a moment, and you will appreciate what an amazing feat that is.

The same is true as you sing either of those songs. Again, rarely will you sing them in the same key unless you are singing to an accompaniment. If you are at a birthday party or out caroling, you will sing the song in the key that is either provided or where the group decides it should be. Still, you are able to sing it with totally new pitches from the last time you performed it.

The reason for this is complicated, but basically it is because the brain remembers the relationships between the pitches and not the pitches themselves. If the first three pitches of a song go up by one step each and then jump down by two steps, that is what is remembered.

The relationships between the pitches create what is called the contour of a melody. You can visualize this fairly easily. Picture a melody printed as notes. They go up and down on the staff. Now imagine that you draw a red line connecting each of the notes, being careful to draw the line *through* the note where it sits on the staff. When you step back and look at the red line, you will see essentially a line graph of melody. This, the melody's contour, is what our brains remember. Any melody that matches this contour, regardless of the starting note, will be recognized as that song.

But wait! This questioner said that he or she often does start singing the melody on the right note. That would seem counter to what I just explained. That is because there is another phenomenon in play.

Some pieces are *always* performed in the same key. This is especially true in classical music, but some standard songs, such as the national anthem, are also often performed in the same key. It is not surprising that the questioner states that he or she mentally sings the piece when the title is heard. This changes everything, because singing involves muscles and muscles have their own memory.

What is happening here is that the person has sung the piece in the past, probably many times, always in the same key. When the title is mentioned, the muscles of the throat can immediately remember how it felt to sing it. At this point, the throat muscles send these messages to the brain, the brain remembers what pitches are associated with the feeling, and the pitch is remembered.

I would venture to say that this same phenomenon does not happen with popular music that has been performed and recorded by multiple artists (and thus most likely is heard repeatedly in different keys). In fact, I see no way it *could* happen with songs of this nature.

There is a fun activity to demonstrate how this all works. Imagine a song, any song, and listen to it in your head. You are hearing it either by remembering the contour or through muscle memory in throat or fingers (if you had ever played it on an instrument). Take a moment and do that now.

Now try hearing the melody again, but this time have it get louder and louder in your memory as the melody goes along. Go ahead and try it.

You were not able to hear it get louder. You may have tried to make it *appear* louder by distorting the sound, but it did not get louder. That is because the volume is not remembered with either the muscles or the contour. Thus, we cannot seem to re-create volume changes in memory.

This is just a glimpse into some of the amazing ways the brain works with music. It truly has its own unique processes for dealing with the music we hear. At the end of the day, developing these critical mental functions is the true reason everyone should have some involvement with music when young. (But that is a completely different topic!)

At different concerts and with different orchestras, I've noticed that sometimes all the violins are on the left of the stage, with the cello section on the right, and other times the first violins are on the left and the seconds are on the right, with the cellos and violas in the middle, surrounded by winds and brasses. Who decides the arrangement of the orchestra, and what are the determining factors? Is it the music to be played? The conductor's wishes? A change in sonority and resonance? The acoustics of the hall?

This can be a very perplexing phenomenon for concert-goers. Just when you think you know your orchestra and where to look for favorite players or instruments, they change it all up. Most audience members are surprised, because it is a common belief that there is one and only one standard way to seat an orchestra. Music appreciation books often further this belief by printing a chart showing how an orchestra should be seated. But there is no official standard. However, the conductor is not altering the seating *just* to confuse you. There are historical, acoustical, and compositional reasons for the shifts.

From the historical perspective, it is important to appreciate that until the twentieth century there was not much interaction between orchestras. Players in the Paris or London or Berlin orchestras would have studied with teachers in those cities, used the instruments common in those cities, and sat in the orchestra in the location that was common in that particular town.

In the twentieth century, orchestras, but especially their conductors, started to become much more international. Orchestras toured other countries, conductors acted as guest conductors to multiple orchestras, and musicians auditioned for orchestras all over the world. Thus, some standardization began.

Today there is an awareness of the importance of trying to be as historically accurate as possible when performing music from earlier eras. One way to help assure this is to have the orchestra seated in the manner it would have been when a composition was first performed.

Next certain composers or compositions suggest a certain seating pattern. One great example is in the last movement of Tchaikovsky's Sixth Symphony, where the melody is divided between the first and second violins. Your brain puts the melody together from the two parts, but if you heard either the first violins or the second violins alone, you would hear the melody in neither. Tchaikovsky orchestrated the melody this way to make it seem broader, more full, than if it were played by just one section.

Separating the first and second violins on stage can expand this effect. Thus, sometimes you will see the orchestra members actually rearrange themselves prior to performing this piece.

Lastly, there are acoustic reasons. Each performance hall has its unique characteristics. An orchestra gets "home team advantage" by arranging itself to take advantage of the hometown acoustics.

The music director or principal conductor is the person who decides all of this for the orchestra. So even if there is a guest conductor, the arrangement will normally not change. However, even this is somewhat negotiable for prominent guest conductors.

Does what instrument a student plays enter into the Thornton School's decision on whether or not to accept him or her?
Admission to a music school is based on a wide range of factors, and yes, instrument type is certainly one of the most important.

All college or university admission procedures are quite fascinating, but the "layers" that music schools need to add make the admission procedures for music one of the most unique and specialized on campus. In fact, years ago I taught at a university that was introducing new software to handle the admission process. They chose the music school to test it out because they felt "if it will work for something as complicated as music, it will work for everyone."

When a school of music accepts its freshman class or graduate class, it has to take into account the needs of the school. The best analogy would be selecting the football team on campus. You can't have all quarterbacks and no linebackers. If in any given year you have too many quarterbacks applying and too few linebackers, you may reject some great quarterbacks and relax the requirement for linebackers.

So too with music schools. We have an orchestra, chamber music ensemble, jazz ensembles, an opera program, and popular music ensembles to create. If we accept too many jazz drummers and not enough jazz bass players in any given year, we will have trouble creating the proper jazz combos. If we have too many flutists and not enough oboists, we can't put together balanced wind quintets. If we have too many sopranos and not enough tenors, we can't stage full operas. This type of decision is true of every instrument in the school. We must keep certain balances or the school will not function, and then we cannot provide the quality experiences the students need.

Therefore, we have strict targets for every instrument in the school every year. Interestingly the students who are applying vary in instruments and quality every year. It almost seems like wine, with vintage years in certain types of grapes. Certain years we see an abundance of excellent cellists, but it might be a lean year, in either quantity or quality, for trumpet. The next year we might see a bumper group of sopranos, and the next year contraltos.

With this ebb and flow, we are constantly altering our targets. If we have a large group of percussionists one year, we accept fewer the next year. If we have two years out of balance in any one instrument or voice, it is very difficult to get the school back in balance, so we try very hard to never have two bumper years or two poor years.

What this means for the applicant is that there is no absolute level for admission to the school that is constant year to year (although there is certainly a minimum level under which we never accept an applicant). The applicant's chances of admission are related to (1) the needs of the school, (2) the size of the previous year's class, and (3) the quality of the other students who apply that year.

As unfair as it sounds, a student who is denied this year might have been accepted last year, and vice versa. To make matters worse, this same phenomenon can influence how large a scholarship offer the student receives as well.

At the highest levels of music schools, the competition for the best students is international. Here it also matters what instrument the applicant plays. All schools seem to have the same areas that are traditionally very competitive. These are violin, cello, bassoon, oboe, horn, and the tenor and baritone voices in the classical area and bass and guitar in the jazz area.

However, it is important to understand that you cannot relax the admission standards just because an instrument is needed. There is an old saying that "you can't hide in a music school." Unlike a more academic area, where a weaker student could sit in the back of the class and earn constant grades of C without affecting the education of the other students in the class, the same is not true of music. All students play in an ensemble and in chamber music groups, and if they are not up to the playing level of the students around them, the entire group will be held back, and everyone will know why.

Therefore, if you are looking to increase your chances of getting into a music school and getting a good scholarship, playing certain instruments will make you more in demand. However, at the end of the day, you have to be able to play at the level of the other students in the school on day one and every day after.

The admission process for a music school, especially the premiere schools, is much more an art than a science. It is a constant, never-ending balancing act to keep the school healthy and the student's musical opportunities intact.

I am curious: how does the USC Thornton School of Music pick which piano to buy for its concert halls and practice rooms? Since taste in tone and touch can be so subjective and varied when it's time to buy a new piano, who picks it out?

You are absolutely correct that an artist's taste in a piano is a very personal thing. Therefore, when we are purchasing a piano for a public area, such as a recital hall or practice room, much thought goes into the selection.

We buy many Steinways, and therefore I will tell you how we purchase those. When we are ready to purchase pianos (we tend to wait until we can buy a few at one time), we send our head piano technician and one member of the piano faculty to New York to Steinway Hall for what is called a selection. Since the pianos are handmade, they are all a bit different. When Steinway feels they have a good number of pianos that fit what we are looking for, they contact us, and we arrange the visit.

The faculty member plays several times the number of pianos that we will ultimately purchase. From those available the faculty member will choose. Since this is such an extreme responsibility on the back of the faculty member, we use a system of rotation for the selection.

While every piano has a specific character, the process of choosing is not as arbitrary as it might seem. During the selection process it is important that the faculty member know exactly where and for what purpose the piano will be used. If the hall or studio where it will live is muffled or dark, a brighter sound in the piano will be sought. Conversely if the hall is alive, a darker sound will be desired.

If the piano will be used primarily for solo performance, as opposed to chamber music, this will be taken into account. The genre of music is also a critical consideration. A piano selected for jazz will probably be drastically different from a piano chosen for chamber music. A piano for popular music will be that different again.

Here is a direct quote from one of the Thornton faculty regarding piano selection. I think he describes what he is looking for beautifully.

> When trying out new pianos I am looking for specific qualities in terms of tone, projection and to a lesser degree, response and feel. I personally prefer a piano with a warm tone, not too brittle or bright, with a capacity for the "pure" strike tone to last as long as possible. If the soundboard of the piano is not so good, the natural sustain tone will not ring or last as long. Therefore, the projection of the piano will not be so great in a concert hall.
>
> Of course all pianos have naturally inherent personalities and qualities. Some are more naturally suited as chamber music and solo recital instruments while others might fare better as

solo instruments with orchestra. That is where taste and specif-
ics come in. A piano may sound wonderful in one hall but be too
brash for another. A piano technician can do "a little" to tweak an
instrument one way or another but the actual inherent qualities
of the instrument will always prevail so it is important to choose
the right instrument for the proposed venue.

Evenness of touch, clarity of sound, sustain of single notes
in different sections of the instrument and the general dynamic
scale are critically important. I want to choose a piano with a
"bouquet" of sound having the greatest amount of colors for per-
formers to bring out and express their music.

How long does the typical concert grand last before it's replaced in a music school?

This is somewhat like asking how long a car will last. A piano is a mechanical device, much like a car, and everything depends on the quality of the instrument when it is new, the amount of use it gets, the environment in which it is used, and the amount and quality of the maintenance it receives.

High-quality instruments can last a lifetime or much more when used in a private home with proper and regular maintenance. When these instruments are put into a professional setting, the wear and tear will greatly reduce the life span. In our school, where the pianos are used almost nonstop from morning until night, we find the practical life span of our concert instruments, even with proper maintenance, is about seven years.

After that, they still may be very good instruments, but the amount of maintenance required to keep them in top-notch shape is not worth the investment. These pianos could last for many more years in a private home or even a private studio but not in a professional or semiprofessional scenario.

***Our piano tuner recommends that we tune our piano
every six months, but it doesn't seem to go out of tune
that quickly. How often do you tune the pianos in the
Thornton School? Just out of curiosity, how many pianos does the school own?***
Pianos are the backbone of any school of music. Every student uses them at some point. Students need pianos for
theory assignments, for accompaniment, or as their major
instrument. Therefore, purchase and maintenance of pianos are extremely important parts of running a school
of music. But because this is an invisible part of a music
school, people are often amazed and intrigued by what
goes on.

First of all, as already noted, our pianos are in almost
constant use from early morning until late at night; in the
practice rooms they are in use *all* night. To accommodate
the needs of the students, we own 157 pianos, and I wish
we had more. Almost all of the pianos are Steinways. We
have other brands as well, and certain faculty members
prefer one to the other, but there is a certain efficiency in
keeping to one brand of piano.

Still, try to picture what 157 pianos look like, and you
get some idea of the magnitude of the undertaking.

It may be shocking, but some of our pianos are tuned
twice a day. That is right, twice a day. These are the instruments that are used in our concert halls.

The normal schedule is that the pianos are tuned in the
morning and then are used for the dress rehearsals. They
are tuned a second time just before the concert. But they
are not only tuned; they are also voiced. A skilled technician can actually change the sound of the instrument with
adjustments, and this is called voicing. Depending on the

desire of the performer and the music that is going to be performed, the technician will voice the instrument to the performer's wishes. So it is not only tuning that is done daily but much more.

Others pianos are tuned every morning, still others once a week, and the rest are on a rotation that can go as long as six weeks between tunings. The once-a-week tunings are for pianos in the studios of the piano faculty and other high-use pianos (in the rehearsal rooms, for example).

To maintain this schedule, we have three full-time piano technicians and also a standing contract with local companies to do basic tunings on some of the pianos, because the three full-timers can't possibly handle the entire inventory. Our piano technicians start their day very early so they can be done by the time classes start at eight a.m.

In your home you certainly don't need anything this elaborate. I don't think you should use a music school's intensively used pianos and the corresponding tuning schedule as any type of indicator for your personal use. Truthfully, the six-month suggestion sounds fine to me. I have friends who get their piano tuned only once per year (these are not professionals). I would hesitate to go longer than that, however. It is not just a matter of the piano being in tune but also being maintained and under the proper pressure so it can last for its full life.

I was a linguist in the service and was taught using the oral-comprehension style of foreign-language training. The students showed up in the classroom, and the instructors just started talking to them in the language they were learning. Later, in college, I learned German the same way.

Why is music not taught that way? In* The Music Man, *Professor Harold Hill proffered the idea of the "think system": music first and theory later. Perhaps we would not have so many dropouts from musical instrument playing if we concentrated on music first.

You have hit upon one of the major areas of debate within the music-teaching profession. Just like the "nature vs. nurture" debate in regard to musical ability, this debate revolves around monikers such as "sound before symbol," "symbol before sound," and "symbol with sound." Like most things in music and education, debates rage about what is best.

The method you describe is in the sound-before-symbol camp, because the child learns the musical sounds before learning the notation, or symbols. This procedure is best exemplified in the methodologies of Suzuki. I find it is often the most misunderstood method around. Suzuki intended the method as a way to develop the natural musical ability in children by helping them learn to play the violin in the way we learn language. It was never meant as a way to solely learn to play violin or learn to read notation.

Suzuki called his method "talent education." Children listen to phrases played by the teacher on his or her violin and repeat them on their own violin. In this way children learn in much the same manner we learn language. Learning notation comes much later after the child can play by ear. In this way, the learning mirrors the way we learn to speak. Opponents of this method say it does not develop violin playing fast enough and learning notation later can be frustrating.

Another method, not as common as Suzuki but still found across the United States, is the Gordon method, commonly referred to by its commercial name "Jump Right In." This can best be described as sound with symbol. Students learn pitch and rhythm phrases that are commonly found in Western music. They see the phrases notated and recite them with certain syllables. Gordon feels that these short phrases, each sometimes two to four beats long, are the equivalent of words in language. If we learn the words, we can combine them into sentences and then into paragraphs. The same is true with music. If we learn the phrases, we can combine them into melodies and expand them into whole works. Opponents of this method say the constant repeating of the phrases outside a musical context is boring and takes the inherent joy out of music making.

The third method is symbol before sound. This method can be seen when a teacher shows a staff and has the students learn the names of the notes or teaches rhythmic notation by referring to a pie (a whole note is the whole pie, a half note is half the pie, etc.). Opponents of this system maintain that it will never lead to fluid reading of music, does not encourage students to listen to themselves playing, and does not transfer well to playing an instrument.

Some teachers feel so strongly that their way is right that if you put three people, one from each camp, in a room and lock the door, most likely only one will emerge when the door is unlocked.

So which way is best? It probably relates to what your goal is. If reading notation is really important, you will choose one way. If performing musically is your main goal, you will choose otherwise.

Which is the most used? Without a doubt most music learning is done in the way you suggest, sound before symbol. Think about songs you know: *I've Been Working on the*

Railroad, It's a Small World (after All), Happy Birthday, the national anthem, and others. You can probably sing them flawlessly but most likely have never seen them notated. In reality, this is how we learn most music throughout our lives.

Standardized tests have become a mainstay of our society. A benefit of this is virtually no one of intellectual excellence is overlooked. I worry that we are still missing many fine potential musicians. Is there any consensus as to the qualities of good musicians? Is there a standardized test for musical ability? If not, could one be developed? What would such a test look like? Could it be put online? Something like "Which of these tones matches the tone you will hear next?" or "Sing into your computer's microphone the following notes" or "Match the following rhythm by tapping on your space key."
I knew it would just be a matter of time until someone brought up standardized testing in music. Whenever we read about education in general, we hear about standardized tests. So are they useful in music?

First of all, let's examine what constitutes a standardized test. This is a test in an area, like intelligence, that is given to a large, a very large, number of people. From the answers, a norm is created. If we plotted all the scores on a graph, we would see what is called a bell curve. Most of the people's scores would fall in the middle, the average area. However, a few would score well above the norm and a few well below the norm. The tests are at their best in identifying these two extremes and don't hold much value in identifying the big area in the middle, because those scores are just basically lumped together as "average."

Theoretically, if a standardized test of musicality could be created, we could identify children at the two extremes, commonly called "gifted" and "at risk." At this point some sort of intervention could take place to challenge the gifted and nurture the at-risk children. This would be appropriate because most education, especially school-based education, is geared toward the great average middle. This is as it should be, as the goal of schools is reaching the most students, and that is where most students are.

For a test to be of value it has to be valid. In other words, there has to be general agreement that what is being tested actually relates to the subject matter. This is where the problems arise in music. What exactly can you test? You can't test playing ability because it would measure only students who play an instrument. You can't test singing ability because it would measure only children who can sing. You can't measure note reading because it would measure only students who know how to read music.

This has been the debate for at least the last century when it comes to standardized testing in music. What makes a valid test?

Still, there are a few accepted standardized tests in music. All of the existing standardized tests follow similar formats. There is always some tonal and rhythm listening. The child hears a series of tones and then hears a second set and has to determine if it is the same or different. More elaborate testing methods have the child pick out the different phrase among four presented. The same is done with rhythm.

There is one test that adds a section where the child hears two short identical musical examples. While the music is the same, the performance is different, with phrasing, tempi, balance, and other musical performance elements varied. From these performances the student is asked to choose the "better" of the two. The right answer is determined by what a panel of "experts" decides is better.

It is not a matter of whether a test can be created or not. The burning question is what do you do with the information the test produces? One test, created by Edwin Gordon, is meant to be used with his teaching materials. The teaching materials have three levels in every lesson, and you gear that musical level to the student's musical level. That is a lot of work, but it is on the right track.

At the other end of the spectrum, when I used to teach elementary school music, the school system I taught in gave every fourth grader a standardized test in music. Then— this was the controversial part—they would encourage the parents of students with "average and above" musical ability to take an instrument. The below-average students were not forbidden from taking music but were not encouraged and maybe not even told of the opportunities.

This is a horrible use of these tests. I don't think this is done much anymore (I taught elementary school in the Dark Ages), but the standardized tests continue for different reasons. I have heard that there is some thought that teacher salaries should be tied to how well their students perform on these tests. This is completely misguided. The tests will always show most students as average. That is actually one of the defining characteristics of a standardized test. If, over time, children start doing better, and more score above average, the test makers refine the test to make it harder. In an ideal test, half of the children taking the test always score above the average and half below.

These tests are meant to identify the two extremes, gifted and at risk. If they ever become common in music, I pray that this will be remembered, understood, and respected.

Why do they call it a treble clef? Are there bass clefs, too? Other clefs?

Yes, there are all types of clefs, but the two most recognizable are the treble and bass clefs. Actually, these are more recent nicknames for these clefs, with the historical names of G clef and F clef being more accurate.

To understand this we need to look at the history of Western music notation. If you ever saw notation in a museum from the Middle Ages, you might have seen a "staff" with only one line or two. Notes were placed above, below, or on these lines to indicate approximately where the pitch should be sung. If it was above the line, it was higher than the note on the line. If it was below the line, it was lower than the note on the line. Unfortunately, this system did not tell you *how much* higher or lower. Still, if you knew the melody (as most people did), it would act as a way to remind you which melody was being sung. If you did not know the melody, the notation was of little use.

As time went on, the system of notation started to become more accurate. With the appearance of staves with several lines, an important convention was begun. At the beginning of the piece of music, a letter was written on the staff to designate a certain line as being a specific pitch. For example, the letter A might be put at the beginning, with the crossbar of the letter on one of the lines of the staff. This informed the performer that this line was the pitch for A, and then the other lines would represent the other corresponding pitches in relation to A.

It is important to realize that any letter, *A* through *G*, can be used at the beginning of a piece of music. If the letter *G* is put on a line, that line represents the pitch G. Likewise if the letter *C* is put at the beginning, the pitch of the line that intersects the letter is C.

Eventually the idea of every line and space representing one pitch became standard, but where this progression started was dictated by the clef, A through G, at the beginning.

This system worked (and still works) very well. Depending on the instrument's or the vocalist's range, the music to be played can be made to fit on the five lines of the staff easily without going much above or below.

Over time, the letters at the beginning of the staff became quite stylized and fancy. This was especially true of the C, the F, and the G clefs. Today these letters look like the clefs in Figure 8.1. These three are still in common use; the one used depends on an instrument's range. They are also still technically movable on the staff. For example, the violin would be notated with the G clef circling the second line of the staff, the bass with the F clef's two dots (which used to be the two horizontal lines of the letter *F*) on the fourth line of the staff (see Figure 8.2).

This system worked just fine until the piano and organ came and messed everything up. These two instruments had such radically extended ranges that they needed eleven or more lines on the staff to accommodate all the notes. This eleven-line staff became very standardized; it is

FIGURE 8.1 The G, F, and C clefs.

FIGURE 8.2 The location of the clefs on the five-line staff for a typical string quartet of two violins, viola, and cello.

FIGURE 8.3 The eleven-line grand staff with a C clef designating the middle line as C.

what is used today for keyboard instruments, with a C clef in the middle, as in Figure 8.3. Since both the organ and piano can play notes above and below these eleven lines, it was decided to insert those lines only when needed and leave them off the rest of time.

At this point those of you who play piano should be saying, "Wait a minute, piano music doesn't have eleven lines, and there is no C clef in the middle." Ah, but it does.

With so many lines the eleven-line staff became too difficult to read. So to make it visually more appealing, the middle line was left out except when needed. This line is where the C clef should be. The result was a staff of five lines on top, a blank space where the C line should be, and five lines below the blank space. This became known as the grand staff.

FIGURE 8.4 The more common grand staff divided into two parts, with the upper half designated with a G clef and the lower half designated with an F clef; the middle C line is inserted only when needed.

To clarify even further, the two staves were moved farther apart, and two new clefs replaced the original C clef. A G clef was put on the second line of the top one, and an F clef was placed on the fourth line of the bottom one.

Figure 8.4 shows how we see it today, but technically it is all one continuous staff. Over time, the G clef became known as the treble clef, because the upper, or treble, notes of the piano are notated there, and the F clef became known as the bass clef, because the lower, or bass, notes of the piano are notated there.

Today publishers are quite casual about whether or not the clefs are actually addressing the correct line of the staff. The grand staff is so accepted and common that few would question what the actual pitches should be, regardless of the actual placement.

As an interesting side note, the fact that there can be and are different clefs in common use and technically any clef is movable leads to the explanation of why so many teachers refuse to use the "Every Good Boy Does Fine" saying to teach the names of the lines of the treble clef. Using this is a bad habit for a youngster or adult to get into because it does not transfer to other clefs or other instruments and can lead to great confusion and frustration later.

Dear Dean Rob: What happens when you answer all the questions that were submitted for this book?
That is when I am finished with the book and simply say "Thanks for reading."

What if I want to hear more answers to more questions?
You can always listen to the live stream of KUSC radio on Saturday mornings. You can listen for the *Ask the Dean* segment around 8:20 a.m. PST. Or you can go to the KUSC website and download podcasts of each week's segment. I hope you do!

SOURCES OF QUOTES

To avoid breaking up the text, I did not insert footnotes for the few quotes I used in the book. Below are the citations for the four quotes that were not attributed to USC faculty members.

Chapter 1

Leonard Bernstein's comments from the stage of Carnegie Hall prior to the performance by Glenn Gould and the New York Philharmonic of the Brahms Piano Concerto no. 1 at the concert of April 25, 1962, were aired live on the orchestra's radio broadcast. The comments were presented on the NPR program *Performance Today* and are accessible at this archive of the radio series: http://www.npr.org/programs/pt/features/gould-bernstein.html.

Chapter 2

Page, Tim. "Maestro and Martinet." *Wall Street Journal*, July 29, 2011. On George Szell. http://www.wsj.com/articles/SB1000142 405270230340610457644591168330 8584.
Melchior, Ib. *Lauritz Melchior: The Golden Years of Bayreuth*. Fort Worth: Baskerville, 2003, p. 179. On Toscanini.

Chapter 3

Gottfried, Martin. *Sondheim*. New York: Abrams, 2000, p. 125.

Chapter 4

Craft, Robert. "*The Rake's Progress*: A Memoir." Naxos CD 8.660 272-73. Program note for Craft's recording of the opera; first published 1994.

INDEX

Note: Page numbers in *italics* indicate illustrations.

and opera, 76
and oratorios, 69–70
hand gestures, 44–45
harmonics, 155–60, *156, 157, 159*
harps, 145–46, 176
harpsichords
  and chamber orchestras, 43
  and changing tastes in
    instruments, 162–65
  and conductorless
    orchestras, 40
  and equal temperament, 172
  and keyboard sizes, 185–86
  and monody, 62
Haydn, Joseph
  and "classical" designation, 211
  and conductorless
    orchestras, 40
  and encores, 268
  and keyboard sizes, 185
  and key designation of
    compositions, 194, 203
  and memorization of
    scores, 120–21
  and Mozart symphonies, 109–11
  and music for Mass, 227–29
  and number of musicians in
    orchestras, 13
  and popular appeal of classical
    music, 259
  volume of work, 204
  and witty music, 220
Haydn, Michael, 108–11
head register, 87–88
hearing loss, 133–36
heckelphones, 15
Herrmann, Bernard, 100, 238
high art, 234
High Middle Ages, 215
Hilliard Ensemble, 118
Hindemith, Paul, 95, 117
Holiday Inn (1942), 277

homophony, 237–38
Hong Kong Cantonese, 102
Hymn and Variations (Cage), 61
hymns, 251–52

ICE (International Contemporary
    Ensemble), 199
immediacy of voice, 86
improvisation, 131–32, 231–32,
    240, 274
Independence Day concerts,
    183, 209–11
inflection, 103
inside players, 6
instrumental makeup of
    orchestras, 143–44
instrument museums, 147
instrument pairings, 112
instrument quality,
    272–74, 296–98
insuring instruments, 177–79
interpretation of compositions,
    199–201, 234–35
introductions, 218
Italian Symphony
    (Mendelssohn), 245
Italy, 62–63, 76–78, *77–78*
Ives, Charles, 116–17, 210,
    220, 235

jazz
  and admissions standards, 293
  and applause conventions, 266
  and "classical"
    designation, 213
  and the double bass, 131–32
  and historical context of
    musical standards, 274
  jazz orchestras, 12
  and modern players ancient
    music, 231–32
  and piano selection, 295

pitch forks, 3, 151
  standards for, 1–3, 3–4
  and vocal vibrato, 60
pit orchestras, 68
Pittsburgh Symphony, 29, 57
pizzicato, 8, 189
plagiarism, 109
Platoon (1986), 240
playing technique, 154–55
political power of music, 232–34
polyphony, 62, 237–38
pops concerts, 212
popular music
  composing for public
    opinion, 113–14
  and composition technique, 97
  contrasted with classical
    music, 220–22
  and memory for pitch, 289
  orchestras, 12, 153
  and percussion, 137
  popular appeal of classical
    music, 222–24, 258–61, 274
  and tonal languages, 102–3
preludes, 218
premiers, 112
pre-performance rituals, 70–73
Previn, André, 35–36
principal conductors, 6, 26,
    27–31, 33, 291
principal guest conductors, 26,
    27, 31–32, 35
principals musicians
  and applause between
    pieces, 46–47
  roles of, 4–7
  and salaries of musicians, 22
  and string section pecking
    order, 25
printing of scores, 223
professional-grade
  instruments, 173–74
professionalism, 120–22, 127–29

professional-quality
  instruments, 190–92
programming decisions,
    28, 278–80
Prokofiev, Sergei, 95, 196
Proper text, 214, 226
proscenium theaters, 186–87
Psycho (1960), 238
"The Psychology of Music"
    (class), 287
public concerts, 121
Puccini, 68, 83
"pulling out all the stops," 286
pure music, 234–35

quality of instruments,
    173–74, 190–92
Quartet for the End of Time
    (Messiaen), 116
quartets, 99

race issues, 49
radio broadcasts, 222–24
Radiolab, 202
The Rake's Progress
    (Stravinsky), 103–4
range of instruments,
    154–55, 304–7
Ravel, Maurice, 98, 104, 202
recitals, 139–40, 269, 283–84
recording of performances, 231
record sales, 113–14
reeds, 1–3, 4, 148–51
Reeling (Wolfe), 152
reference pitch, 1–3, 3–4, 150–51
regional traditions, 10
register shifts, 88
rehearsals
  and autocratic
    conductors, 56–58
  and chamber orchestras, 45
  and composer notations, 200
  and conductor duties, 30–32